# THE SIGNED ENGLISH SCHOOL BOOK

Harry Bornstein and Karen L. Saulnier
illustrated by Ralph R. Miller, Sr.

**The Signed English Series**
KENDALL GREEN PUBLICATIONS
Gallaudet University Press
Washington, D.C.

KENDALL GREEN PUBLICATIONS
An imprint of Gallaudet University Press
Washington, DC 20002
http://gupress.gallaudet.edu


Fourth printing 2009
Printed in the United States of America

Library of Congress Cataloging-in-Publication Data
Bornstein, Harry.
The signed English schoolbook.

(The signed English series)
Bibliography: p.
Includes index.
1. Sign language-Study and teaching. 2. Deaf-Education-English language. I. Saulnier, Karen Luczak. II. Title. III. Series. [DNLM: 1. Deafness-rehabilitation. 2. Manual Communications. 3. Teaching Materials. HV 2474 B736s]
HV2474.B667 1987 419 87-15042
ISBN 0-930323-30-0

# CONTENTS

# PREFACE

*The Signed English Schoolbook* is the latest in our continuing effort to make Signed English a more useful tool. This book may be considered a second course in learning Signed English and is intended to follow *The Signed English Starter.* We believe that these books will provide the most benefit to you if you study them in the recommended order. However, as with the other materials in the Signed English series, *The Signed English Schoolbook* is self-contained and can be used alone as you may desire.

The *Signed English Schoolbook* includes about 100 signs taken from *Signs for Instructional Purposes,* which was published in 1969 and is now out of print. As far as we know *Signs for Instructional Purposes* was the first book especially prepared for post-secondary education. The signs were developed with the active cooperation of Gallaudet University's faculty and were subsequently used in a large number of other post-secondary programs. The signs have been reviewed again recently by Gallaudet faculty for currency and appropriateness.

The illustrations for the signs from *Signs for Instructional Purposes* are modifications of drawings originally made by Betty Miller. The remaining illustrations in this book have been taken from other books in the Signed English Series and include signs drawn by Linda C. Tom, Nancy L. Lundborg, Ann Silver, Jack Fennell, Jan Skrobisz, and Ralph R. Miller, Sr.

Ralph R. Miller, Sr., our late principal artist, drew the largest number of the illustrations contained in this book. Even more than we feel the lost of his talent, we miss this sweet and good gentleman. Therefore, in his memory, we and Lillian B. Hamilton have established the Ralph R. Miller, Sr. Award. This award is given annually to the Gallaudet University graduating senior who shows the most promise in the field of art. Hopefully, that promise will result in comparable contributions to deaf and hearing children.

# INTRODUCTION

*The Signed English Schoolbook* is intended to be the "second course" in the Signed English Series. It is designed to provide Signed English vocabulary and sentence patterns related to school activities and the classroom environment.

The "first course" for home or class study of Signed English is *The Signed English Starter.* It was designed to provide a comfortable and reasonable start to learning Signed English. *The Starter* includes a basic functional sign vocabulary and exercises using those signs. In addition it presents a systematic progression for learning to use the fourteen Signed English markers, a discussion of the unique features of a manual English system, and a section on how to develop name signs.

## THE PURPOSE OF THIS BOOK

*The Signed English Schoolbook* is designed to serve two purposes. First, for those of you who are teachers or otherwise serve school-aged children and adolescents, it provides the vocabulary, in a topical arrangement, that you will need for the full range of school activities.

Second, for those of you who are parents, *The Schoolbook* gives the language tools that will enable you to be actively involved in your child's education at home and at school. It is structured in a manner which will help you achieve speed and smoothness in the use of signs with speech.

By design, the vocabulary in *The Schoolbook* is largely different from *The Starter.* However, some overlap does exist for continuity and completeness. Neither *The Starter* nor *The Schoolbook* should be considered reference books; they are texts. *The Comprehensive Signed English Dictionary* is the primary reference book for the Signed English Series. The Signed English Series continues to grow and presently consists of approximately 60 story books, coloring books, poems, songs, posters, and flash cards. A complete list of available titles is given in the back of this book.

## THE SIGNS IN THIS BOOK

Since this book is a second course in Signed English, it is assumed that you know the basics of Signed English and are ready to learn some more about the complexities of using a Signed English system for communication.

The signs in this text come from the Signed English corpus which has been codified in one or another of the books we have published in the Signed English Series over the past fifteen years. We have tried to cover the full range of classroom and other campus activities in which young school children and adolescents are engaged. Signs are included for sports and play as well as for academic subjects. Signs are also provided related to children and adolescents learning to deal with their feelings and developing sexuality, to groom and dress themselves, and to cope with health issues.

## REGIONAL VARIATION OF SIGNS

Some of the signs in this book are highly specialized and infrequently used. When signs such as these have limited exposure, they are more apt to vary in their formation in different regions across the United States. In fact, many signs will vary even within a state. This phenomenon of regional variation is clearly illustrated in Shroyer and Shroyer's book *Signs Across America.* Because regional variations may confuse a young child who is learning to sign, some schools and states have produced their own sign books showing those signs used in their programs.

Depending on where you live and travel, it is likely that you will encounter people who use different signs than those presented in this book, or who feel that a word should be fingerspelled rather than use a sign at all. You can deal with this situation in a number of ways. First, you should understand that there is no authoritative person or dictionary that can give you the "right" sign for a given English word. Sign language is simply not a language that has only one right way to communicate an idea.

Second, you should understand that the signs or words that people use regularly are often very important to them. For hearing-impaired people, or those who identify closely with hearing-impaired people, specific signs may become an important part of their identity. Professionals for whom the skill of signing may have been hard won, may feel strongly about the specific signs they learned. They may also have a psychic investment in what they have learned.

As a matter of respect for those who prefer the signs they know and have learned, it makes little sense to insist on the "rightness" or use of any given sign. Instead, we suggest that you view alternate signs as synonyms and treat them very much as you would synonyms in English, i.e., more or less equally appropriate. Further, respect those people who prefer to fingerspell a given word, especially in an academic setting. They may have a specialized meaning in mind and prefer not to use a given sign in a specific instructional context.

## HOW TO USE THIS BOOK

In addition to providing the appropriate vocabulary, this *Schoolbook* is designed to help you achieve speed and smoothness in your use of signs while speaking. On the average, it takes longer to form a sign than it does to speak the corresponding English word. Consequently, you should attend to trying to parallel your speech with signs, at least in the beginning. Consciously try to form each sign at the same time you speak the English counterpart. To assist you in learning the skill of paralleling your signs and speech, we have included a number of sentences and incomplete phrases at the end of each chapter in this book. After you have learned the individual signs in the chapter, repeat each phrase or sentence several times while speaking. Try to synchronize the beginnings of the sign with the spoken word. When you feel you are able to do this comfortably, pair each incomplete phrase with every appropriate sign in the chapter. We believe that this type of exercise will permit you to sign more comfortably and, at the same time, enable you to offer a more complete model of English to the child.

A time may come when you do not feel a need to supply a child with a complete manual model of English. This may be true when communication is your only purpose. It may also happen when you have reason to believe that the child is able to unconsciously fill in many features of English from the sound of your voice, the shape of your lips, and/or his or her own knowledge of the English language. When you determine that it is not necessary to provide a complete manual model of English, you may not need to sign all or most of the markers and many of the function words of English. You will find that when you don't sign every marker or function word, you will be able to sign in parallel with your speech more easily. You should be sure, however, that the child has really mastered these features of English before you begin skipping signs.

You may also elect to substitute signs from American Sign Language, the sign language used by deaf people when they communicate with each other. Many of these signs represent whole ideas rather than individual English words. When you are using Signed English but omit some signs and markers and substitute signs from American Sign Language, you are in effect using a Pidgin Sign English which is a combination of the two languages. In those instances that you choose not to model English manually, it may be perfectly appropriate and effective to use Pidgin Sign English, especially with older students.

We wish you the best of luck in your use of Signed English. You will find it to be a challenging, but useful, language tool.

# SIGN MARKERS

Signed English uses two kinds of gestures or signs: sign words and sign markers. Each sign word stands for one English word, such as *mother, shoe, horse,* etc. These sign words should be signed in the same order as words are used in an English sentence.

The sign markers should be used when you wish to change the form and the meaning of some words in a sentence. This includes such things as changes in number, possession, degree, verb tense, etc. We recommend that you use the 14 sign markers pictured here.

All but one of these markers are signed after the basic sign word. The marker that stands for "opposite of" is the only marker that is signed before the sign word.

In Signed English you use either a sign word alone or a sign word and one sign marker to represent a given English word. When this does not adequately represent the word you have in mind, use the manual alphabet and fingerspell the word.

If you use these markers properly, you will provide a better and more complete model of English.

**regular plural nouns: -s**
bear*s*, house*s*

mice

**irregular plural nouns:**
(sign the word twice)
children, sheep, mice

**regular past verbs: -ed**
talk*ed*, want*ed*,
learn*ed*

**irregular past verbs:**
(sweep RH open B, tips out, to the right) *saw*,
hea*r*d, bl*ew*

**3rd person singular: -s**
walk*s*, eat*s*, sing*s*

**possessive: -'s**
cat*'s*, daddy*'s*, chair*'s*

**verb form: -ing**
climb*ing*, play*ing*, runn*ing*

**participle:**
fall*en*, g*one*, grow*n*

**adjective: -y**
sleep*y*, sunn*y*, cloud*y*

**adverb: -ly**
beautiful*ly*, happ*ily*, nice*ly*

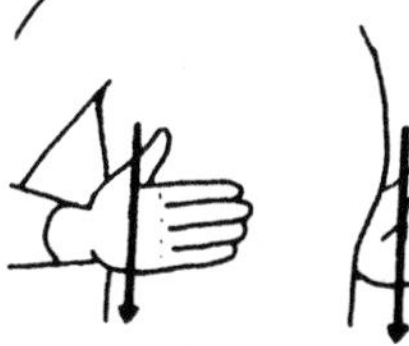

**agent (person):**
(sign made near the body) teach*er*, act*or*, art*ist*

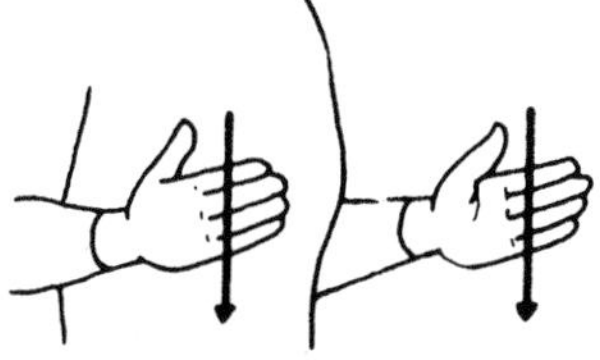

**agent (thing):**
(sign made away from the body) wash*er*, dry*er*, plant*er*

**comparative: -er**
small*er*, fast*er*, long*er*

**superlative: -est**
small*est*, fast*est*, long*est*

**opposite of: un-**
(made before the sign word, as a prefix) *un*happy, *un*important

# AMERICAN MANUAL ALPHABET

Fingerspelling is an important part of Signed English. It fills in the "sign gaps" in your sentences if you do not know the sign for a particular word.

Fingerspelling is a letter-by-letter manual representation of English words. Each letter of the alphabet is represented by a specific handshape. Form the letters with your hand held up comfortably about chest level, the palm facing outward, i.e., toward your audience.

Make your letters in a smooth, clear manner. Pause slightly between words but do not drop your hand. Avoid bouncing or pushing letters forward in an attempt to be clear.

Do not move your hand position while fingerspelling. However, when fingerspelling a word that contains a double letter (e.g., *soon, hall*) you may move your hand slightly to the right when forming the second letter.

Remember always to say words, not individual letters, while signing and fingerspelling words. Do not let your hands obscure your lip movements.

Most formal names for people, places, and things, as well as addresses, are fingerspelled.

A
B
C
D
E
F
G
H
I
J
K
L
M
N
O
P
Q
R
S
T
U
V
W
X
Y
Z

# NUMBERS

**number**
Flat O shape both hands, left palm in, right down, tips touching. Reverse positions.

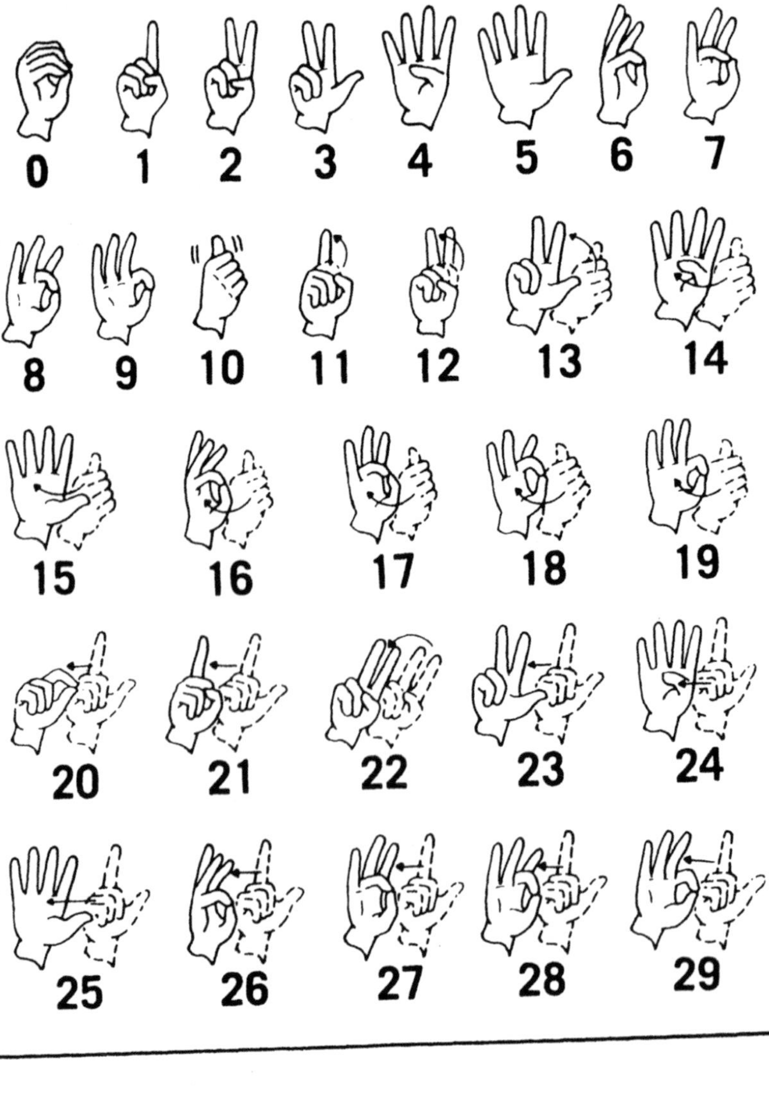

0 1 2 3 4 5 6 7

8 9 10 11 12 13 14

15 16 17 18 19

20 21 22 23 24

25 26 27 28 29

## 30–99

**Thirty through ninety-nine:**
Sign by forming the two figures that comprise the number.

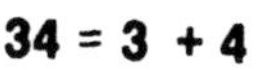

34 = 3 + 4   60 = 6 + 0

## 100

**One hundred:**
Form the number 1, then C with right hand.

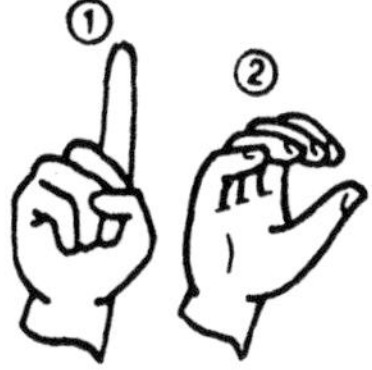

## 1,000

**One thousand:**
Form the number 1 with RH. Then place tips of right M in left palm.

## 1,000,000

**One million:**
Form the number 1 with RH. Then place tips of right M in left palm. Bounce tips forward once (twice for billion).

## Ordinal Numbers

Sign 1st through 9th by signing the number (palm out) then twisting to palm in.

8th

## Fractions

Sign the numerator then lower hand slightly and sign the denominator.

1/4

3/8

# KEY to WORD DESCRIPTIONS

In order to use this book easily and effectively, you should be familiar with the names of your fingers, the manual alphabet, the signs for the numbers one through ten, and certain handshapes that are frequently used when making the base signs.

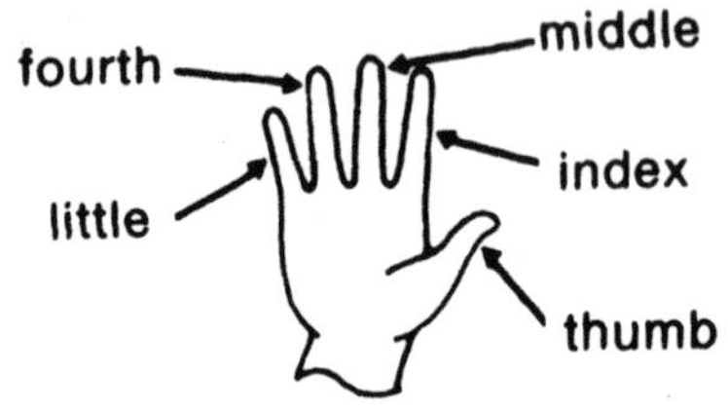


- **RH = right hand**
- **LH = left hand**

### ILLUSTRATIONS

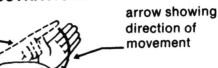

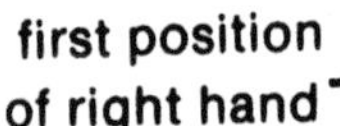


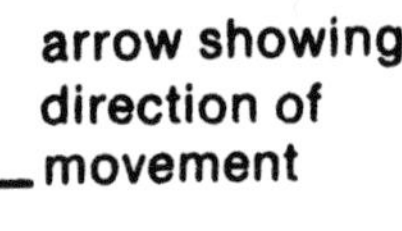


final position
of right hand

### HANDSHAPES

Sample letter shape A. See complete alphabet on page xiii.

Sample number shape 1. See numbers 1–29 on pages xiv and xv.

**open B**

**bent B**

**bent V**

**claw shape**

**flat O**

# KEY to ARROWS

The dotted line shows the starting point of a sign. The directional arrow shows the movement toward the solid-line (or final) hand position.

Arrows indicate single, double, or repeated movement as described below:

single movement, once toward point

double movement, twice toward point

repeated movement, back and forth

repeated movement, forward, back, and forward

right arc (directions are from the perspective of the signer in the drawings)

left arc

clockwise, counterclockwise

motion markers indicate a slight wiggling movement

# 1.
# THE CLASSROOM

**book**
Palms together thumbs up. Open as if opening book.

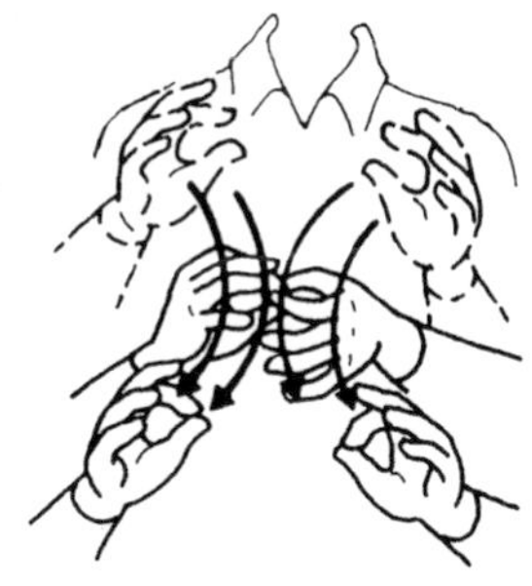

**story**
Open 9 shape both hands. Move down, link thumbs and index fingers, then pull apart, ending in 9 shapes. Repeat motion.

**shelf**
Open B both hands held high, palms down, tips out. Hold together then move apart in straight line.

**calendar**
LH open B palm in. C shape RH palm and tips left. Place RH in left palm then slide over tips and down back of LH.

## pencil sharpener

Place tips of right thumb and index finger on mouth, then slide across upturned left palm. Then form S shape LH palm down. Mime turning handle of sharpener with modified A shape RH.

## staple

Open B both hands, left palm up, tips out; right palm down, tips left and slightly bent. Strike base of left palm with base of right.

## scotch tape

Make a cross on upper left arm with fingers of 4 shape RH. Then form H shape both hands, palms down, tips touching. Draw apart in straight line.

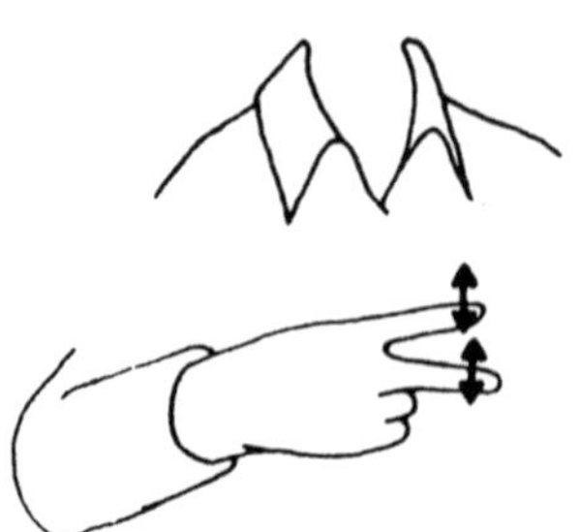

## scissors

V shape RH palm in, tips left. Open and close fingers like scissor blades.

## ruler

R shape both hands, thumbs extended. Tap thumbs together.

**pen**
LH open B palm up, tips out. "Write" in palm with middle tip of right P.

**pencil**
Place tips of right thumb and index finger on mouth then slide across upturned left palm.

**crayon**
LH open B palm up, tips out. C shape RH. Move right thumb forward on left palm with small wave-like motion.

**paper**
Open B both hands, left palm up, tips out; right palm down, tips left. Brush base of right palm across base of left palm toward body twice.

**chalk**
Mime writing on blackboard with chalk.

**erase**
LH open B palm right, tips out. Rub knuckles of right E back and forth on left palm once or twice.

**blinds (window)**
B shape both hands, palms in, left tips right, right tips left. Hold in front of face then drop and spread fingers.

**bulletin**
A shape both hands, palms facing, thumbs extended. Hold before chest, punch forward, drop, and punch again.

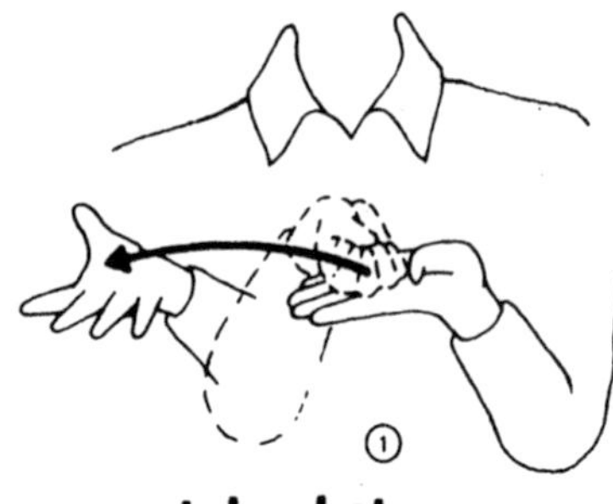

**wastebasket**
LH open B palm up. RH flat O palm and tips up. Place RH in left palm then slide out into 5 shape palm up, tips out. Place index finger of right B under left wrist and arc to elbow, ending with little finger side touching.

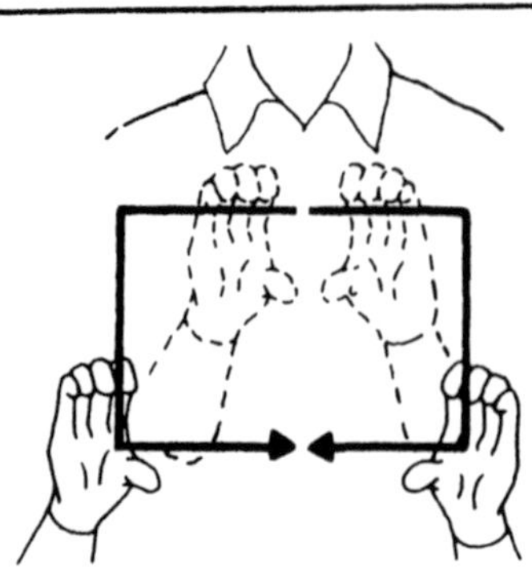

**chart**
C shape both hands held close together. Move apart, down, then back together.

**flag**
Place right elbow on back of left hand which is held before you. Wave right hand back and forth.

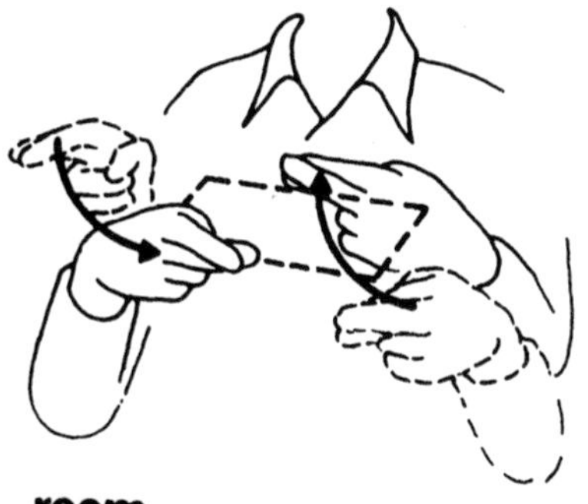

**room**

R shape both hands, tips out. Turn right R left and left R right to form box shape.

**chair**

C shape LH palm right. Hang right N over left thumb.

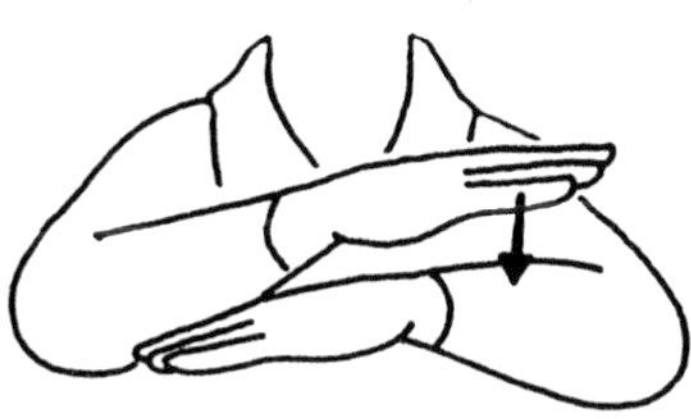

**table**

LH open B palm down, tips right, held across front of body. Lower forearm of right open B down on left forearm.

**desk**

Extend left forearm before body, palm down, tips right. Tap inside of left elbow with fingertips of right D.

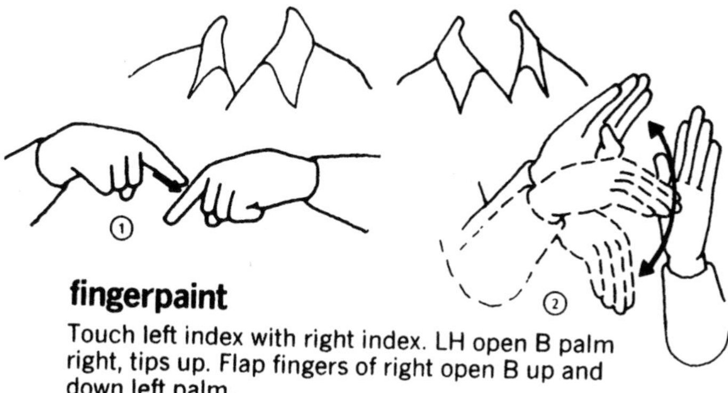


**fingerpaint**

Touch left index with right index. LH open B palm right, tips up. Flap fingers of right open B up and down left palm.

**computer**
LH open B palm down, tips out. Place base of right C on left wrist and move up arm in short bouncing motions.

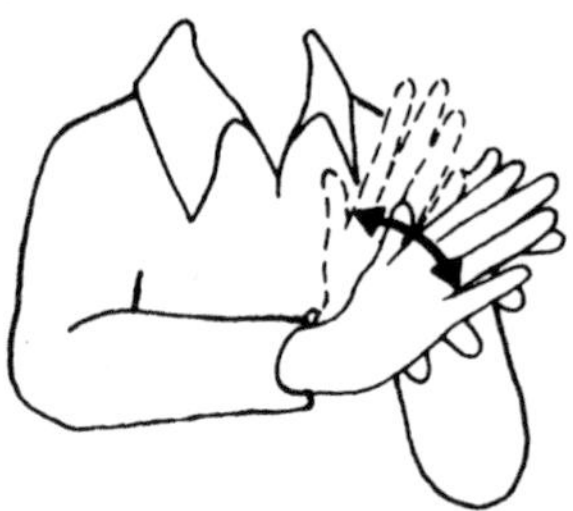

**movie**
Five shape LH palm right, tips out. Five shape RH palm left, tips up. Place palms together then gently shake right fingertips back and forth (to indicate flickering motion).

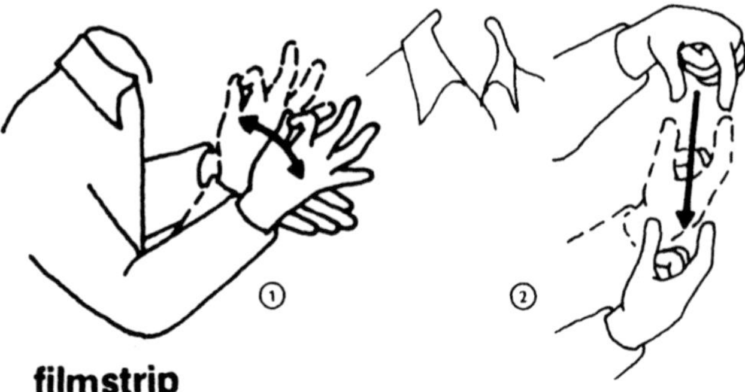


**filmstrip**
LH open B palm and tips slanted right. Place base of right F in left palm and move back and forth. G shape both hands, left tips down, right tips up. Place right G under left G, then drop down.

**picture**
LH open B palm right, tips up. Place thumb and index finger of right C against right eye then move down to left palm.

**camera**
Mime holding camera in front of face and clicking shutter.

**string**

S shape LH palm out. Place tip of right I on left S then shake away to the right.

**rubber band**

Rub right X down side of cheek twice. Then move X shape hands, palms in, apart and back, as if stretching rubber band.

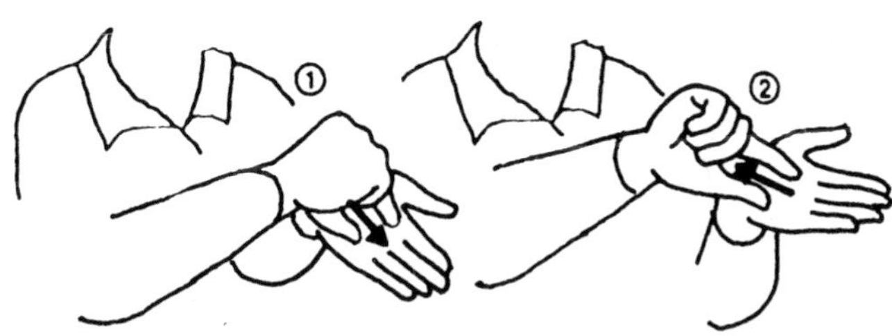

**glue**

LH open B palm up, tips out. Place right G on left palm, slide forward, flip over, and slide back.

**clay**

Put hands together and move slightly as if molding clay.

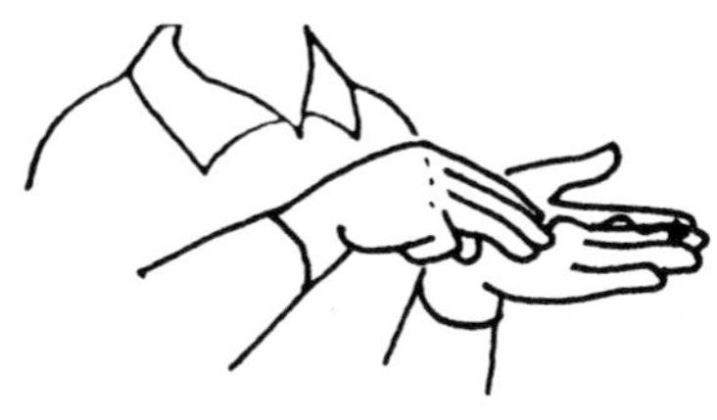

**Magic Marker**

LH open B palm up, tips out. Write across left palm with tips of M shape RH.

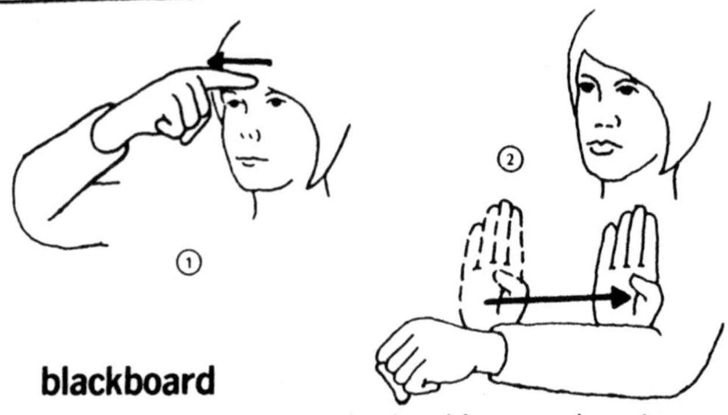

## blackboard

Draw index finger across forehead from one brow to the other. Run base of right B up left arm from wrist to elbow.

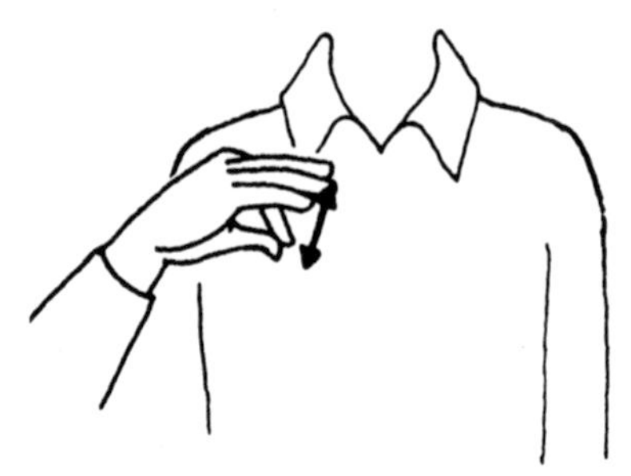

## flannel

Brush thumb and index tips of right F on upper right chest.

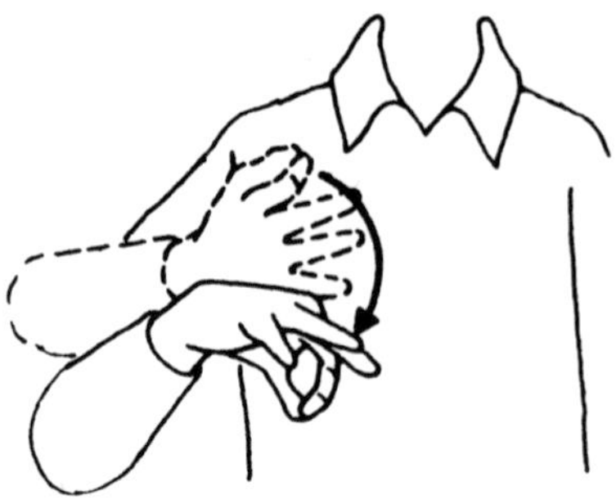

## pin

Mime sticking pin in dress or shirt with right thumb and forefinger.

## clip (noun)

LH open B palm in, tips right. Snap right index, middle finger, and thumb over left index.

## tack

A shape both hands, thumbs extended. Press thumbs into an imaginary bulletin board.

**cardboard**

LH open B palm in, tips right. Grasp left fingers with right fingers and wiggle back and forth.

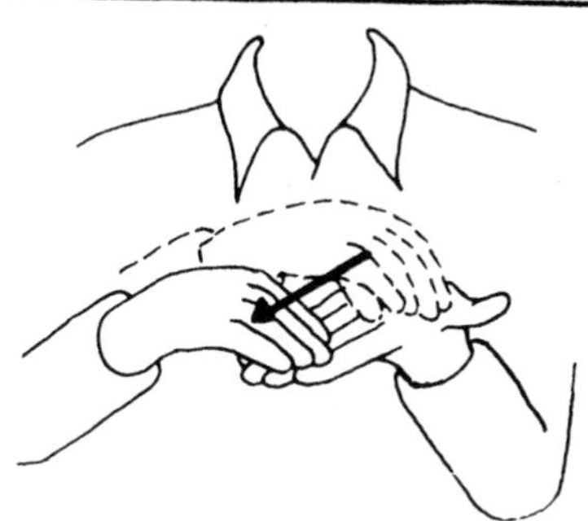

**card**

LH open B palm up, tips out. C shape RH palm down. Slide RH off left palm.

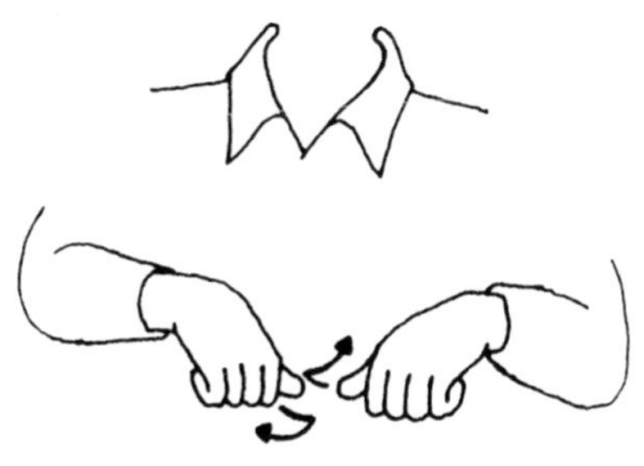

**puzzle (noun)**

A shape both hands, thumbs down. Make motion of fitting together.

**puppet**

RH flat O palm out. Snap thumb and fingertips together several times, as if operating hand puppet.

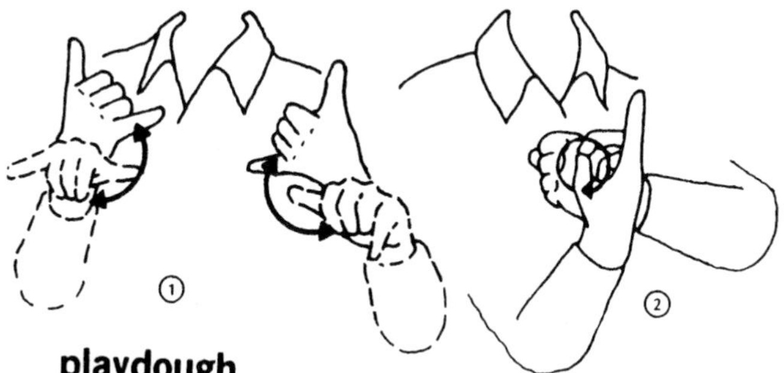

**playdough**

Y shape both hands, palms in. Simultaneously twist back and forth. S shape LH palm in, knuckles right. D shape RH palm in. Circle RH clockwise on back of left S.

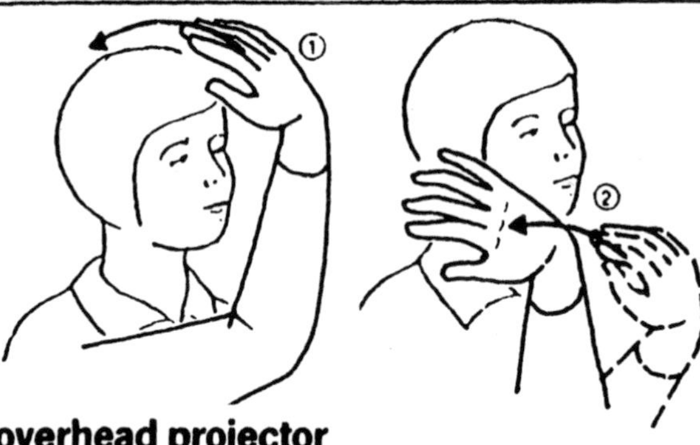


**overhead projector**

Pass right open B, palm down, over top of head. Form right flat O, palm in, and place at right shoulder. Open quickly into 5 shape palm in.

**screen**

Hold hands in front of body, palms out, tips up. Draw apart, down, and back again, outlining shape of screen.

**letter (alphabet)**

One shape LH palm right, tip out. Place tips of right G on base of left index then move forward one or two times.

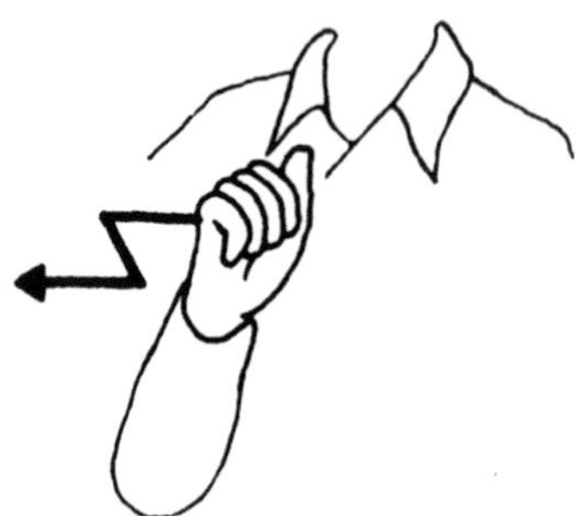

**alphabet**

A shape RH. Move down in Z motion.

**class**

C shape both hands held close together. Draw apart and around to front ending in 5 shapes, little fingers touching.

## PRACTICE SENTENCES

Repeat each of the following phrases or sentences several times. Start forming each sign at the same time you begin to speak its corresponding word.

After you can sign, and simultaneously say, each phrase or sentence comfortably, pair each incomplete phrase with every appropriate sign in this chapter.

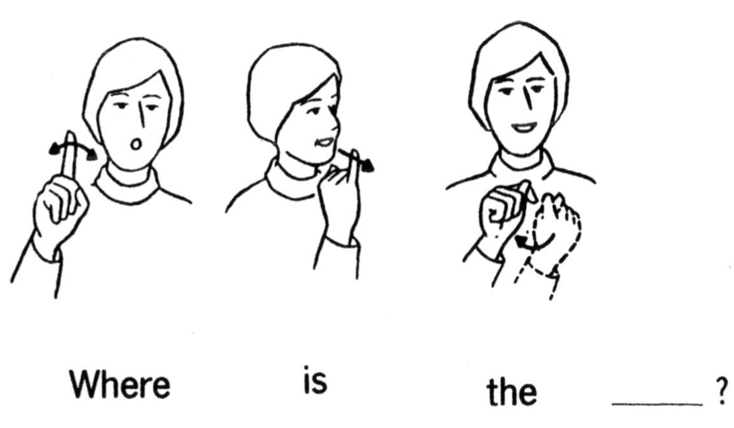
Where
is
the
_____ ?

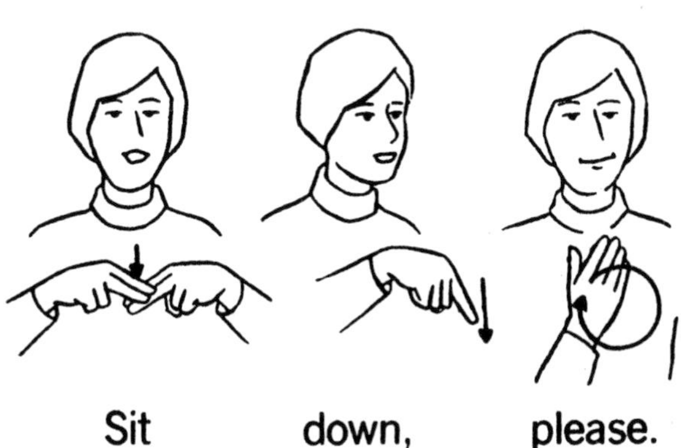
Sit
down,
please.

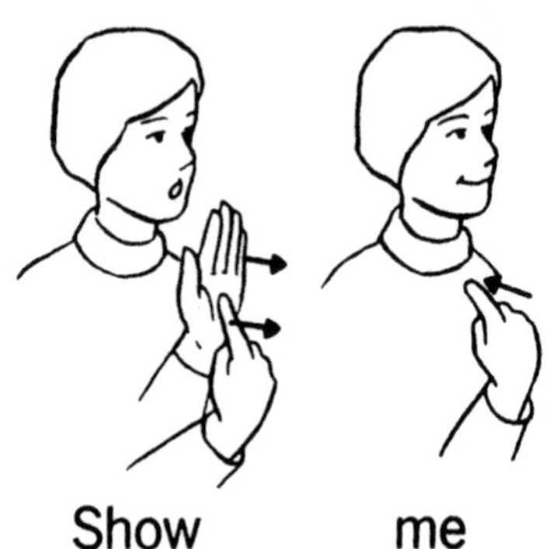

Show me ____.

Put that away.

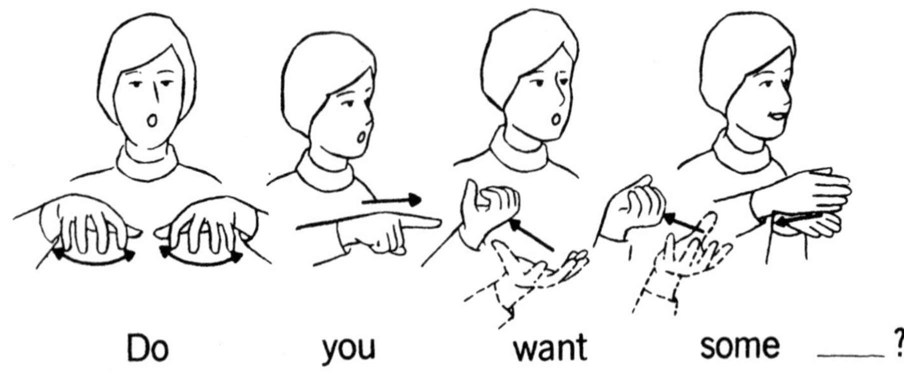

Do you want some ____?

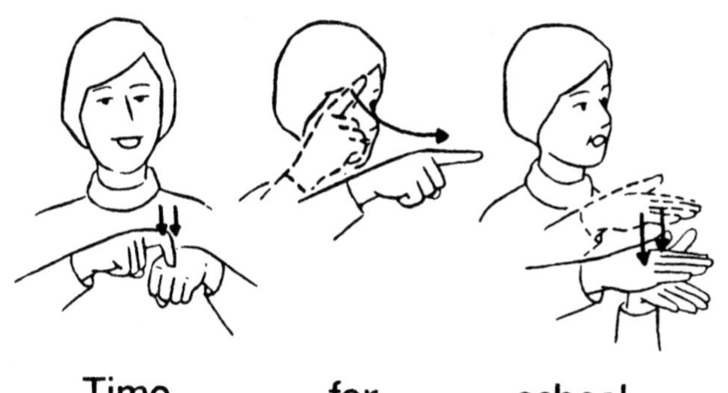

Time for school.

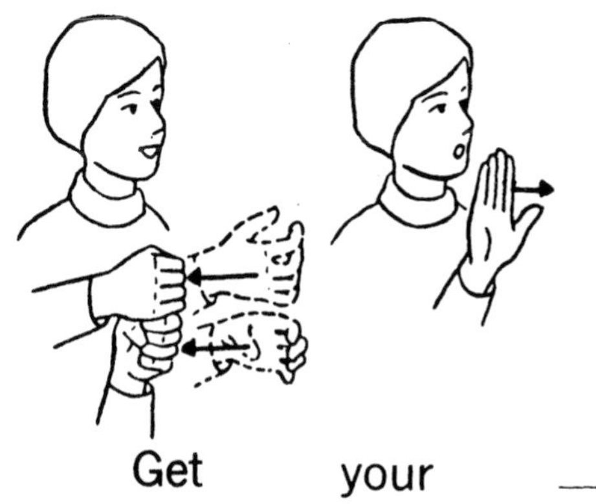

Get your ____ .

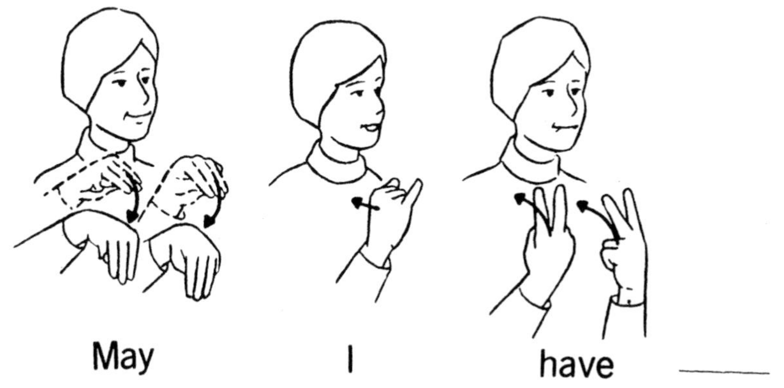

May I have ____ ?

# 2.
# HEARING LOSS

**otologist**
LH open B palm up, tips out. Tap left wrist with base of right O.

**audiology**
Circle right A clockwise at right ear.

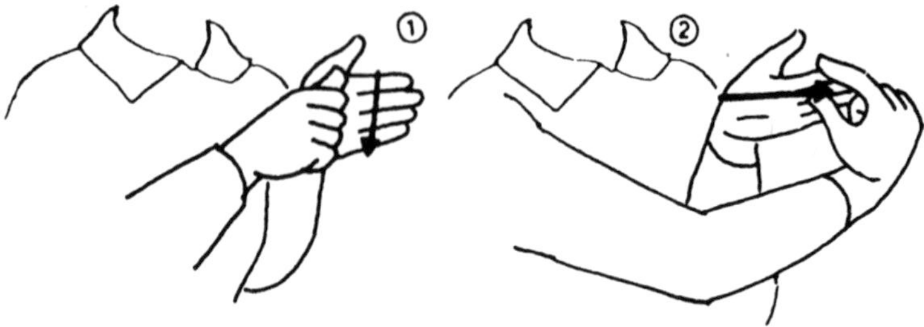


**audiogram**
LH open B palm slanted right. Draw right A down left palm, change into G shape, then move forward on left palm.

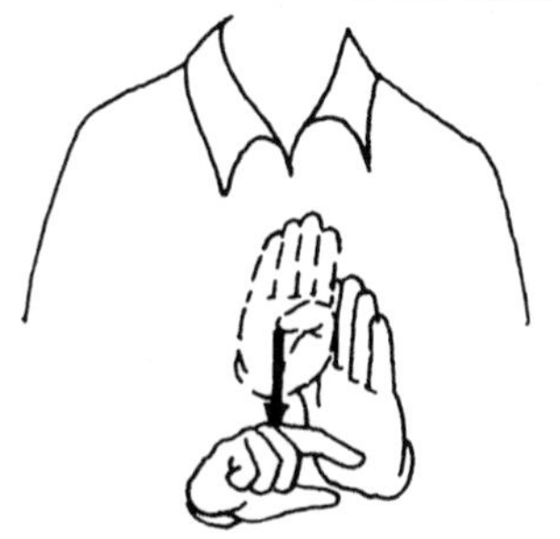

**background**
Open B shape LH, palm out. Place B shape RH against left palm then drop down slightly, changing to G shape.

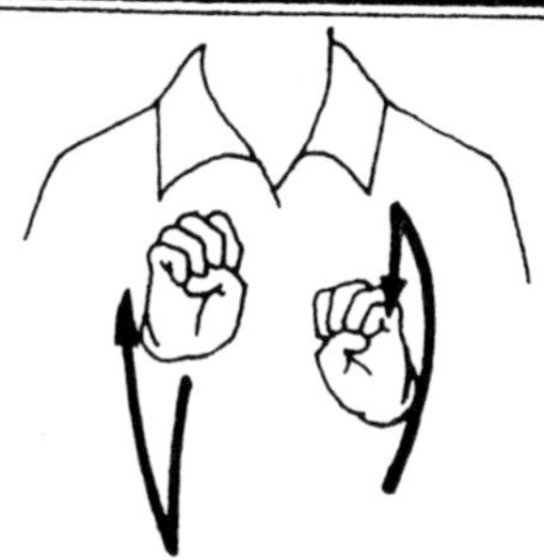

**evaluate**
E shape both hands, palms out. Move up and down alternately.

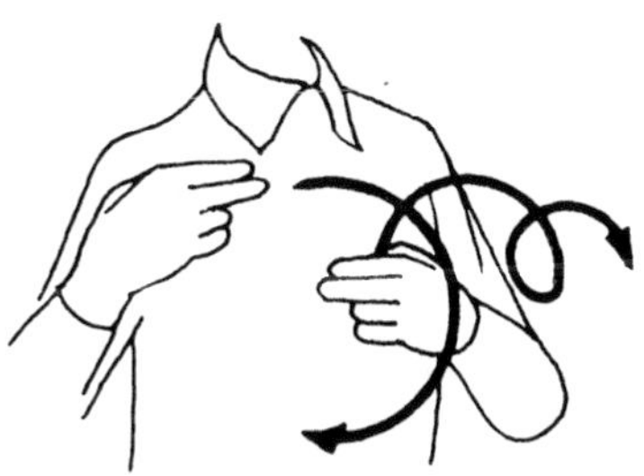

**hereditary**
Place H shape hands, palms down, at right shoulder, RH above LH. Roll down over each other in forward motion.

**intensity**
Form fist with LH, palm up. Outline left bicep with little finger of *I* shape RH.

**threshold**
I shape both hands, palms in, little fingers touching. Pull apart.

**frequency**
Right index finger, tip pointing outward, curves up and then down.

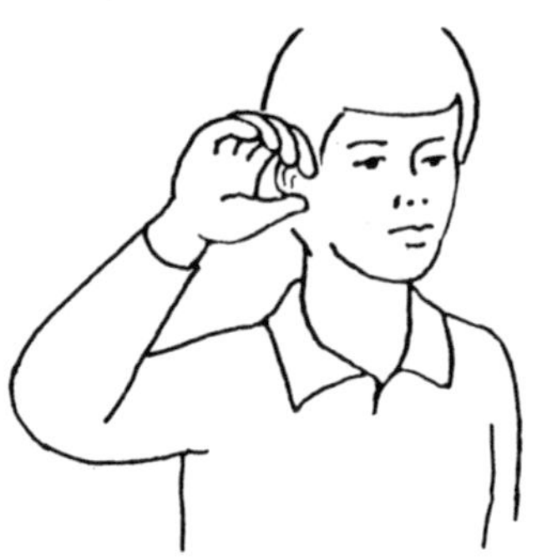

**listen**
Cup hand over ear.

**sound**
Tap right ear with right S.

**breathe**
Place tips of claw hands on chest, left below right, then move in and out.

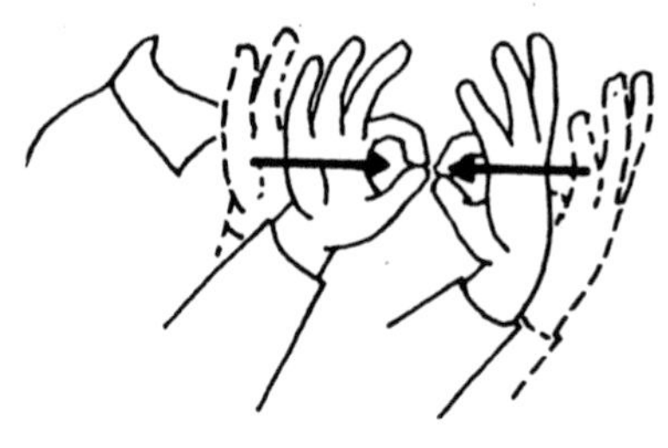

**fit**
F shape both hands, left palm slanted in. Touch tips of left index and thumb with tips of right index and thumb.

**microphone**
S shape RH palm in. Hold in front of mouth as if holding microphone.

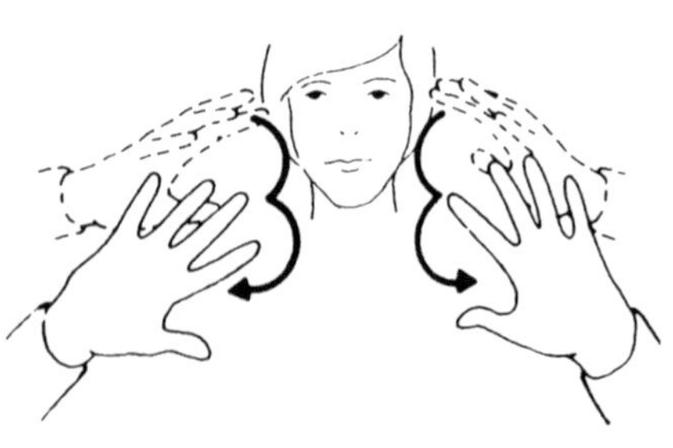

**noise**
Five shape both hands, index fingers held at ears. Shake hands outward.

**deaf**
Point index finger to ear, then place index fingers of double B shapes together, palms down.

**hearing impaired**
Place right H, palm in, at ear. Move out, changing to I shape.

**hearing aid**
Place right thumb, index, and middle finger on right ear (as if inserting aid).

**ear mold**
Place right index finger and thumb in right ear (other fingers spread).

**cord**
C shape LH palm out. Place tip of right little finger on side of right C and draw away to right in wiggly motion.

**battery**
B shape LH. Strike left index finger with knuckle of right index finger twice.

**lipread (speechread)**

V shape RH palm in. Place in front of lips and move back and forth from right to left several times.

**oral**

O shape RH palm and tips left. Circle clockwise at mouth.

**speech**

S shape RH. Change to bent V, palm in, and circle at mouth.

**pronounce**

P shape RH palm down. Hold index tip at mouth and make small circle forward.

**vowel**

One shape LH palm right, tip out. Place base of right V on tip of left index.

**consonant**

Place base of right C, fingers closed except for index, on top of left index.

**communicate**
C shape both hands, palms facing. Move back and forth alternately at sides of mouth.

**voice**
V shape RH palm in. Place tips on throat then arc upward and out.

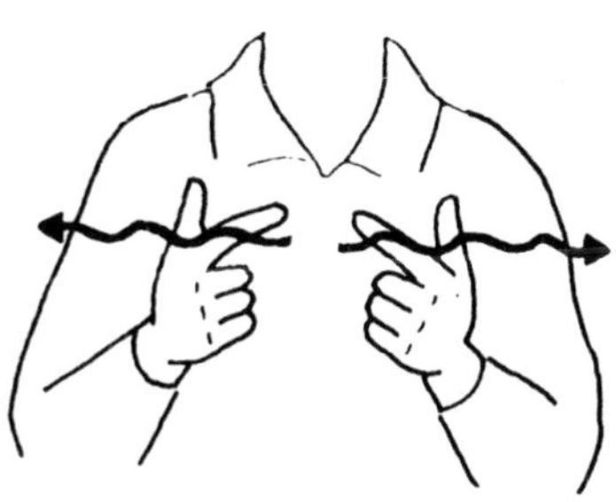

**language**
L shape both hands, palms facing, index tips out. Place hands close together then wiggle apart.

**public speaking**
Form a P shape with RH. Change to open B shape, palm left. Place at right side of head, pivoting wrist up and down several times.

**expressive**
Hold S shape hands, palms in, against chest. Thrust forward into open 5 shapes, palms up.

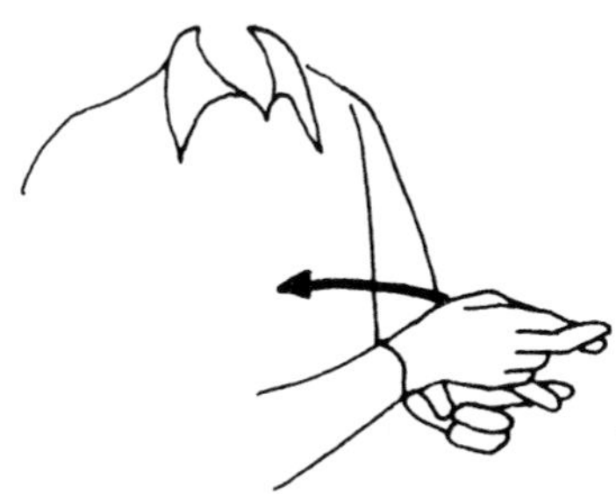

**receptive**
R shape both hands, right on top of left. Move both hands against body, keeping right on top of left.

**bell**
LH open B palm right, tips up. Strike right S against left palm and pull away. Repeat motion.

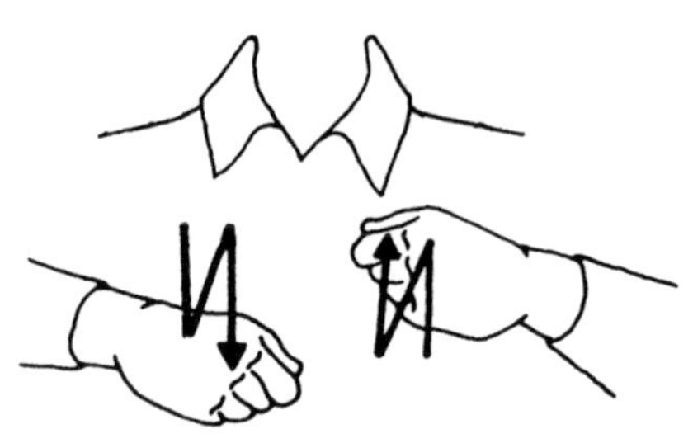

**drum**
Mime holding drumsticks and beating drum.

**horn**
C shape LH palm and tips right. S shape RH palm left. Hold RH at mouth and blow.

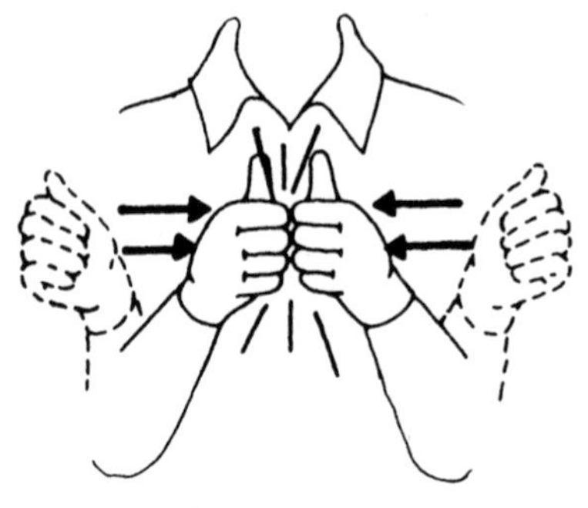

**cymbal**
A shape both hands, knuckles facing, thumbs extended. Hit together as if banging cymbals.

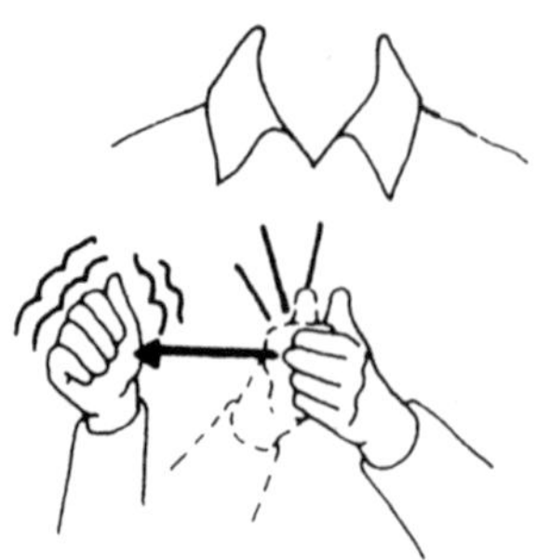

**tambourine**
LH open B palm right, tips out. Hit left palm with right A then shake RH away to the right.

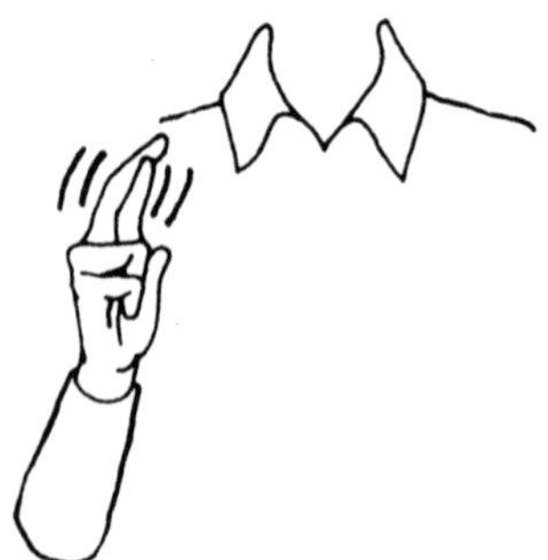

**rattle**
R shape RH. Shake back and forth.

**music**
LH open B palm up, tips slightly right. Swing right M back and forth over left palm and forearm without touching.

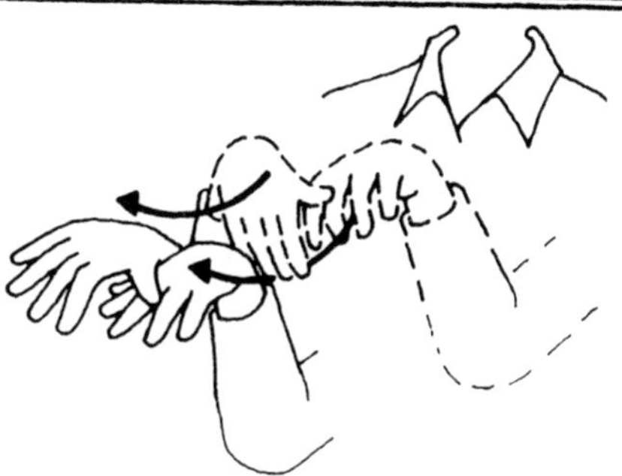

**march (verb)**
Five shape both hands, palms in, tips down. LH in front of right. Swing fingers back and forth while moving both hands forward.

**rhythm**
R shape RH palm down, tips out. Move in rhythmic motion to the right.

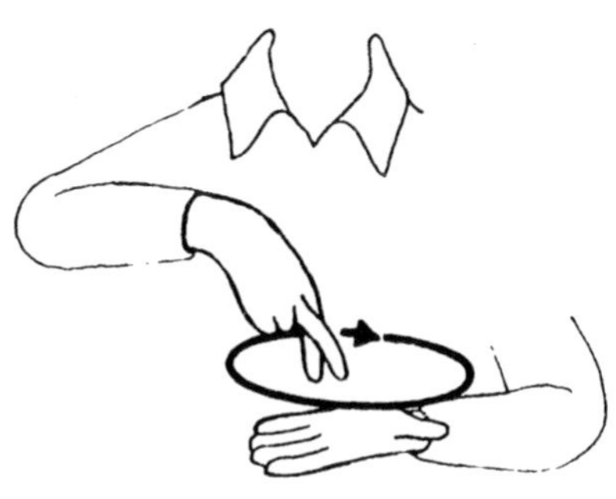

**record**
LH open B palm up, tips out. Circle tips of right R clockwise over left palm.

**sing**
LH open B palm up. Swing fingers of right open B above left forearm and palm in rhythmic motion.

**dance**
LH open B palm up, tips out. Sweep right V over left palm several times.

**fast**
L shape both hands, palms facing, index tips out. Draw back quickly into S shapes.

**slow**
Draw palm of RH slowly up back of LH.

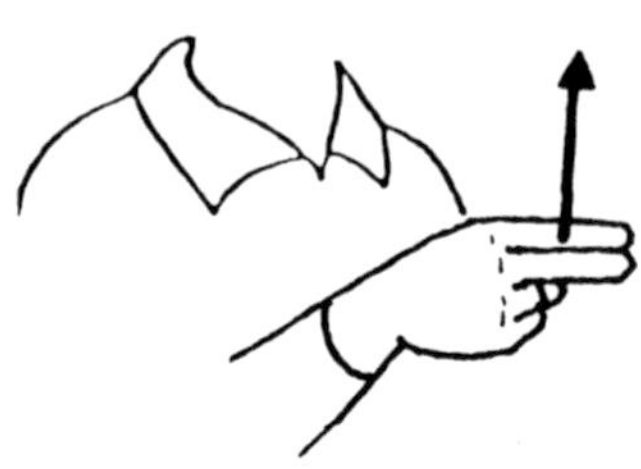

**high**
H shape RH tips out. Move up several inches.

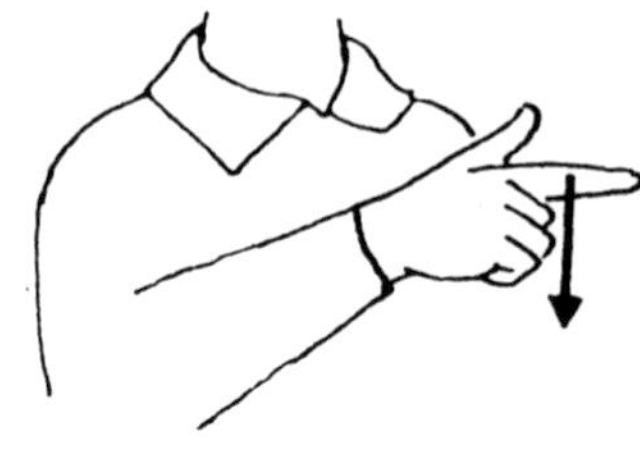

**low**
L shape RH palm down. Move down.

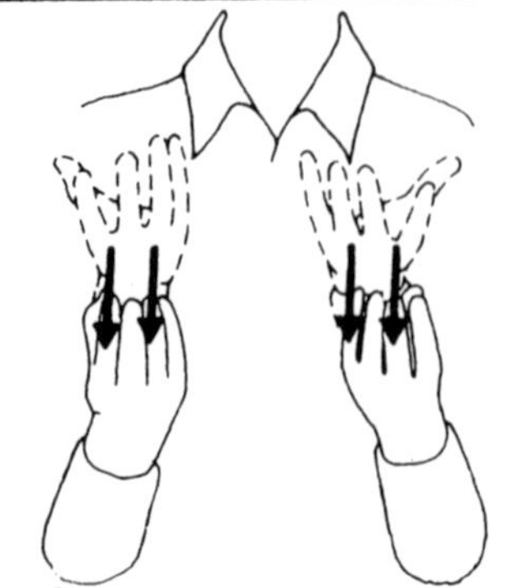

**soft**
Claw shape both hands, palms up. Lower into flat O shapes palms up. Repeat.

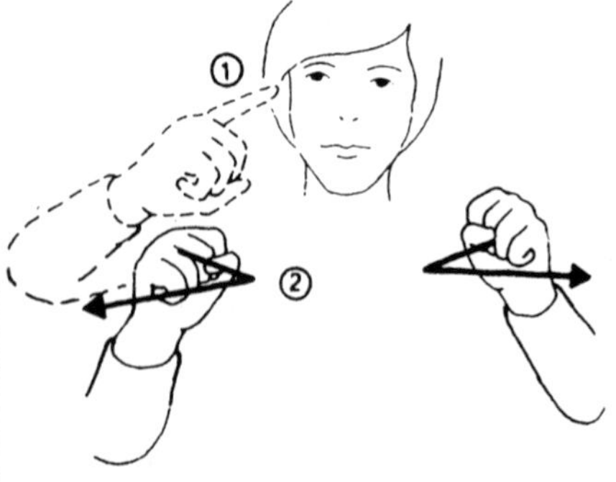


**loud**
Place right index at right ear, then shake S shape both hands in front of body.

## PRACTICE SENTENCES

Repeat each of the following phrases or sentences several times. Start forming each sign at the same time you begin to speak its corresponding word.

After you can sign, and simultaneously say, each phrase or sentence comfortably, pair each incomplete phrase with every appropriate sign in this chapter.

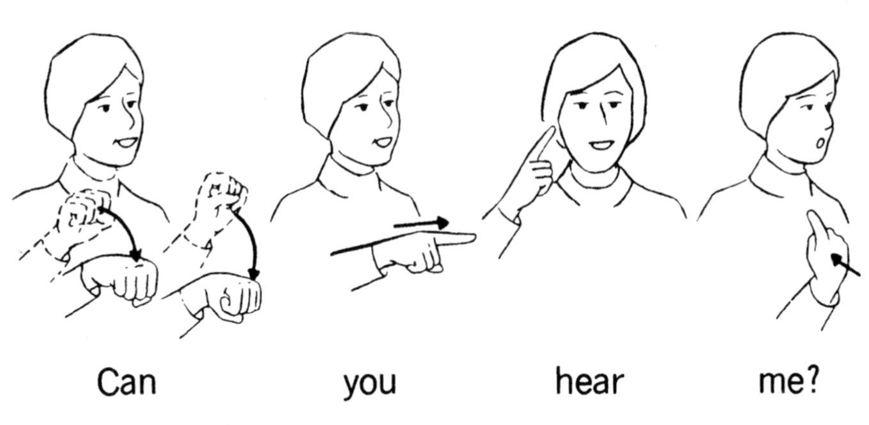

Can you hear me?

Your voice is too _____ .

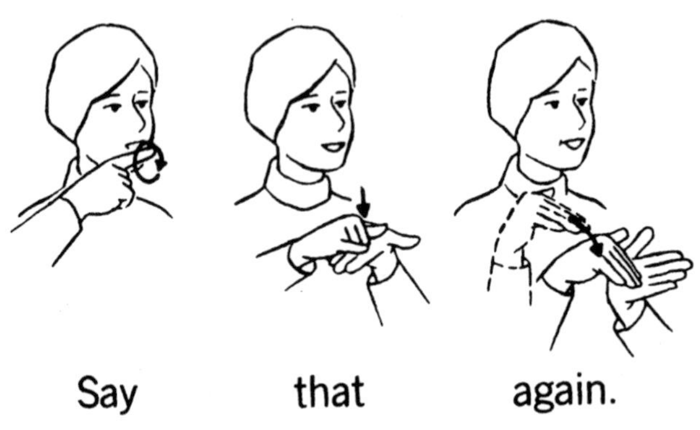

Say that again.

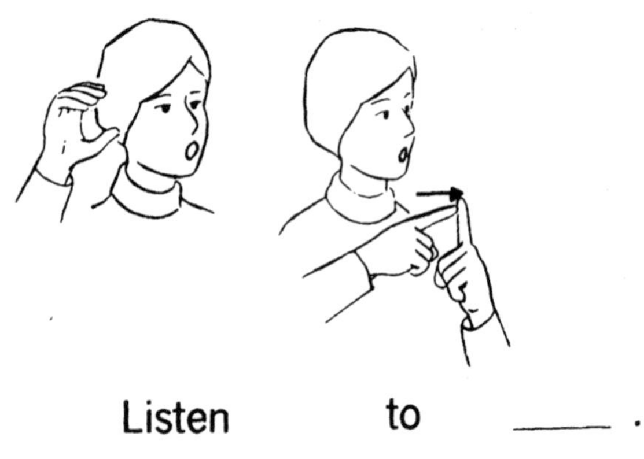

Listen to ____ .

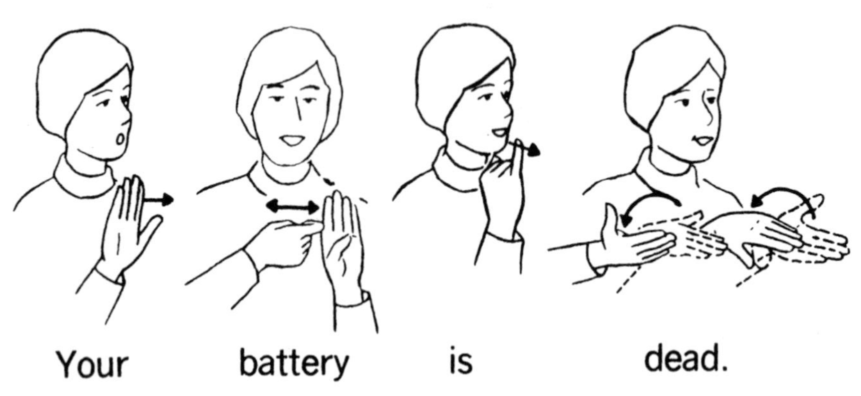

Your battery is dead.

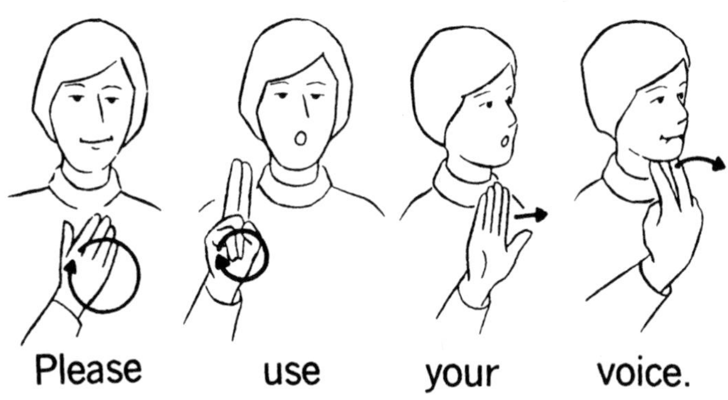

Please use your voice.

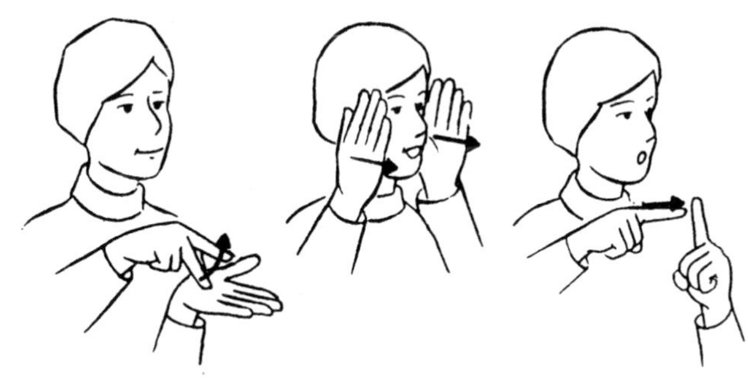

Pay attention to ____ .

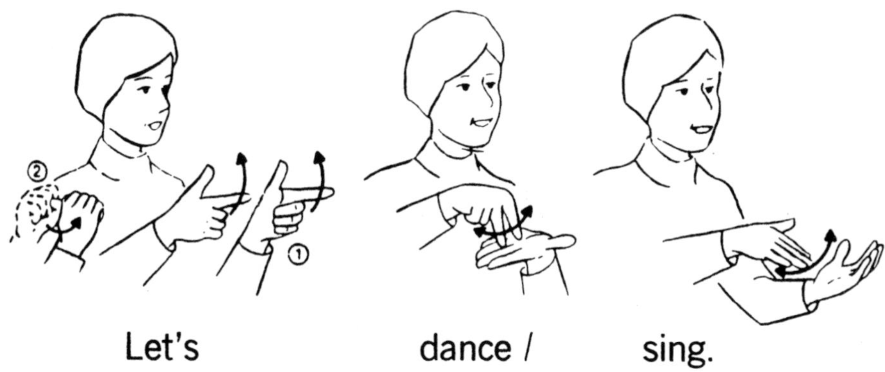


Let's dance / sing.

# 3. SCHOOL PEOPLE and PLACES

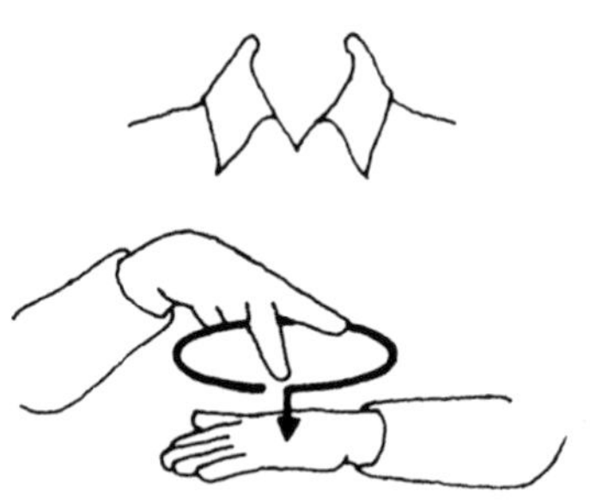

**principal**
LH open B palm down. Circle right P over back of left hand, then drop middle fingertip on back of LH.

**secretary**
LH open B palm up, tips out. K shape RH. Place middle finger on right cheek, then move down to left palm and slide forward.

**police**
Tap right C just below left shoulder (indicating badge).

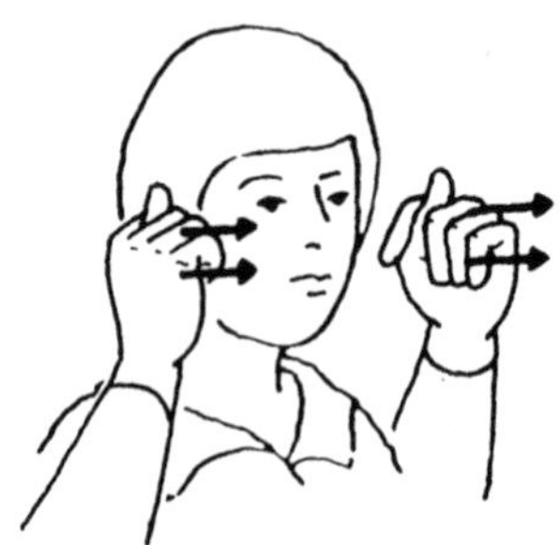

**tutor**
T shape both hands. Hold at temples and move out twice.

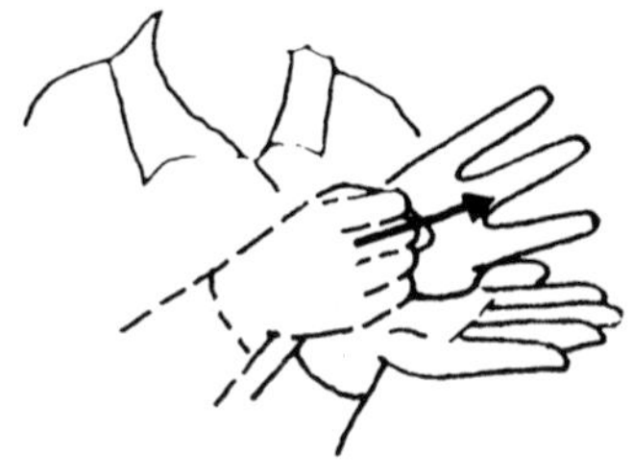

**social work**

LH open B palm up, tips out. Put little finger side of right S in left palm then change to W shape.

**coach**

One shape LH knuckles down, tips slanted right. Rub right C back and forth on left index.

**superintendent**

Place C shape hands at temples and move out into S shapes. Then circle right open B, palm down, over hand and forearm of left S, palm down.

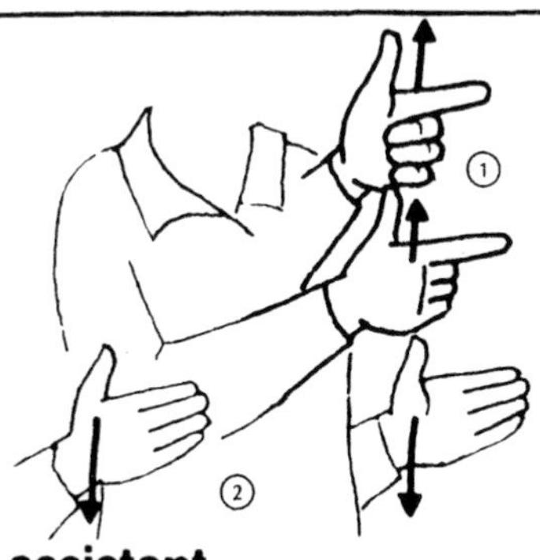


**assistant**

L shape both hands, index tips out, left palm right, right palm left. Place right L under left and push up. Follow with agent marker.

**aid**

A shape both hands, knuckles facing, right thumb extended. Place right A under left and push up.

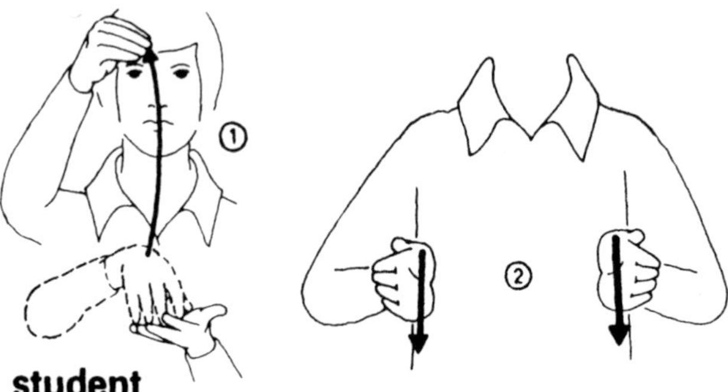


**student**
LH open B palm up, tips slanted right. Place right tips in left palm then lift up to forehead closing into flat o. Follow with agent marker.

**athlete**
A shape both hands. Push up above shoulders, as if pushing up weights. (Make sign twice for athletic).

**scout (noun)**
Place together index, middle, and fourth fingers of RH. Hold up near right shoulder, palm out.

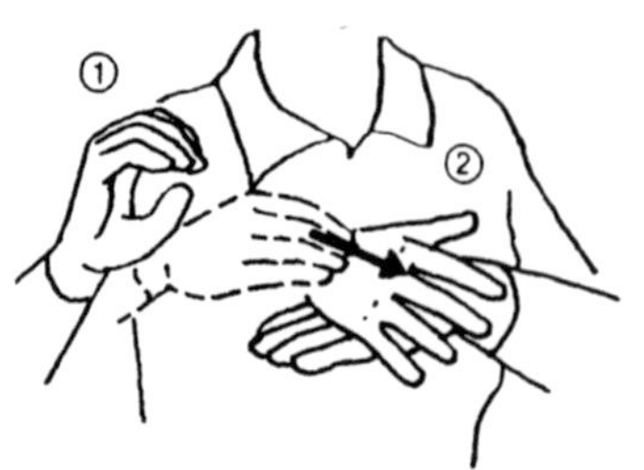


**counsel**
B shape LH palm down, tips slanted right. Place right C on back of LH then open into 5 shape.

**custodian**
Hold LH palm up, tips out. Slide right C across left palm twice. Follow with agent marker.

**advise**
Place right A on back of LH then spread out into 5 shape.

**administration**
Fingerspell A-D-M.

**coordinate**
F shape both hands, thumbs locked. Both hands move clockwise away from body.

**interpret**
F shape both hands, fingers curved, palms facing, thumb and index tips touching. Twist RH forward. Repeat motion.

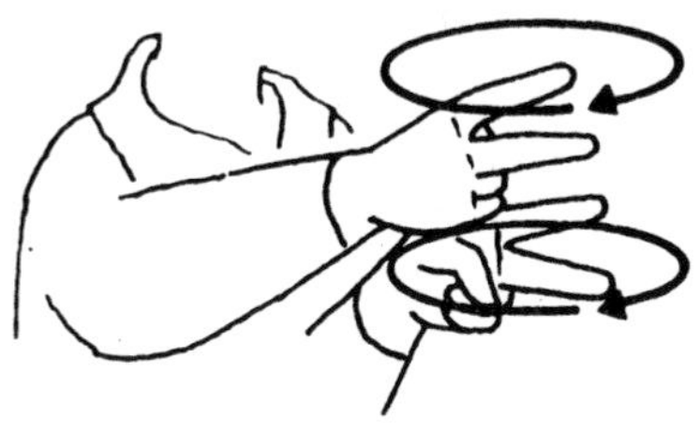

**supervise**
V shape both hands, tips out, right on top of left. Move both hands in horizontal clockwise circle.

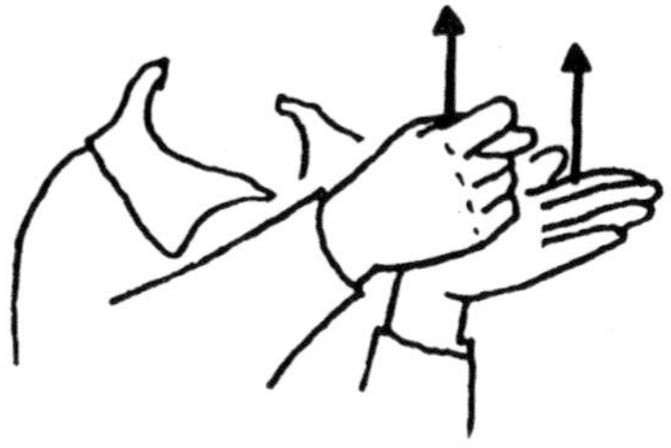

**therapy**
T shape RH little finger side down. Place on left palm and move both hands up.

**primary**
LH open B palm down, tips right. Circle right P counterclockwise under left palm.

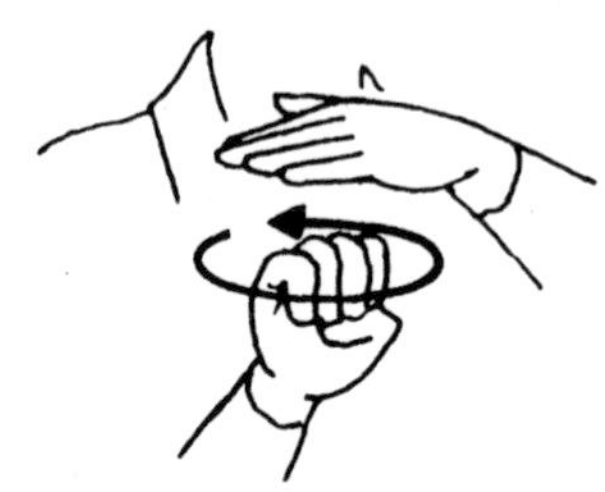

**elementary**
LH open B, palm down, tips right. Circle right E counterclockwise under left palm.

**middle**
LH open B palm up, tips out. Circle right M over LH, then drop tips in center of left palm.

**intermediate**
LH open B palm up, tips out. I shape RH little finger down. Circle right little finger over left palm then place in center of palm.

**lower**
LH open B, palm down, tips right. Circle right L counterclockwise under left palm.

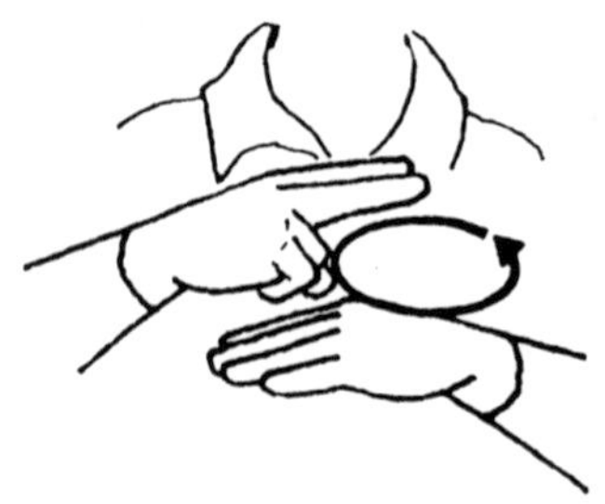

**upper**
LH open B palm down. Circle right U, palm down, over back of LH.

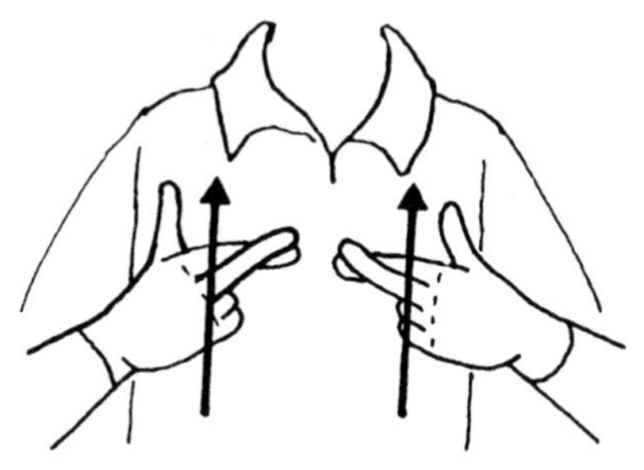

**residence**

R shape both hands, tips facing, thumbs extended. Move up body.

**dormitory**

Place middle finger and thumb of right D on right edge of mouth then move to upper cheek.

**apartment**

A shape both hands. Change into P shapes while bringing left P behind right P, outlining shape of room.

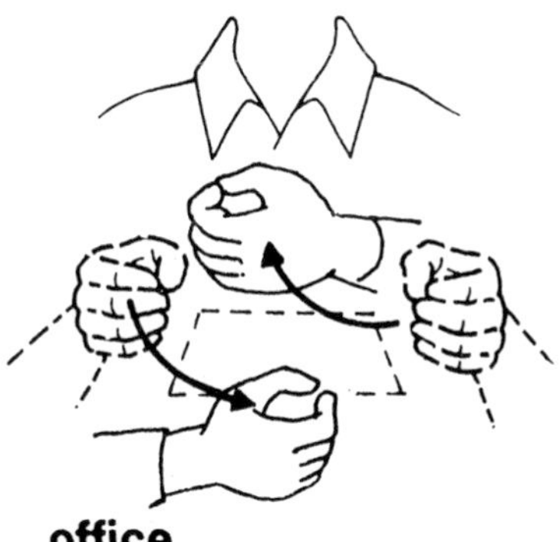

**office**

O shape both hands, tips out. Move right O left and left O right, indicating square shape.

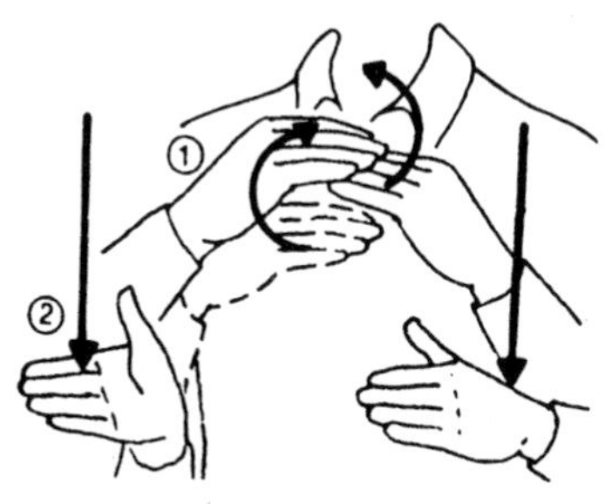


**building**

Open B both hands, palms down, tips facing. Alternately place one on top of other, moving upward. Then form sides of building, palms facing.

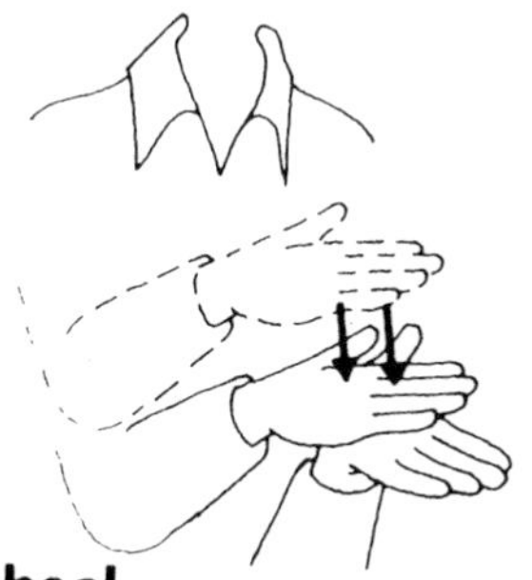

**school**

Open B both hands, left palm up, tips out; right palm down, tips left. Clap hands twice.

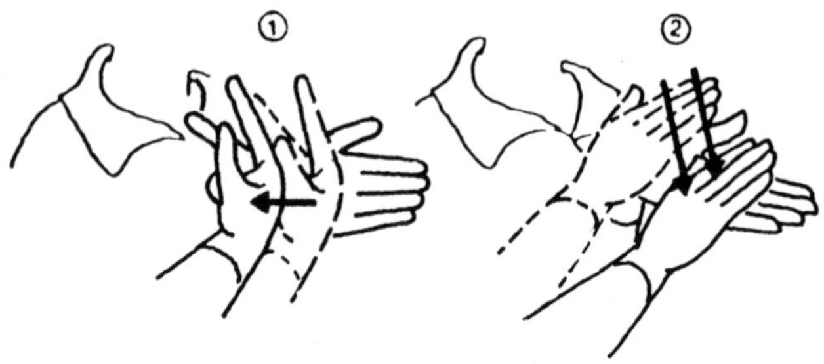


**preschool**

LH open B tips right. Place back of right P against left palm then move right P toward body. Clap right palm against left palm twice.

**auditorium**

A shape both hands, thumbs touching. Draw apart and around to front, ending in M shapes tips up. (Sometimes this word is fingerspelled A-U-D.)

**department**

D shape both hands, palms facing. Touch tips, move out in semicircles, and come together with little fingers touching.

**campus**

Circle right C clockwise over back of LH which is held palm down, tips out.

**library**

L shape RH. Circle in front of body.

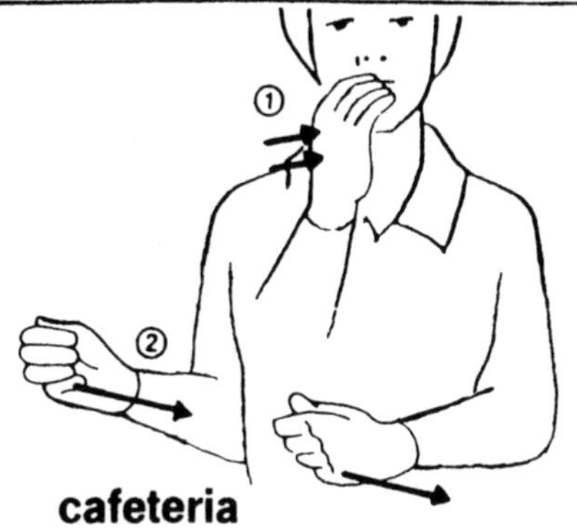

**cafeteria**

Place tips of flat O on mouth. Then form A shapes both hands, palms facing, and move from right to left.

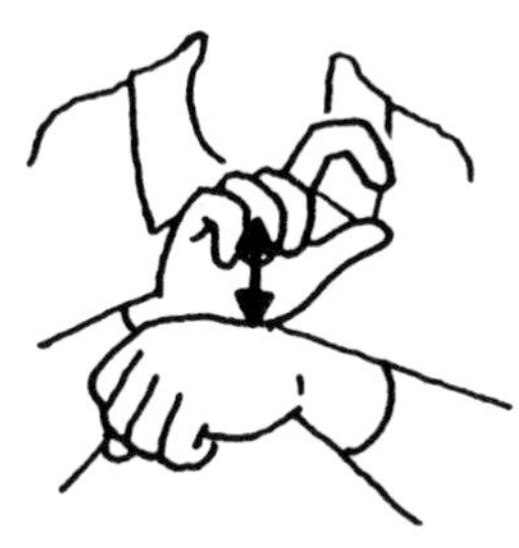

**chapel**

S shape LH knuckles down. Form C shape with index and thumb of RH and tap back of left S twice.

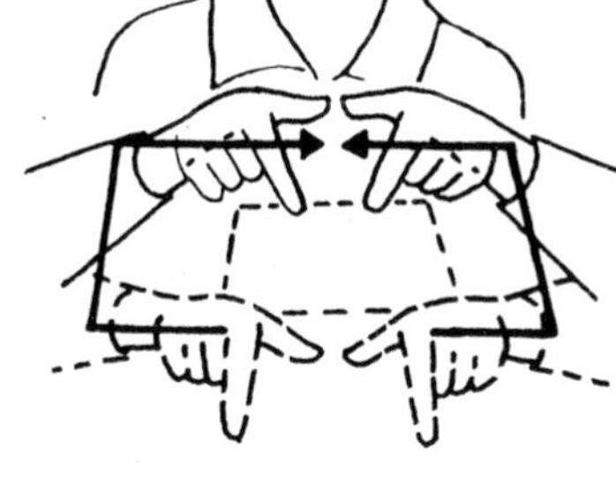

**parking lot**

Place base of 3 shape RH in left palm. Follow with -ing marker. Then form L shapes both hands, palms down, thumb tips almost touching. Move back toward signer while outlining square shape with thumbs.

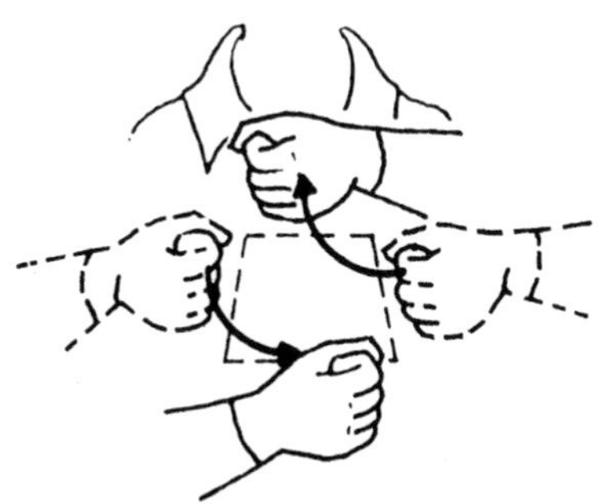

**shop (noun)**

S shape both hands, palms facing. Turn right S left and left S right to form box shape.

**store (noun)**

Flat O shape both hands, tips down. Swing out twice.

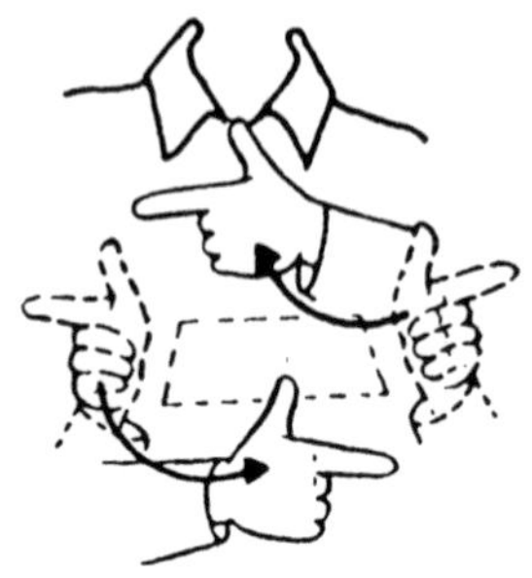

**lounge**
L shape both hands. Turn right L left and left L right to form box shape.

**lobby**
L shape RH, palm down. Move RH under LH and form large circle moving counterclockwise.

**waiting room**
Hold open hands palms up in front of body, left a little ahead of right. Wiggle fingers slightly. Follow with -ing marker. R shape both hands, tips out. Turn right R left and left R right to form box shape.

**rest room**
R shape RH palm down. Bounce to right.

**post office**
Fingerspell P-O.

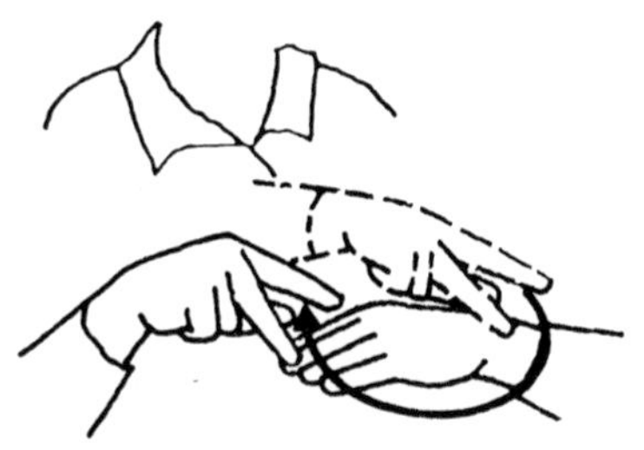

**patio**

B shape LH palm down. Place middle fingertip of right P on outer left wrist then arc out to tip of left middle finger.

**hall**

H shape both hands, tips up. Move forward and out from sides of face.

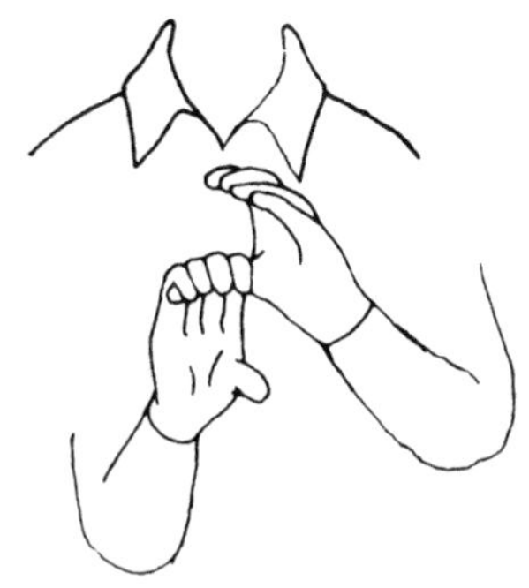

**couch**

C shape both hands, left palm out, right palm left. Hook right C over thumb of left C.

**bed**

Place right palm on right cheek and tilt head slightly.

**door**

B shape both hands, palms out slightly, tips a little up. Place index fingers together then turn RH to the right, ending with palm up. Return to starting position.

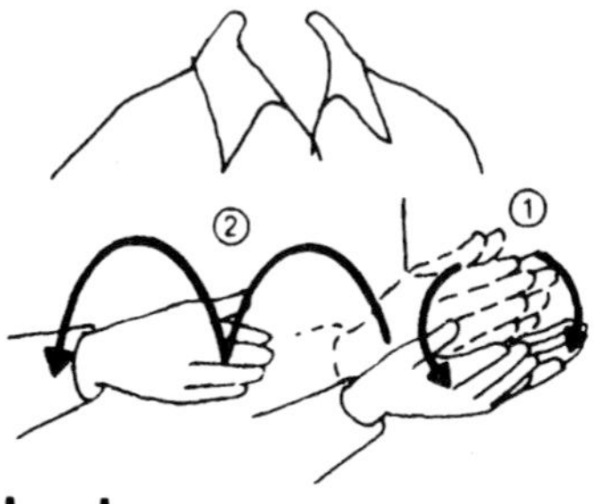


**bookcase**

Place palms together, thumbs up, and open as if opening book. Then form right open B, palm left, tips out, and move to right while dipping up and down.

**wall**
W shape both hands, palms in, held close together. Move hands apart then back, outlining shape of wall.

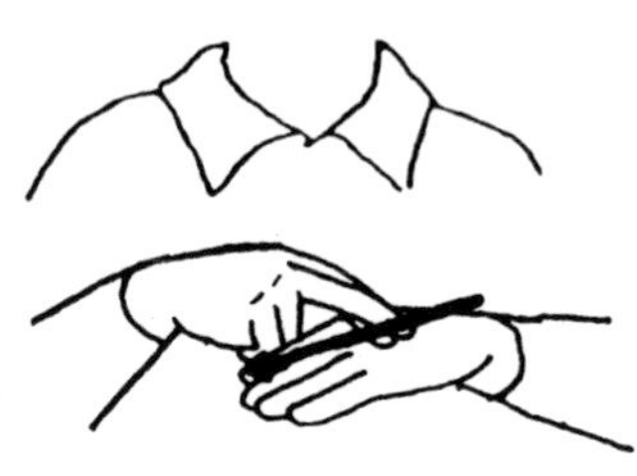

**rug**
LH open B palm down, tips out. R shape RH palm down, tips left. Place RH on left wrist and slide to fingertips.

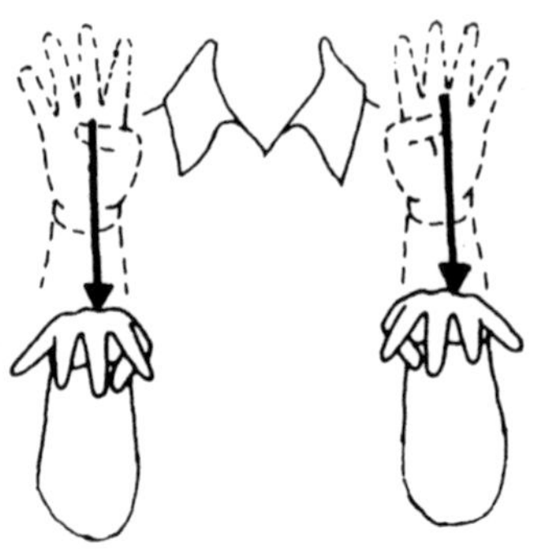

**curtain**
Four shape both hands. Drop forward and down, ending with palms down.

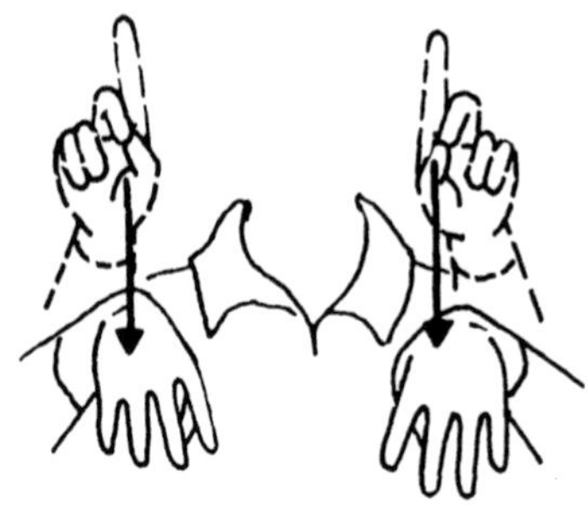

**drapes**
D shape both hands. Change to 4 shapes while dropping down.

**lamp**
RH flat O palm down. Rest right elbow in left palm. Drop right flat O into 5 shape, palm down.

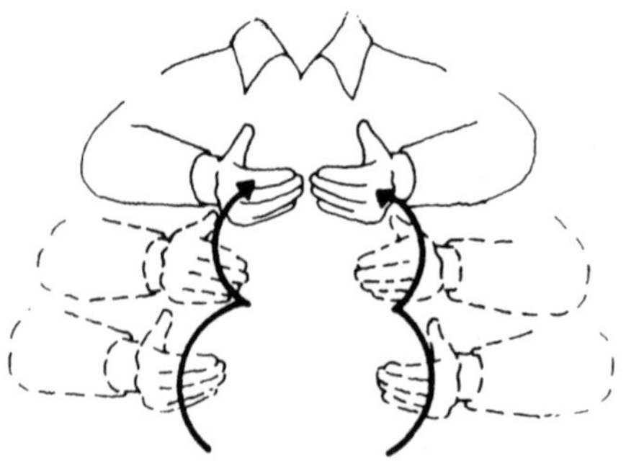

**vase**
Curved open B shape both hands, palms and tips facing. Move up, outlining shape of vase.

**kitchen**
K shape RH. Shake back and forth.

**menu**
LH open B palm right, tips up. Bounce tips of right M down left palm.

**cook**
Open B both hands, left palm up, right palm down. Place right palm on left and flip over, as if flipping pancakes.

**snack**
LH open B palm up, tips out. Place thumb and index tips of right F in left palm, then raise to mouth.

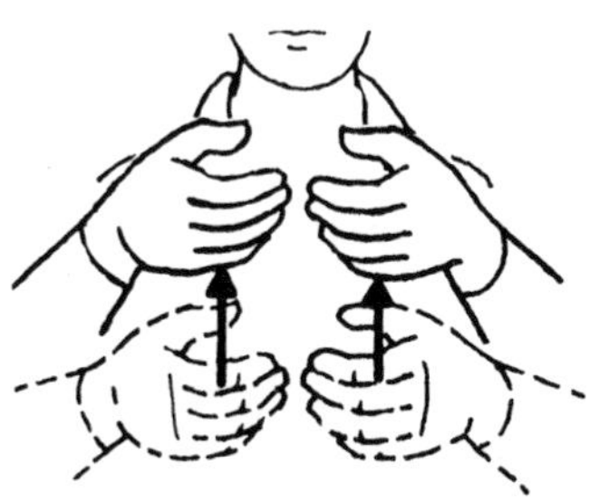

**can (noun)**
C shape both hands, palms facing. Move up, outlining shape of can.

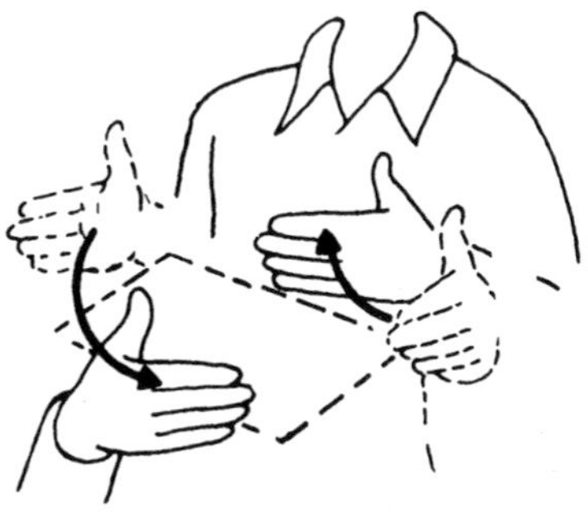

**box**
Open B both hands, palms facing, thumbs up. Turn LH right and RH left to form shape of box.

**luggage**
S shape RH knuckles down. Mime carrying suitcase.

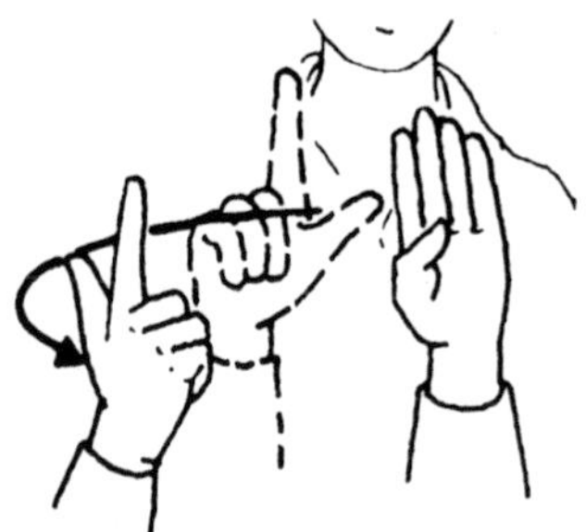

**locker**
B shape LH palm out but lowered slightly. Place thumb of right L on side of left index. Then twist to right ending with palm up.

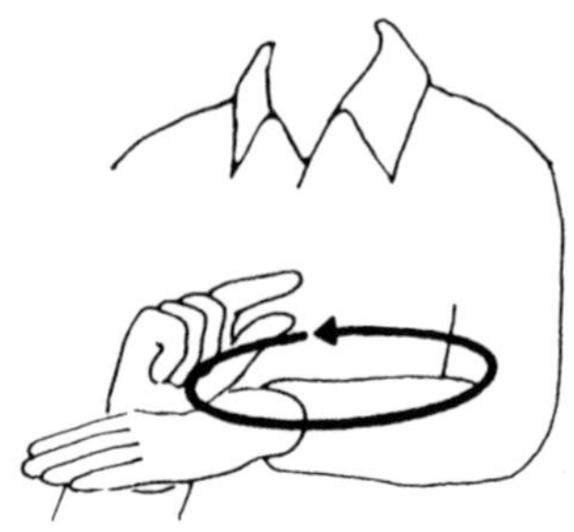

**ground**
LH open B palm down, tips right. Place base of right G on back of left wrist, then circle counterclockwise over elbow and return to original position.

**telecommunication device for the deaf (TDD)**
Fingerspell T-D-D.

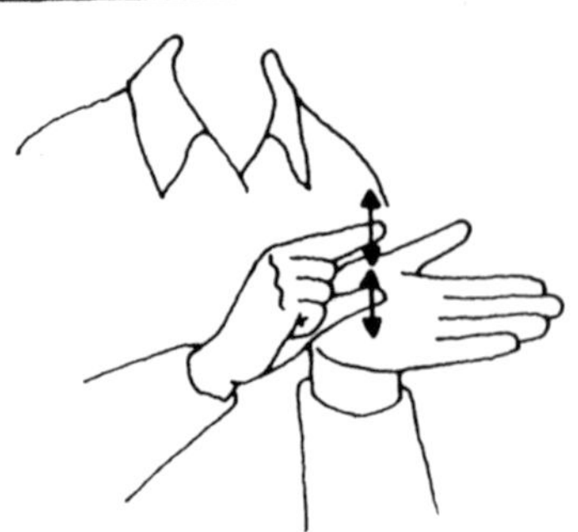

**newspaper**
LH open B palm up, tips out. Place thumb of right G in left palm then snap tips together two or three times.

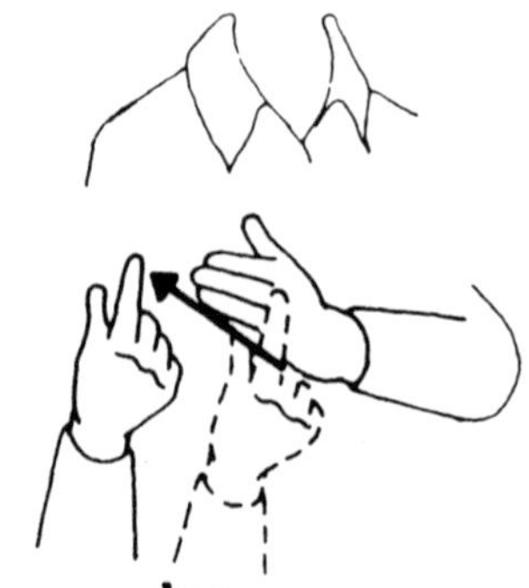

**magazine**
LH open B palm right, tips out. Grasp bottom of LH with right index and thumb and slide RH forward.

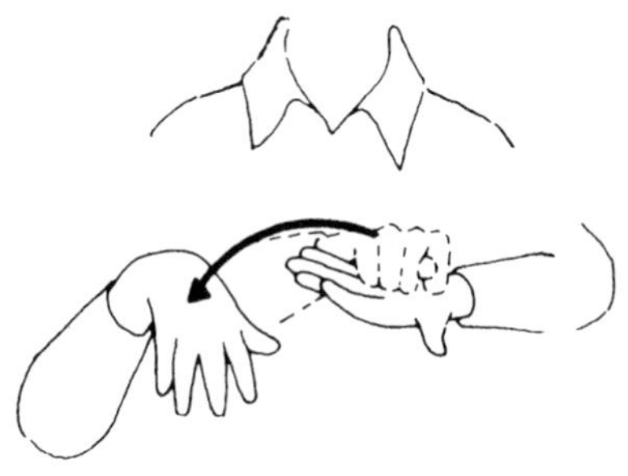

**trash**
LH open B palm up. Place palm of right T in left palm, lift out, then drop into 5 shape palm down.

**sanitation**
LH open B palm up, tips out. Rub knuckles of right S twice across left palm.

**laundry**
L shape both hands, left palm up, tips slanted right; right palm down, tips slanted left. Twist hands back and forth.

**linen**
L shape RH, palm in. Rub up and down on right upper chest.

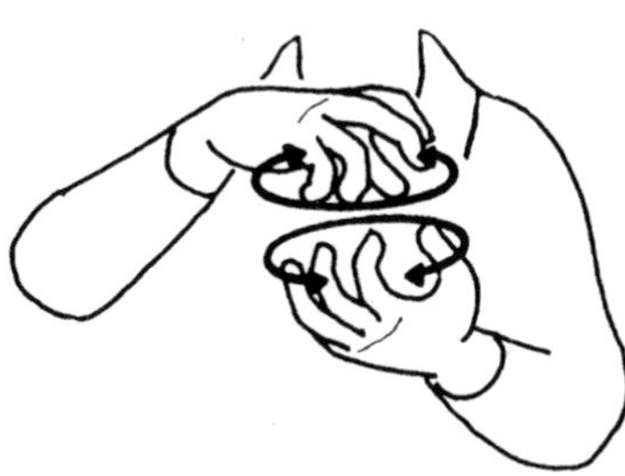

**washing machine**
Claw shape both hands, right held above left. Twist hands back and forth at wrists, indicating churning motion of machine.

**toilet**
Shake right T from left to right several times.

**work**
S shape both hands, palms down. Hit back of left S with right S. Repeat motion.

**teach**
Flat O shape both hands. Hold at temples and move out twice.

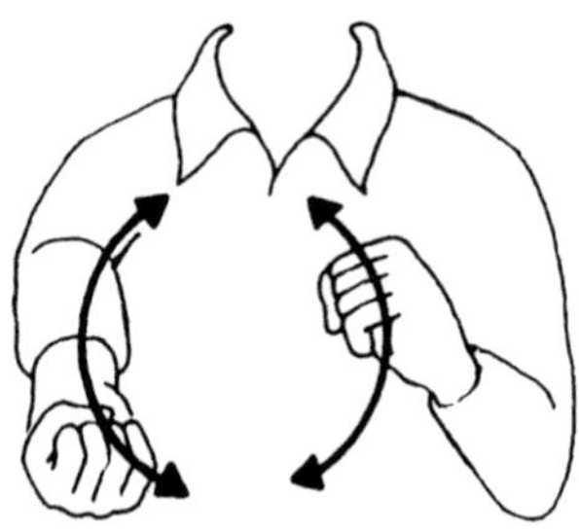

**drive**
A shape both hands. Move as if turning steering wheel of car. (Sometimes made with two D shapes.)

**fountain**
Flat O shape both hands, palms facing, tips touching. Move out and apart while wiggling fingertips.

**driveway**
Place right 3 shape in left palm then change both hands to open B shapes, palms facing, tips out. Move out in straight line. (A compound of *drive* and *way* may also be used.)

## PRACTICE SENTENCES

Repeat each of the following phrases or sentences several times. Start forming each sign at the same time you begin to speak its corresponding word.

After you can sign, and simultaneously say, each phrase or sentence comfortably, pair each incomplete phrase with every appropriate sign in this chapter.

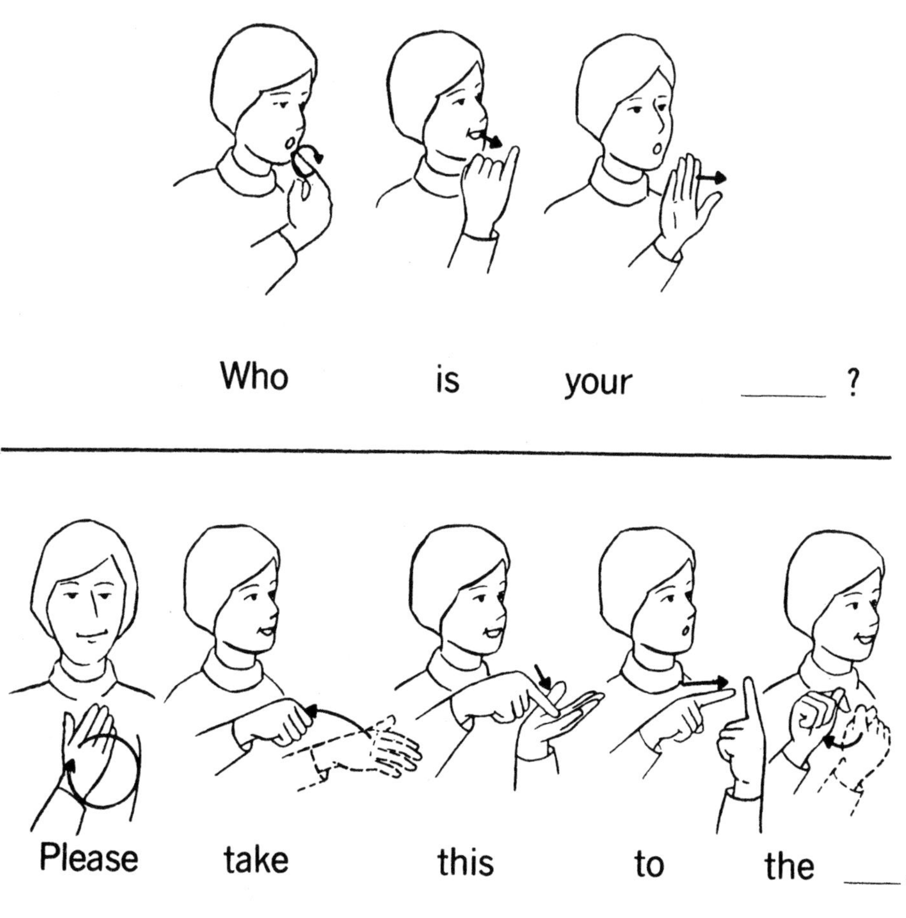

Who is your ___ ?
Please take this to the ___.

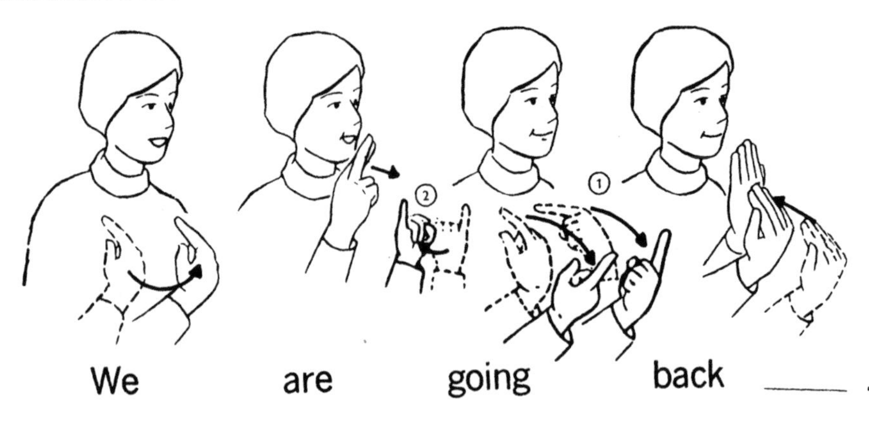

We are going back ______ .

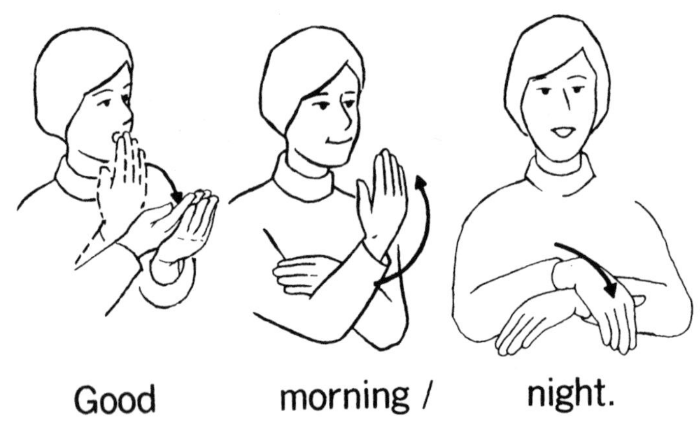

Good morning / night.

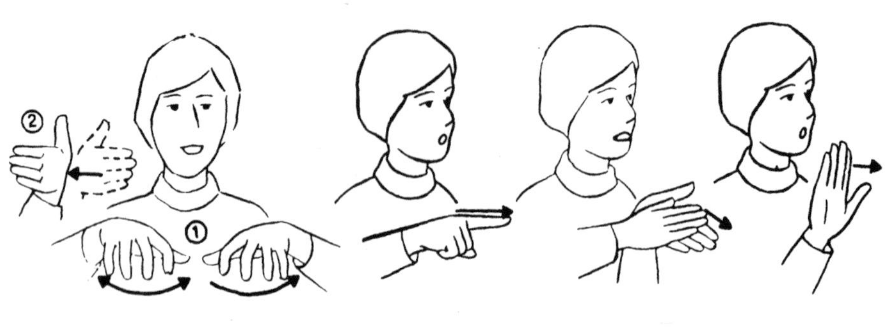

Did you clean your ______ ?

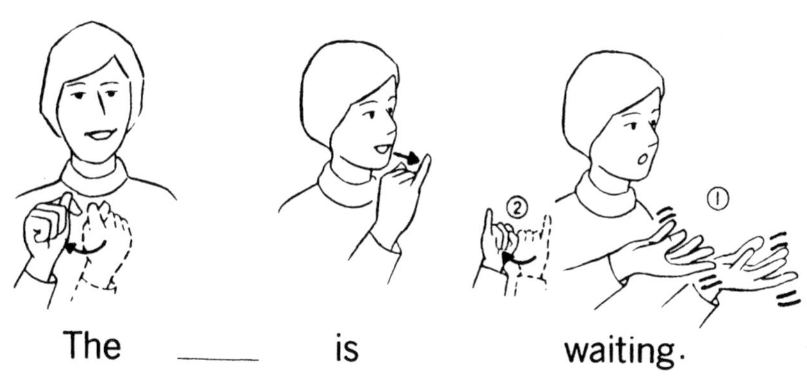

The ____ is waiting.

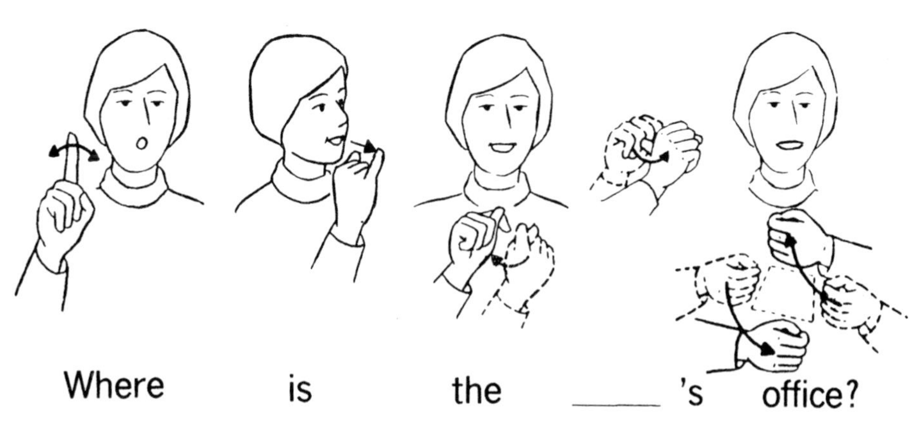

Where is the ____'s office?

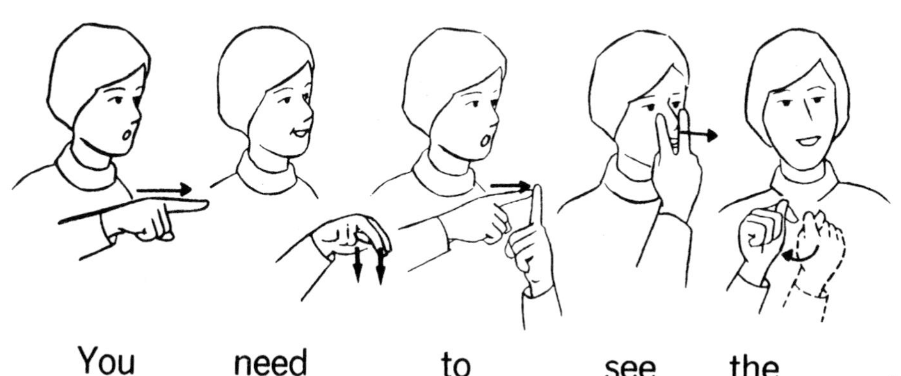

You need to see the ____.

# 4. THINKING and LEARNING

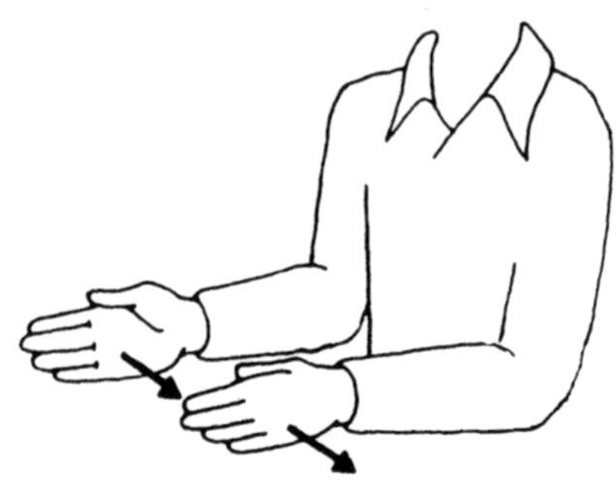

**plan**
Open B both hands, palms facing, tips out. Move to left or right.

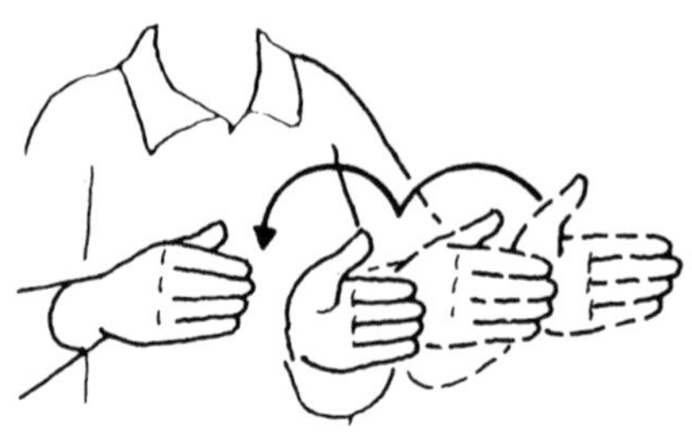

**organize**
Open B shape both hands, palms facing, tips out. Bounce from left to right keeping hands parallel.

**examine**
LH open B palm up, tips out. One shape RH palm down. Slide right index forward on left palm.

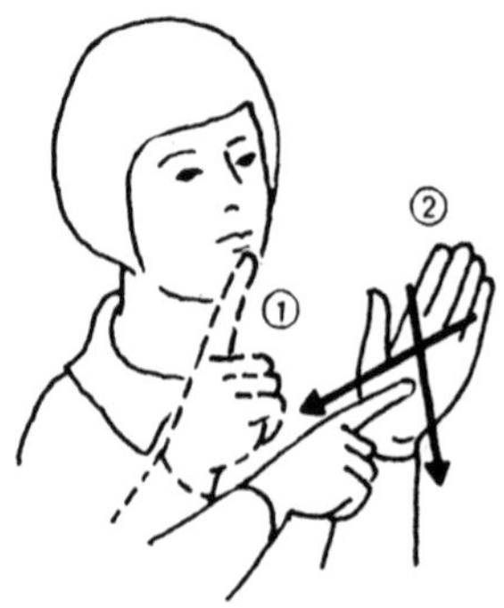


**criticize**
Touch lips with right index finger, then make a cross mark in left palm which faces right, tips up.

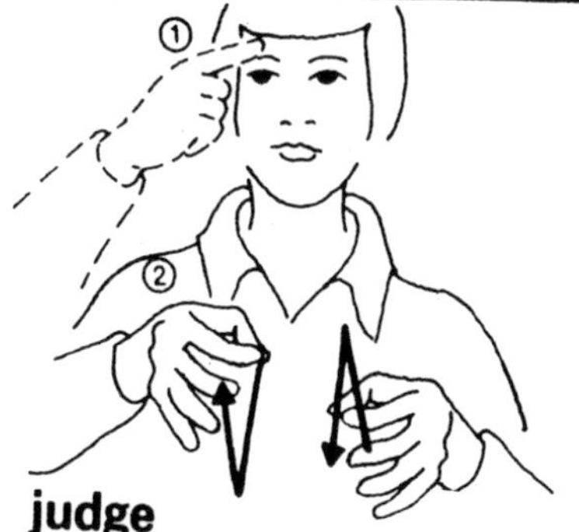


**judge**

Tap forehead with right index then form F shapes, palms facing, tips out, fingers spread. Move up and down alternately.

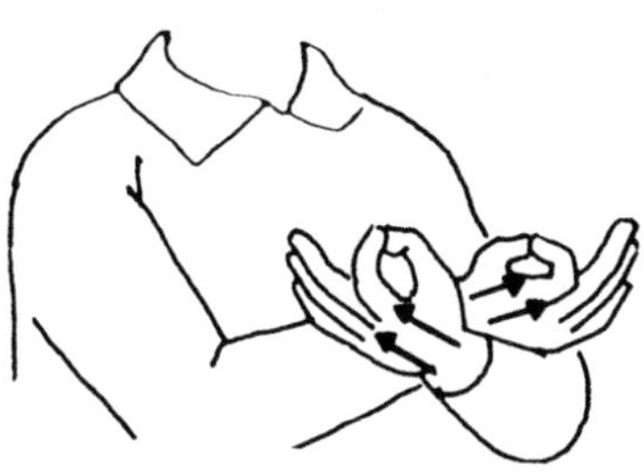

**figure out**

F shape both hands, palms up, left tips right, right tips left. Pass back of right F across left wrist. Repeat motion.

**find out**

C shape LH palm right. Place tips of right F in left C then pull out.

**look up (in a book)**

LH open B palm up, tips out. Brush tip of right thumb on left palm several times.

**guess**

Cupped RH palm left. Move in quick grasping motion across face, closing into S shape.

**investigate**

X shape both hands, palms out, right behind left. Nod hands while crooking index fingers.

**recognize**
Place tips of right R at right eye then place in upturned left palm.

**reason**
Circle right R, palm in, clockwise at middle of forehead.

**memorize**
Place tips of claw shape RH on forehead then move out into S shape keeping palm in.

**remember**
Place thumb of right A on forehead, then drop down and touch thumb of A shape LH palm right.

**opinion**
O shape RH palm and tips left. Place at right side of forehead and nod to left twice.

**idea**
I shape RH palm in. Place little fingertip on right temple then move out.

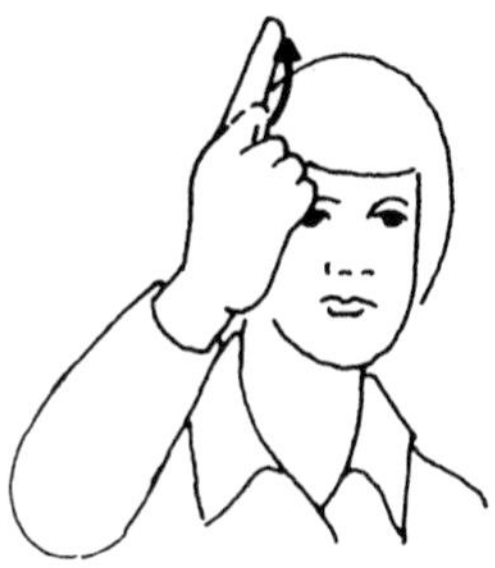

**understand**
S shape RH palm in. Place on or near right temple then snap index finger up.

**misunderstand**
V shape RH palm left. Place index tip on forehead. Twist inward, ending with middle fingertip on forehead.

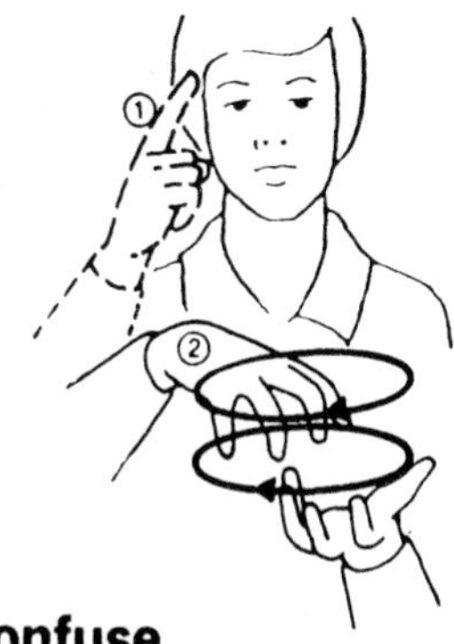


**confuse**
Place right index on temple. Alternately circle claw shape hands, right over left, in a clockwise motion.

**pretend**
P shape RH palm out. Place index finger of right P on right side of forehead then circle forward.

**believe**
Place right index on forehead then clasp both hands together.

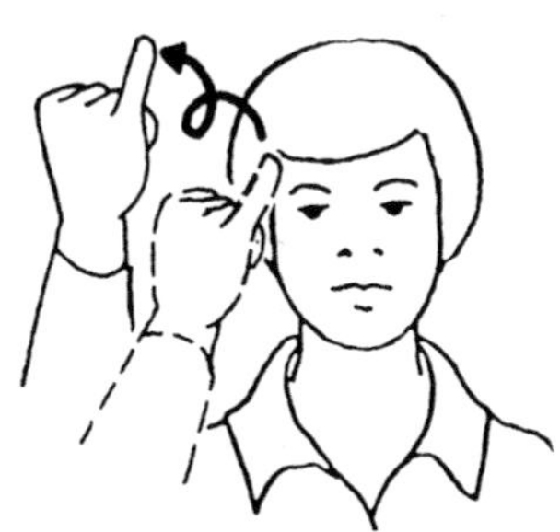

**imagine**
Place tip of right I on forehead. Circle it upward and away from the head.

**suppose**
Tap right temple gently with right little finger.

**concentrate**
C shape both hands, palms facing, held at temples. Move forward parallel to one another.

**try**
T shape both hands, palms facing. Move forward while arcing downward.

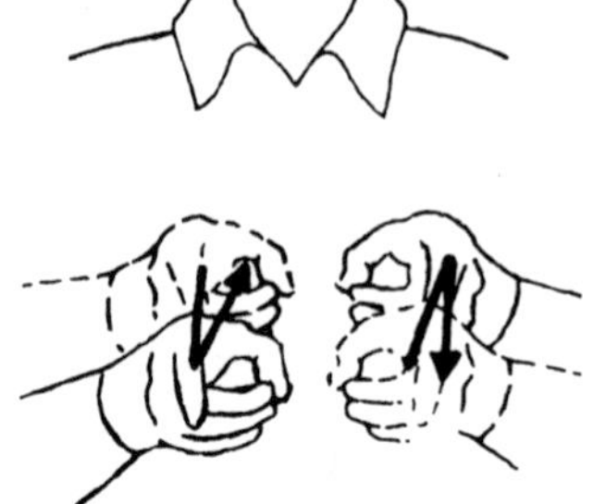

**describe**
D shape both hands, palms facing. Move back and forth alternately.

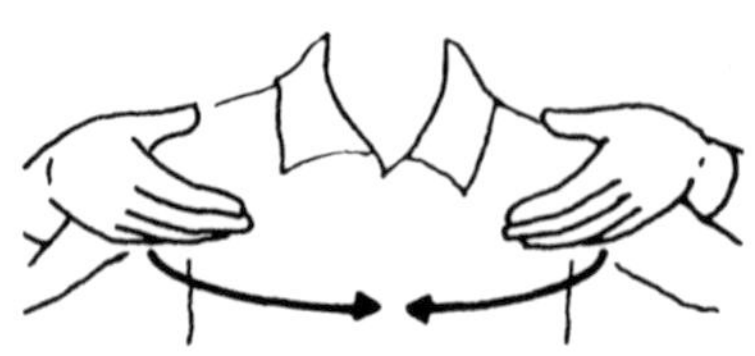

**introduce**
Cupped open B shape both hands, palms in. Hold out at sides of body then move in toward each other.

**discuss**
Tap right index finger several times on upturned palm of LH.

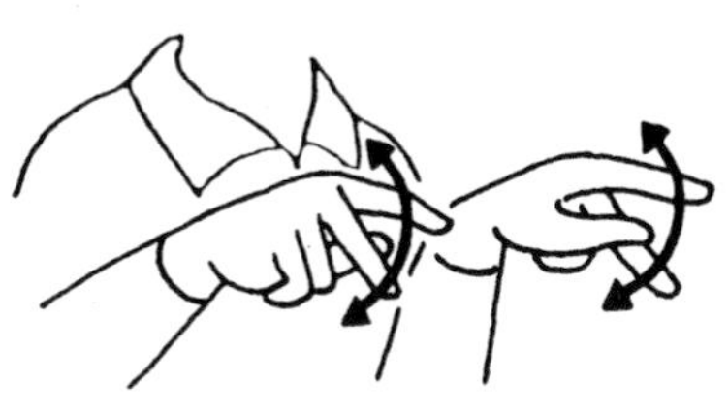

**probable**
P shape both hands, palms down. Shake up and down at wrists.

**false**
One shape RH palm left. Brush across lips, ending with index tip pointing left.

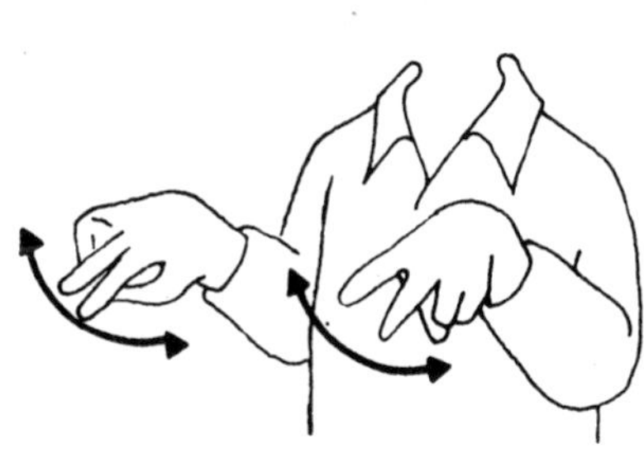

**observe**
V shape both hands, palms down, tips out. Swing back and forth from left to right.

**notice**
Place tip of right index at right eye then move down into palm of LH open B.

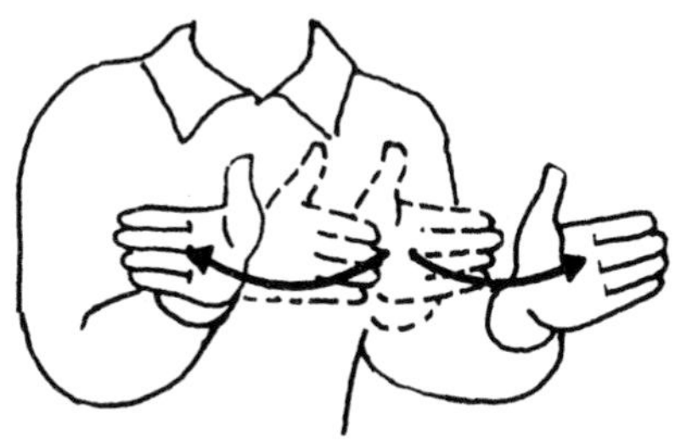

**general**
Open B both hands held parallel to one another. Move forward and spread apart.

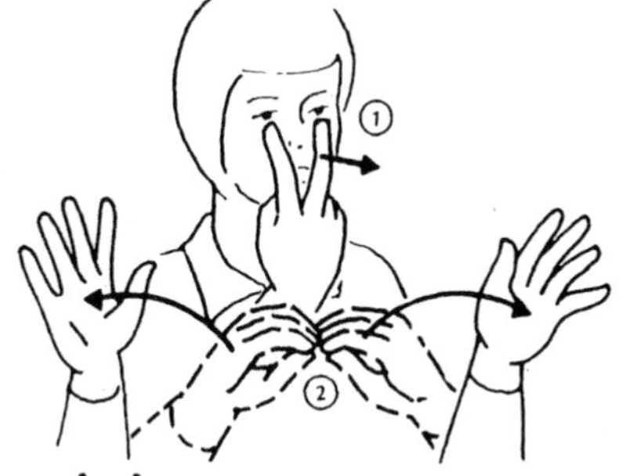


**obvious**
Place tips of right V at eyes and move forward. Then touch together tips of flat O shapes and spread apart, ending in 5 shapes palms out.

**cooperate**
Hook right index and thumb into left index and thumb then circle counterclockwise.

**practice**
One shape LH palm down, tip out. Brush knuckles of right A back and forth on left index.

**order**
Place tip of right index on lips, then turn it outward and down in forceful manner.

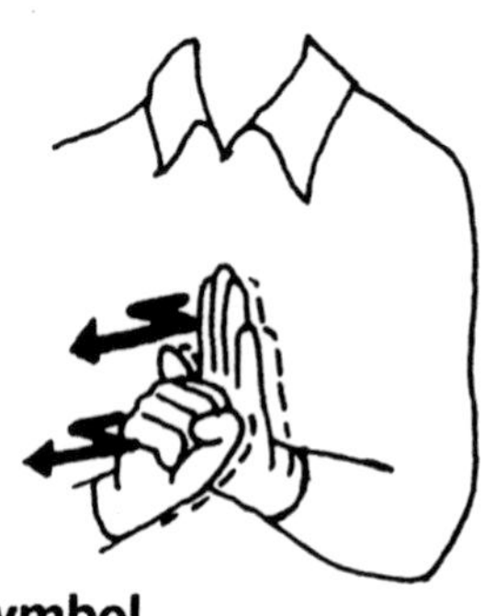

**symbol**
Open B shape LH, palm out. Place thumb side of S shape in left palm and shake both hands slightly forward.

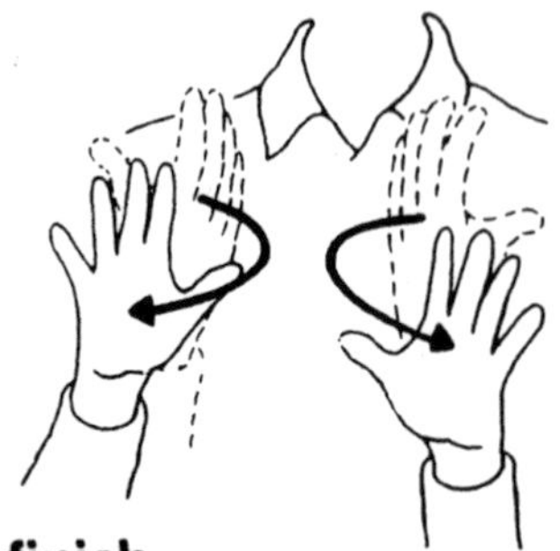

**finish**
Five shape both hands, palms in. Turn suddenly so that palms and tips face out.

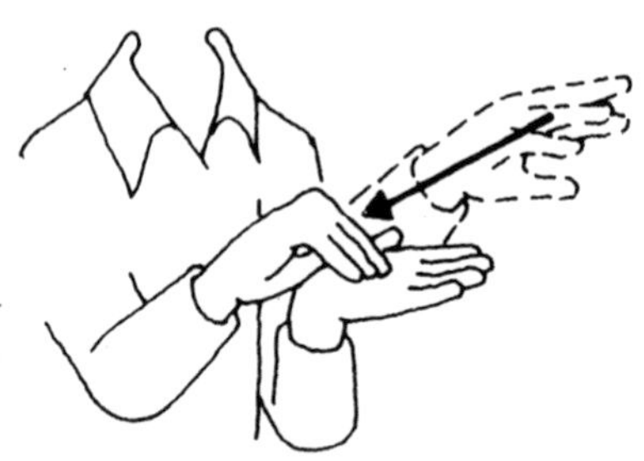

**copy**
LH open B palm up, tips out. Hold right hand palm down, fingers spread, above and slightly ahead of LH. Draw RH back into flat O shape and place in left palm.

**educate**

E shape both hands, palms facing, held at temples. Move forward twice.

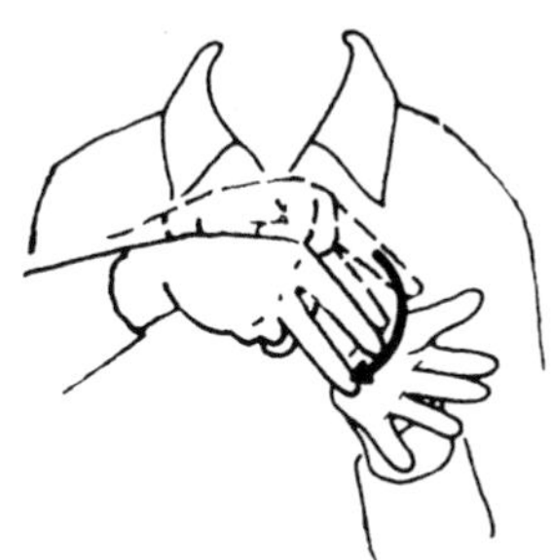

**mean (verb)**

LH open B palm right, tips out. V shape RH palm down. Place tips of V on left palm then reverse, ending with right palm up.

**however**

One shape both hands. Cross index tips and pull apart twice with short, small movements.

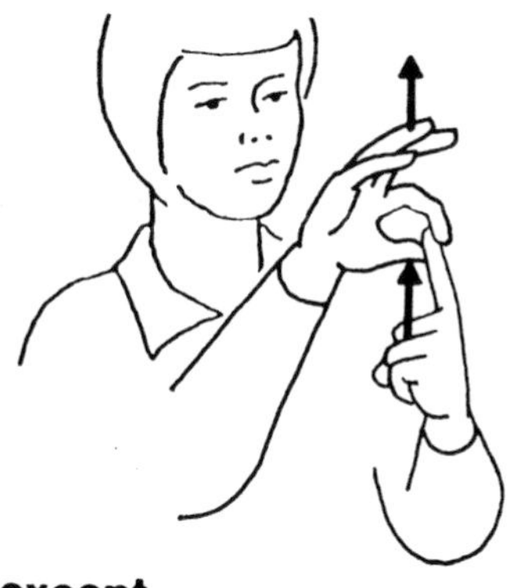

**except**

Grasp left index finger with right thumb and index finger and pull up.

**excellent**

F shape both hands, left palm in, right palm out. Jerk both hands forward slightly.

**curious**

F shape RH palm in. Place thumb and forefinger on the throat and wiggle.

**read**
LH open B palm right, tips up. Move tips of right V down left palm in back and forth motion.

**write**
Mime writing in upturned left palm with thumb and index finger of RH (other fingers closed).

**lesson**
Open B both hands, RH fingers bent. Place little finger side of RH on fingertips, then heel, of left palm.

**test**
X shape both hands, palms out. Crook and uncrook index fingers several times while moving hands downward.

**question**
Outline question mark in air with right index finger.

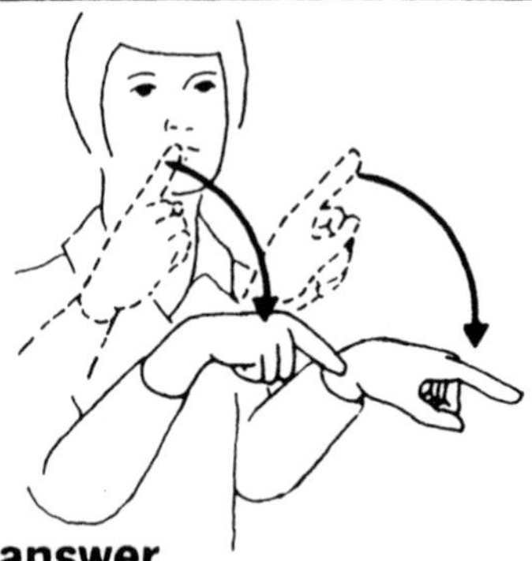

**answer**
One shape both hands, right index on mouth, left index a little in front of face. Move both forward ending with palms down.

# PRACTICE SENTENCES

Repeat each of the following phrases or sentences several times. Start forming each sign at the same time you begin to speak its corresponding word.

After you can sign, and simultaneously say, each phrase or sentence comfortably, pair each incomplete phrase with every appropriate sign in this chapter.

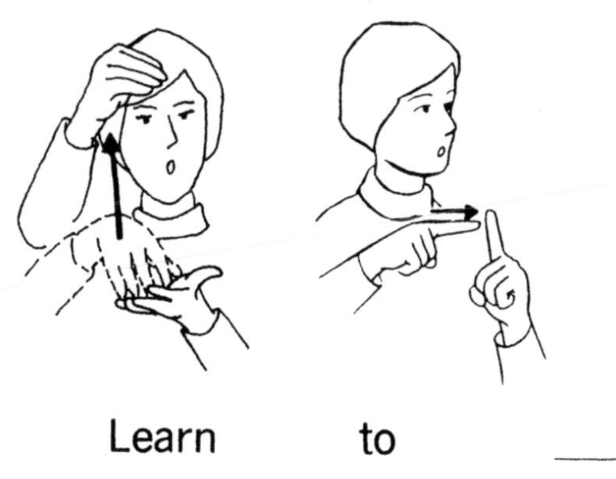

Learn to ____ .

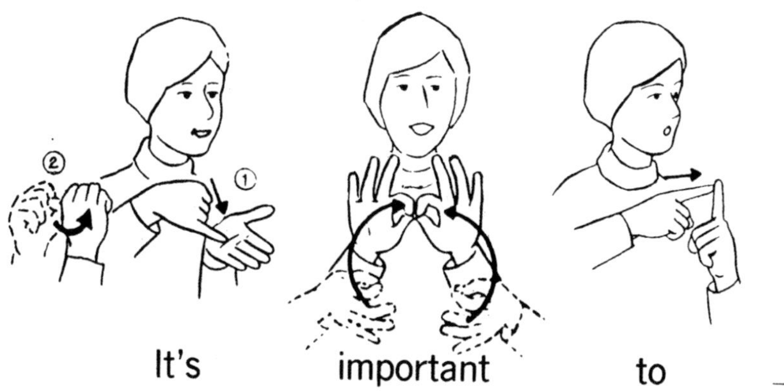

It's important to ____ .

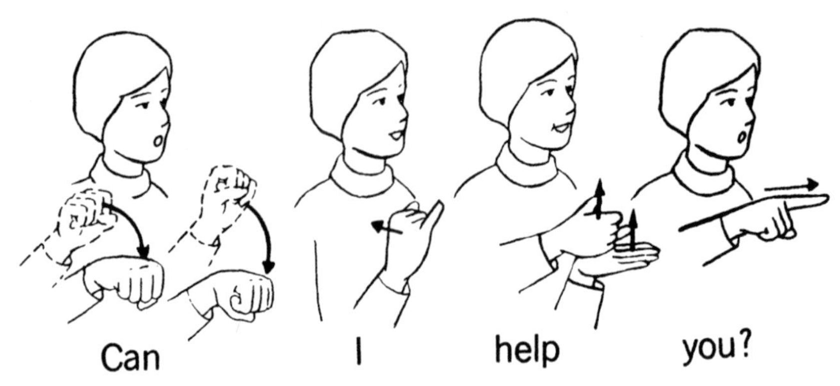

Can I help you?

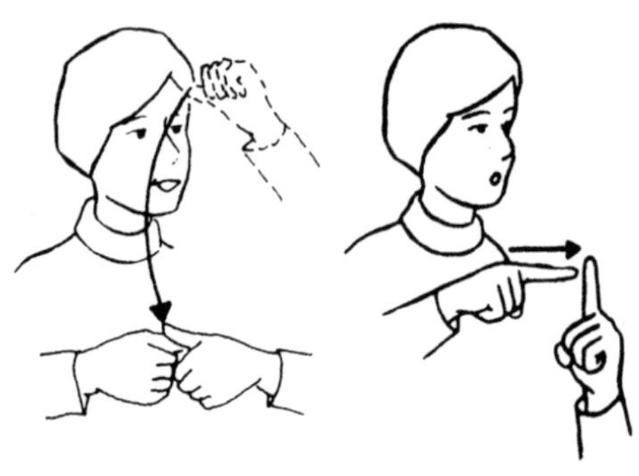

Remember to ______ .

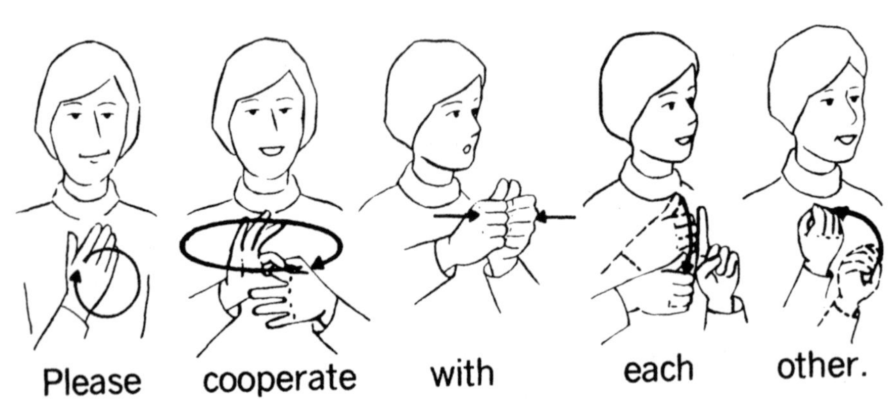

Please cooperate with each other.

# 5.
# MATHEMATICS

**mathematics (math)**
M shape both hands, palms in. Brush little finger side of right M on index finger of left M while moving hands in opposite directions. Repeat motion.

**percent**
O shape RH palm out. Move to right, then down, outlining percent sign.

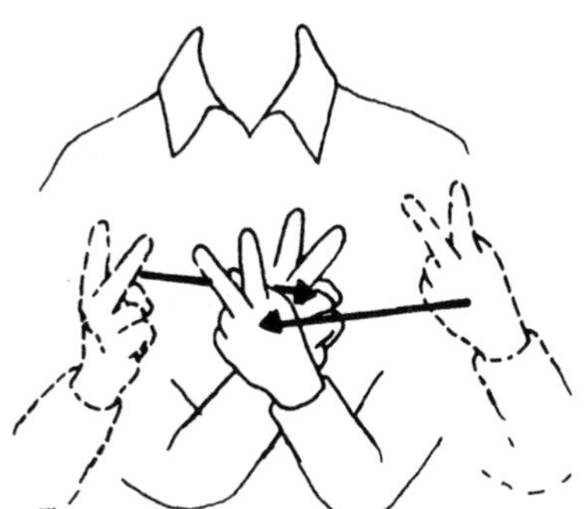

**arithmetic**
V shape both hands, palms in, tips up. Cross one another twice.

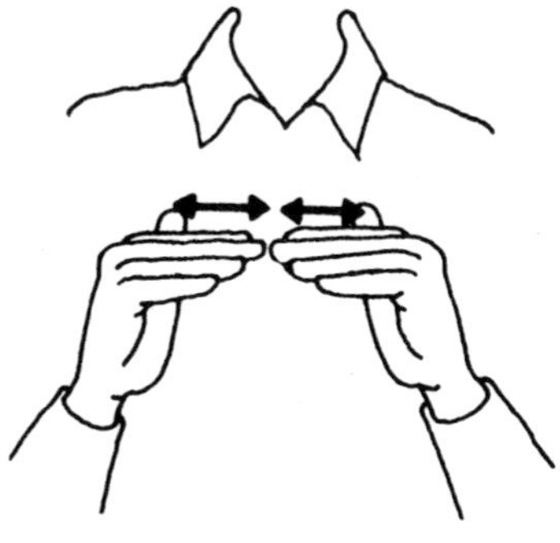

**equal**
Bent open B shape both hands, palms down. Tap tips together.

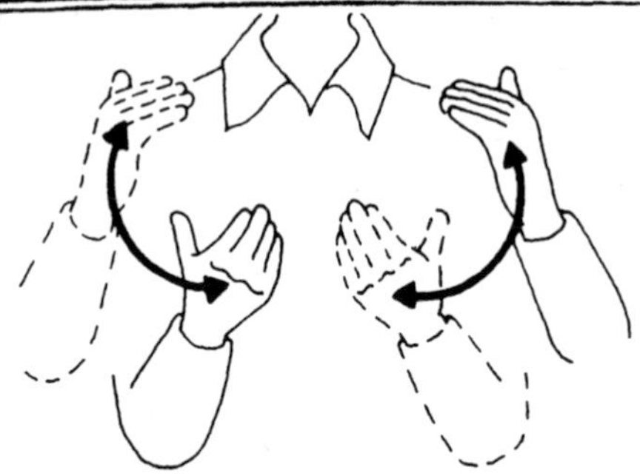

**compare**
Curved open B both hands, tips out, left palm up, right palm down. Turn each over, reversing positions. Repeat motion.

**diagonal**
Form D shape with RH. Move diagonally from upper RH corner to lower LH corner.

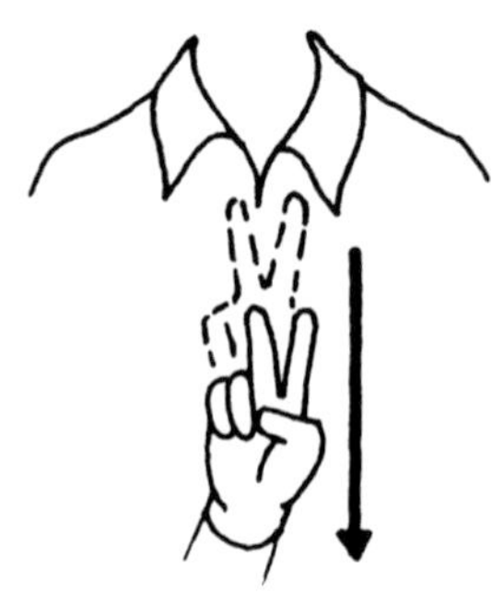

**vertical**
V shape RH, palm out. Move straight down.

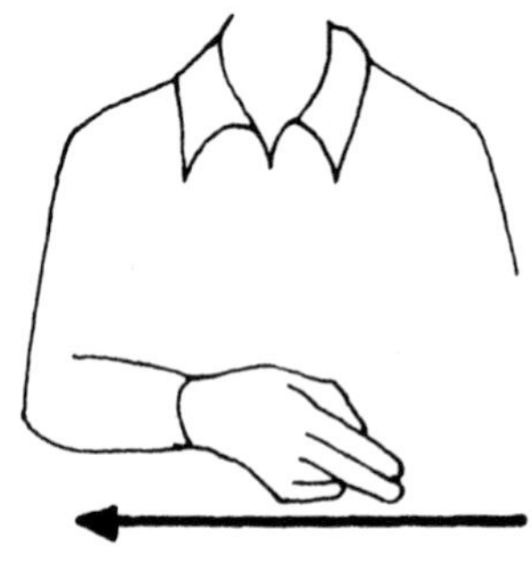

**horizontal**
H shape RH, palm facing left. Move to the right.

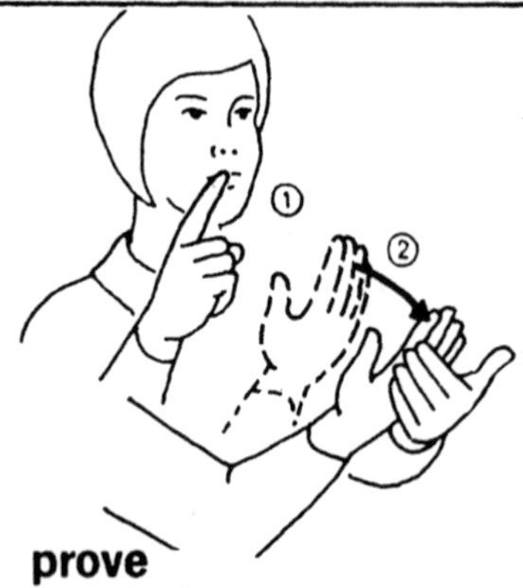


**prove**
Place tip of right index at lips. Then slap back of right open B into palm of left open B.

**example**
LH open B palm slanted out. Place thumb side of right E against left palm and push both hands out.

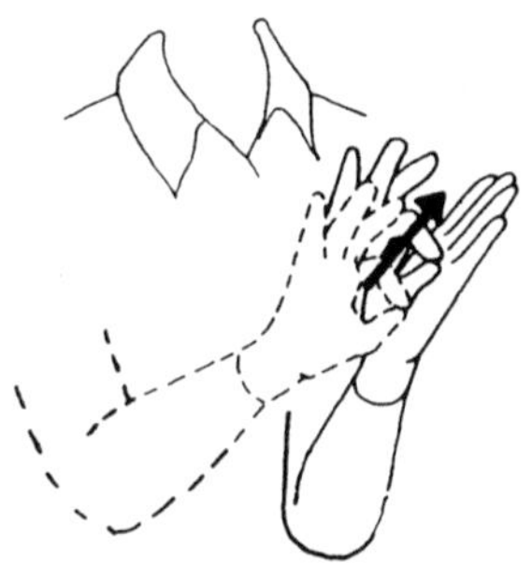

## count

LH open B palm right, tips up. Run thumb and index finger of right 9 shape up left palm.

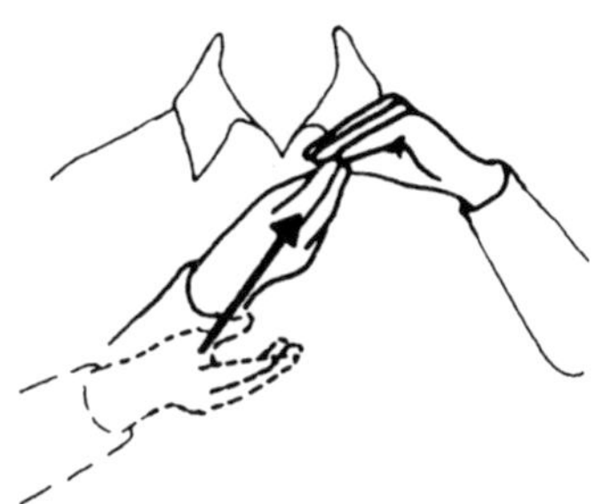

## add

Hold left flat O, tips down, over right open palm. Close RH into flat O and bring up to left tips.

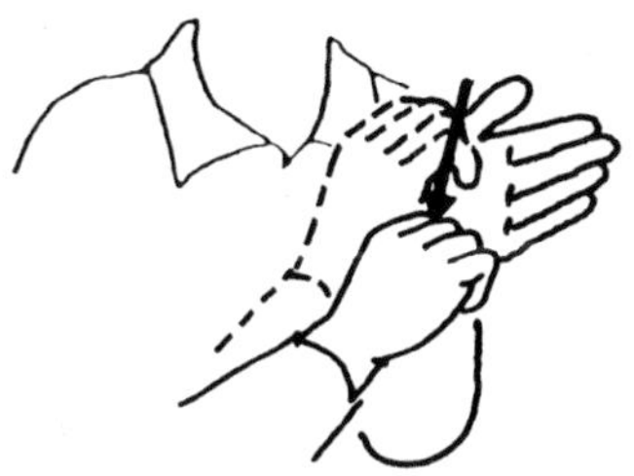

## subtract

LH open B palm right, tips out. Scratch fingertips of right C downward on left palm, ending in A shape RH.

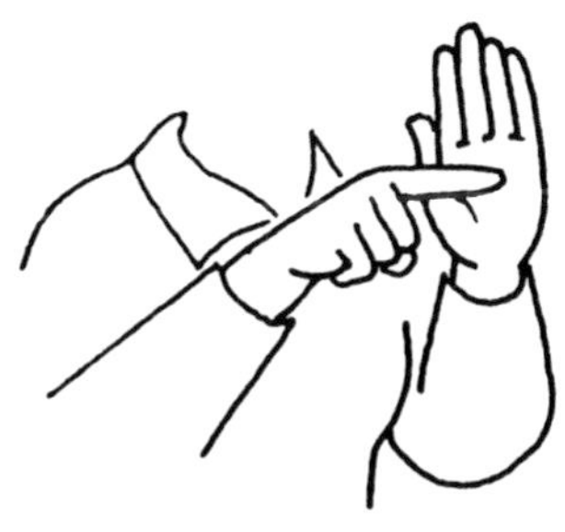

## minus

LH open B palm out. Place side of right index horizontally across left palm.

## multiply

V shape both hands, palms in. Brush little finger side of right V on index finger side of left V while moving hands in opposite directions. Repeat motion.

## divide

Open B both hands, palms and tips slanted toward one another. Place little finger side of RH on left index. Swing hands apart, ending with palms down.

**correct (adj.)**
One shape both hands, tips out, left palm right, right palm left. Place right 1 on top of left. Repeat.

**right (correct)**
One shape both hands, tips out. Strike base of left index with little finger side of RH.

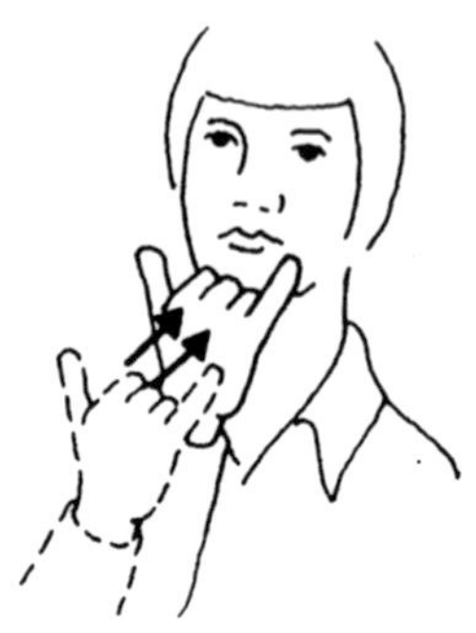

**mistake**
Tap chin with knuckles of right Y twice.

**wrong**
Strike chin with knuckles of Y shape RH.

**error**
Y shape both hands, palms in. Hit chin alternately with each hand.

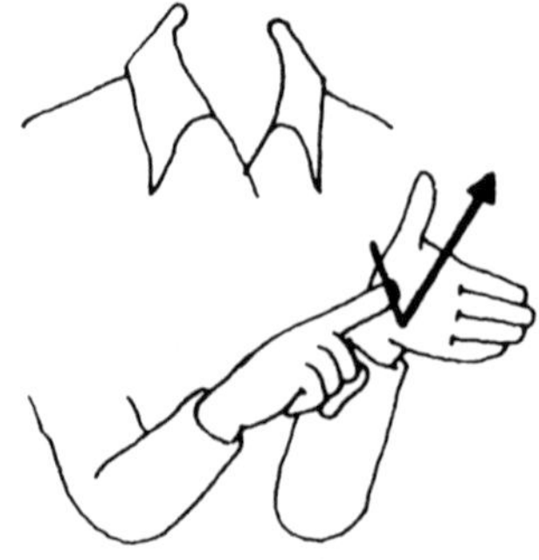

**check**
LH open B palm up, tips out. Outline check mark in left palm with right index.

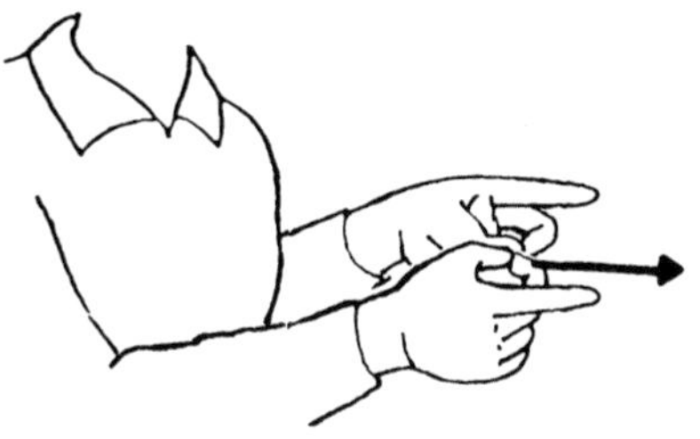

## direction

D shape both hands, palms facing, index tips out, thumbs and middle fingers touching. Move right D forward.

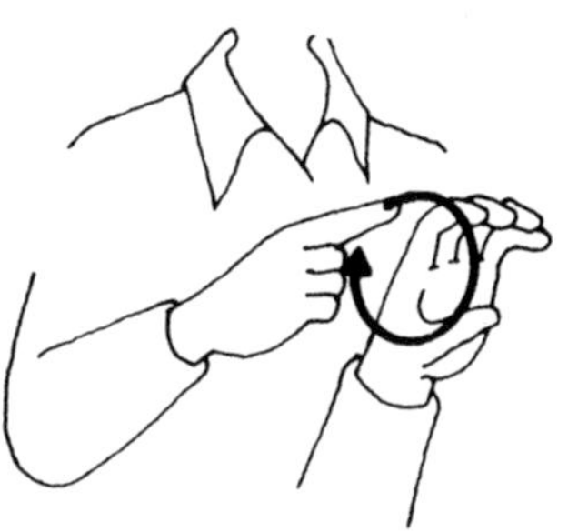

## circle

C shape LH. Circle thumb side with right index finger clockwise. (Sometimes made without left C.)

## frequent

LH open B palm up, tips out. Bounce tips of right F forward on left palm.

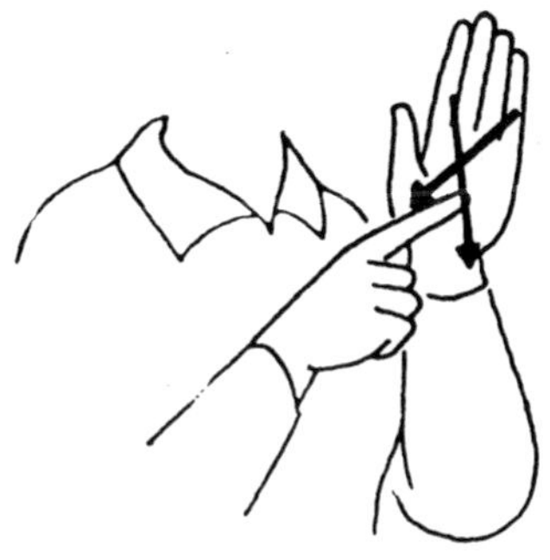

## cancel

Make cross mark in palm of left open B with tip of right index finger.

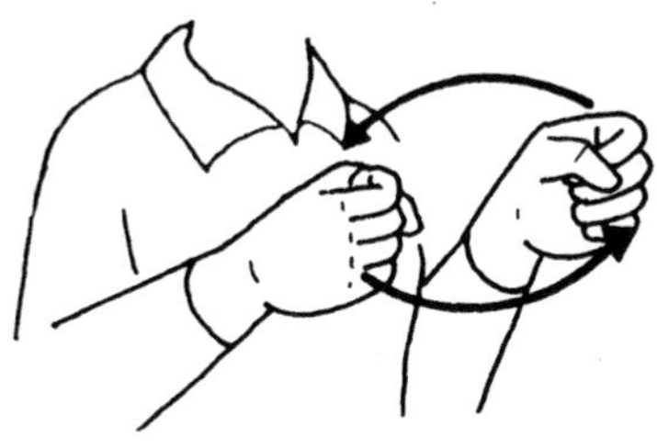

## substitute

S shape both hands, right behind left. Simultaneously arc right S under left and left S over right.

## complete

B shape LH palm right, tips out. Slide right C off left index finger and drop down.

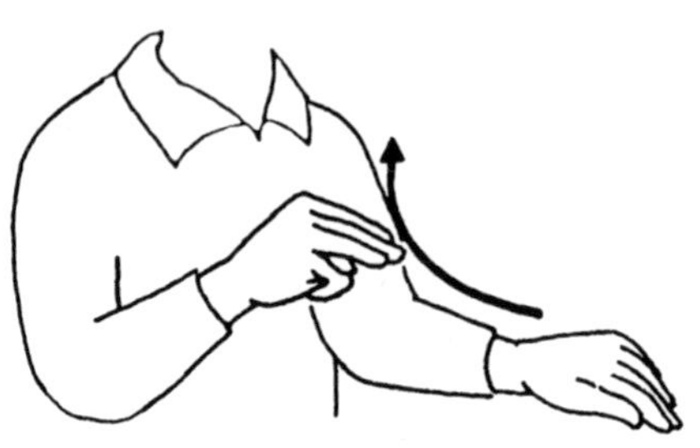

**mile**
LH open B palm down, arm extended. Place tips of right M on left wrist then move up arm.

**yard (measurement)**
Slide knuckles of right Y up left arm.

**foot**
LH open B palm down, tips slanted right. Brush thumb and index tips of right F down inside of left wrist.

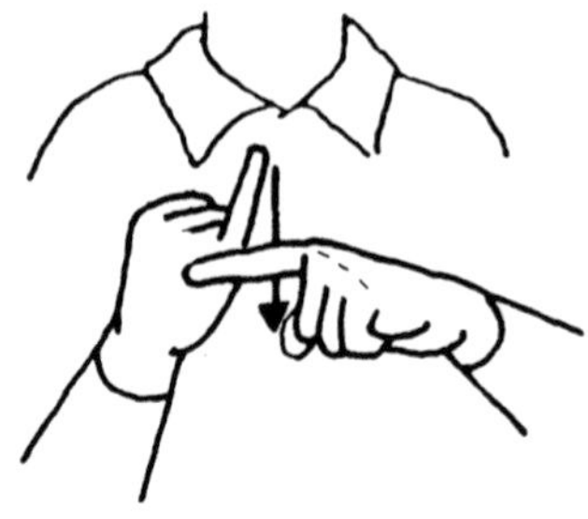

**inch**
One shape LH palm down. Slice down left index finger with right little finger.

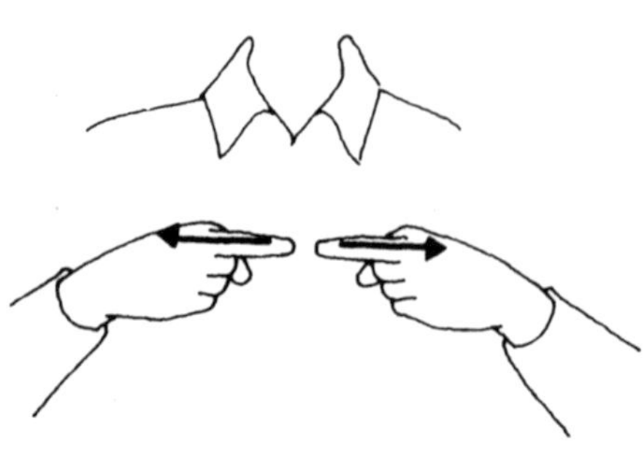

**opposite**
One shape both hands, palms in, tips facing. Draw apart.

**alike**
Y shape both hands, thumbs almost touching. Move apart and back again.

**zero**
O shape RH tips left. Move forward sharply.

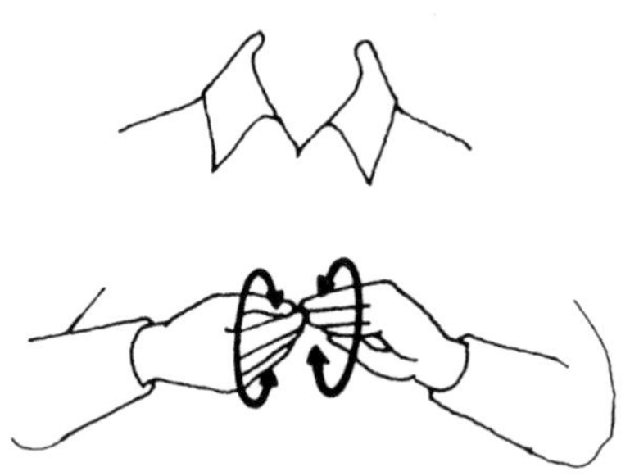

**number**
Flat O shape both hands, left palm in, right down, tips touching. Reverse positions.

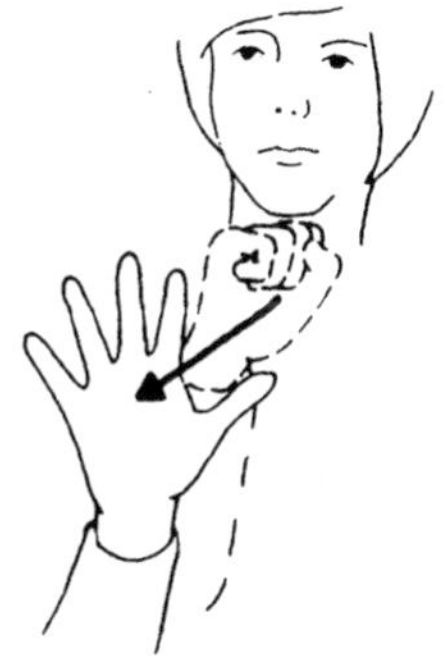

**nothing**
S shape RH. Place knuckles under chin and flick out into 5 shape palm out.

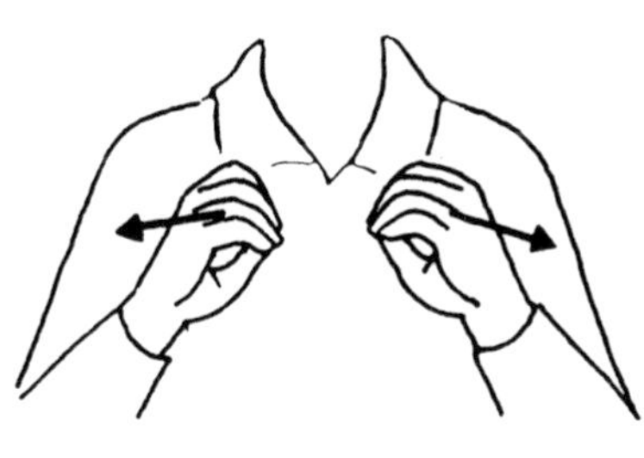

**none**
O shape both hands, palms and tips facing. Move forward and to the sides.

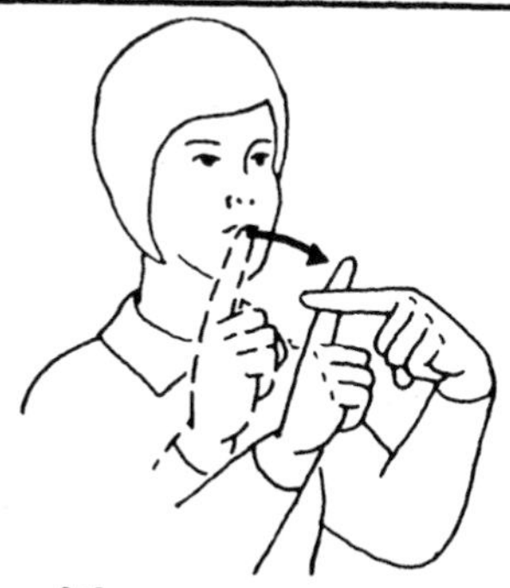

**positive**
One shape LH palm down, tip right. Place tip of right index at mouth then strike against side of left index.

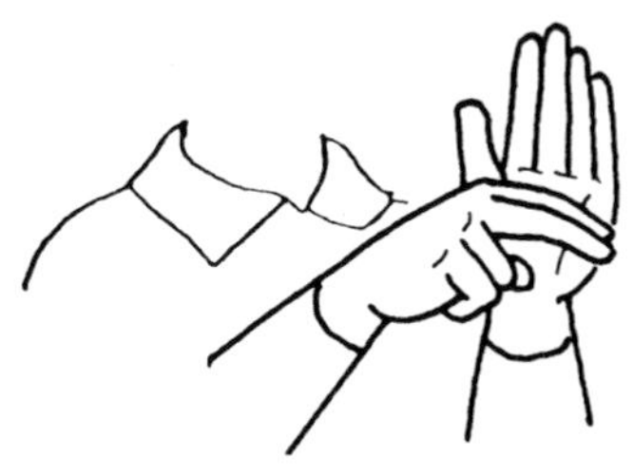

**negative**
LH open B palm out. N shape RH tips left. Strike left palm with the index finger side of right N.

## PRACTICE SENTENCES

Repeat each of the following phrases or sentences several times. Start forming each sign at the same time you begin to speak its corresponding word.

After you can sign, and simultaneously say, each phrase or sentence comfortably, pair each incomplete phrase with every appropriate sign in this chapter.

Copy this ____ .

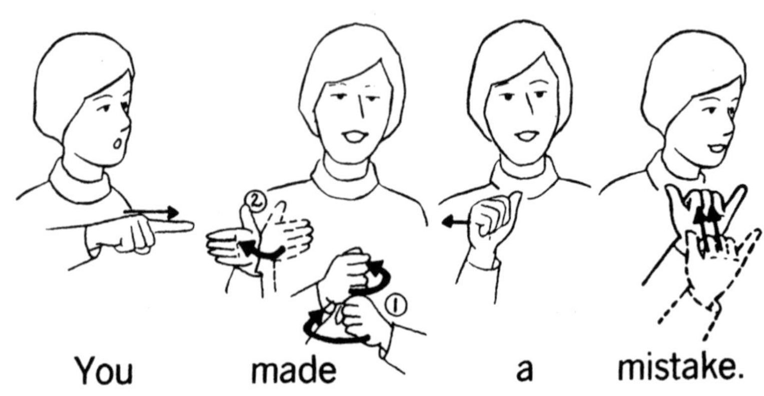

You made a mistake.

Please be careful.

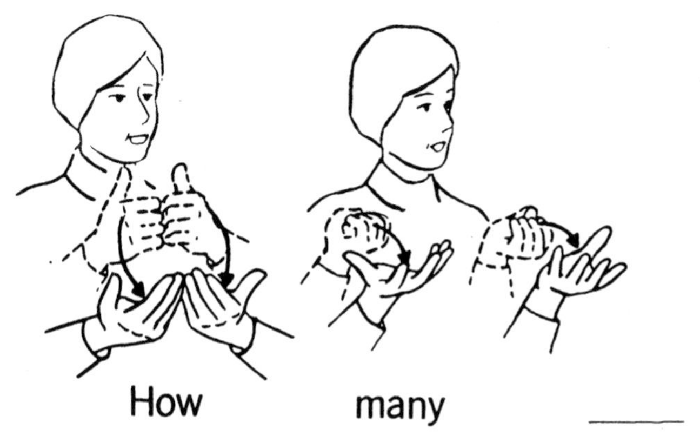

How many _____ ?

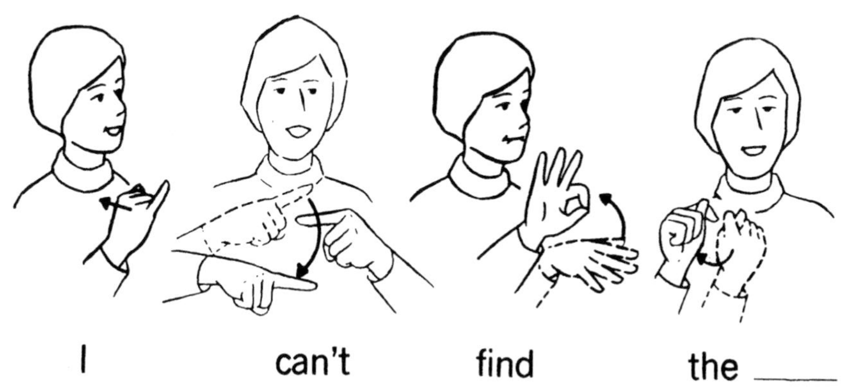

I can't find the _____ .

# 6. SCIENCE

**experiment**

E shape both hands. Circle toward one another alternately, as if pouring from vials.

**invent**

Four shape RH palm left. Place right index tip on forehead then move up.

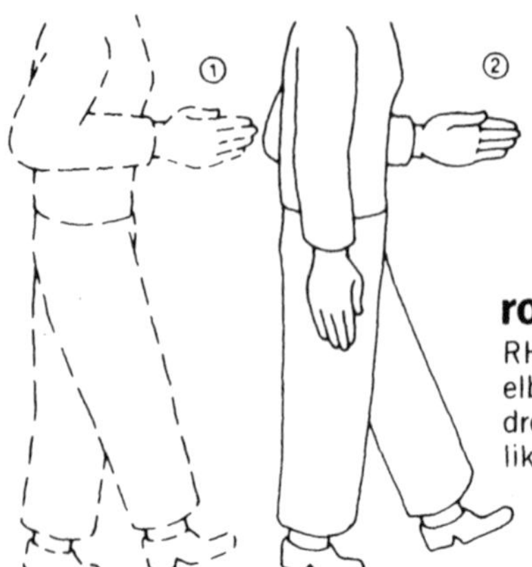


**robot**

RH open B palm left, tips out, elbows held at side. Walk forward, drop RH, then raise left open B in like motion.

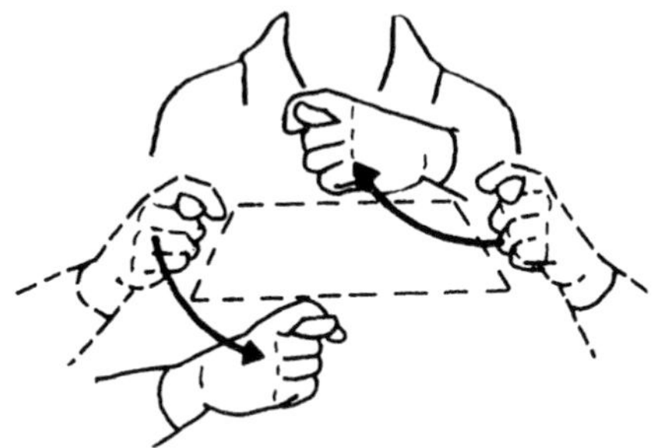

**tank (container)**
T shape both hands, thumb tips out. Swing right T to left and left T to right, outlining square shape.

**model**
LH open B palm out. Place index finger side of right M horizontally against left palm. Move both hands out.

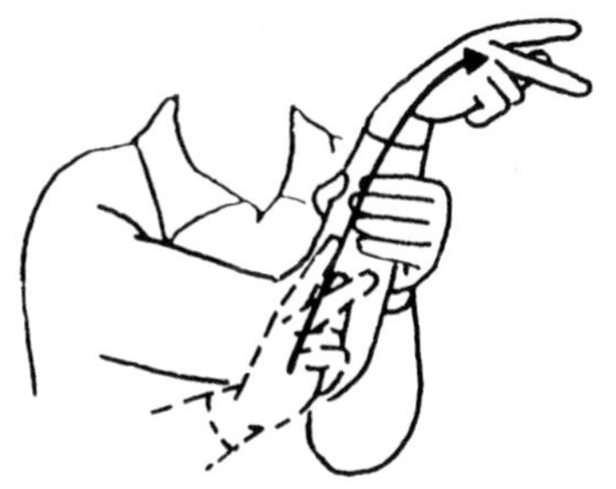

**plant**
Pass right P up, through, and over C shape LH palm right. (Sometimes *plant,* the verb, is signed by passing the tips of right P down through C shape LH.)

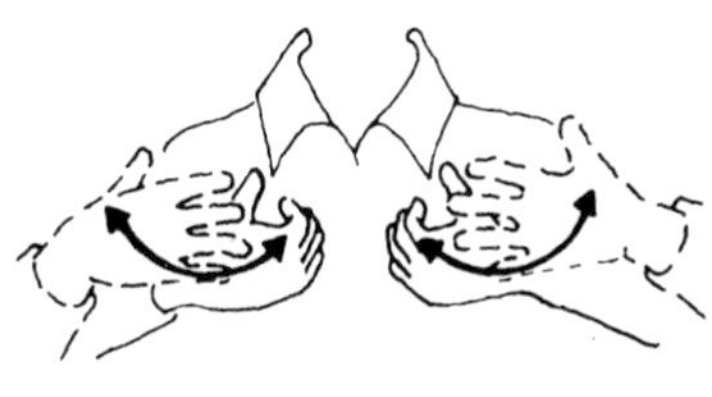

**animal**
Place tips of claw hands on upper chest and move back and forth toward one another.

**texture**
Place back of RH in palm of LH, then rub RH fingers together several times.

**surface**
Open B both hands, palms down. Rub right palm across back of LH.

**metal**
B shape LH, tips slanted right. Strike tip of left index with tips of right M.

**mineral**
Tap back of left fist several times with back of M shape RH.

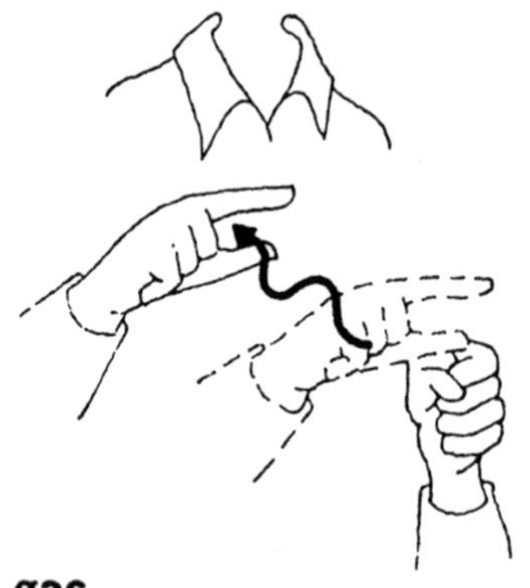

**gas**
S shape LH palm right. Place thumb of right G on top of left S, then move up in wavy motion.

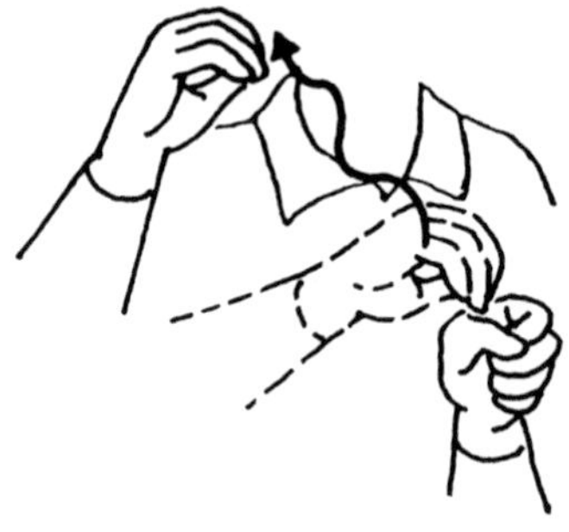

**oxygen**
S shape LH palm right. Place tips of right O on top of left S then move up in wavy motion.

**rubber**
X shape RH palm out. Rub down side of right cheek twice.

**liquid**
C shape LH palm and tips right. Arc thumb of right L into left C.

**vacuum (noun)**
LH open B palm down, tips out. Place base of right V on back of left B then slide forward.

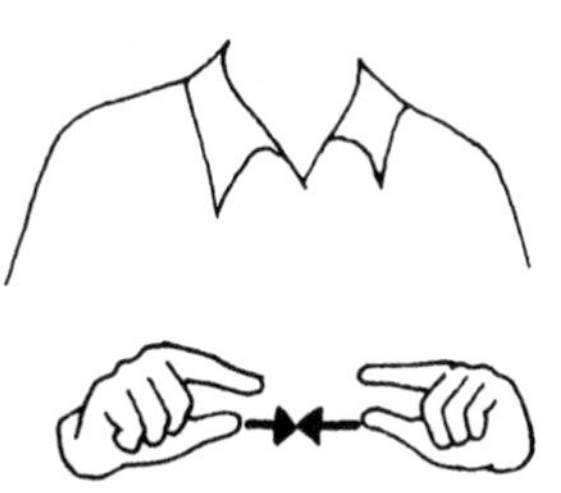

**gravity**
G shape both hands, palms out. Slowly draw hands together, ending with thumbs of G shapes touching.

**energy**
Outline muscle of left arm with right E.

**reflex**
Tap back of left wrist with right R then quickly flip up LH.

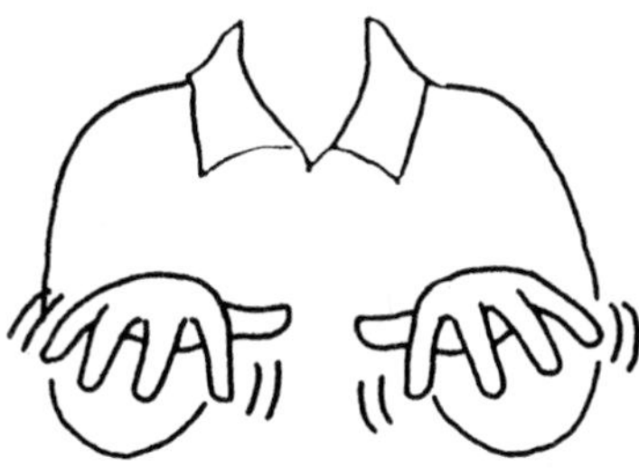

**vibrate**
Five shape both hands, palms down. Wiggle slightly.

**function**
S shape LH, palm down. Brush base of F shape RH back and forth against back of left wrist.

**stimulus**
Flick index finger of RH toward back of left fist. Repeat motion.

**response**
R shape both hands, RH at mouth, LH slightly forward. Arc both hands forward, ending with palms down.

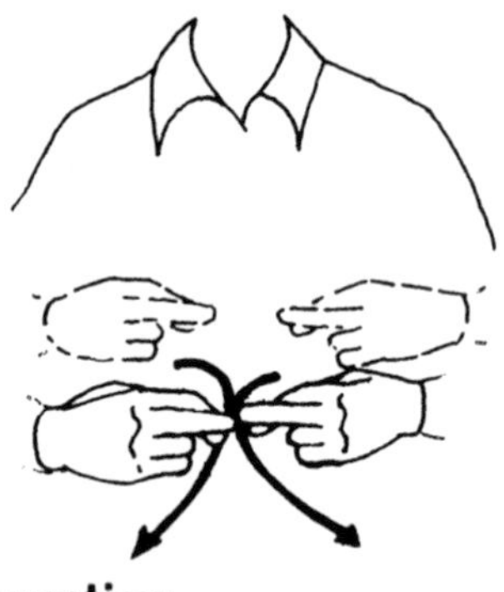

**reaction**
R shape both hands, tips facing. Strike tips together, then move outward in opposite directions.

**theory**
Circle right T shape, palm left, clockwise at right side of forehead.

**correlation**
Interlock thumb and index fingers of both hands. Move back and forth from right to left.

**constant**
Thumb tips of C shape hands touch and then move forward.

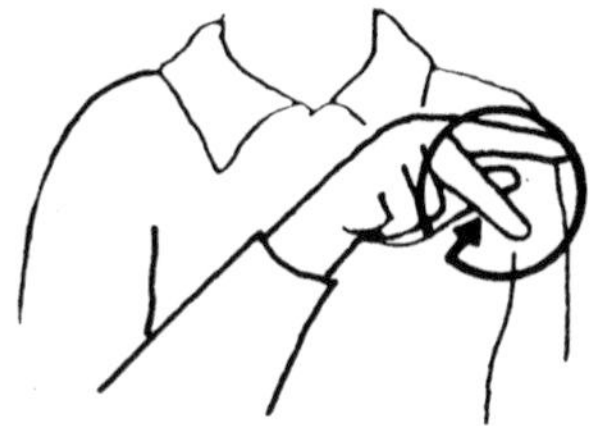

**personality**
Circle, then tap, upper left shoulder with thumb of right P.

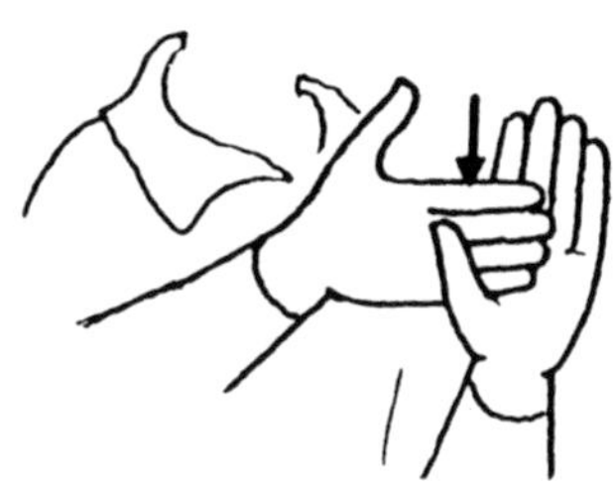

**psychology**
LH open B palm out. Strike LH between thumb and index with little finger side of right open B.

**brain**
Place thumb of right C on forehead.

**adapt**
A shape both hands thumbs up, palms touching. Twist hands in opposite directions, RH moving left, LH moving right.

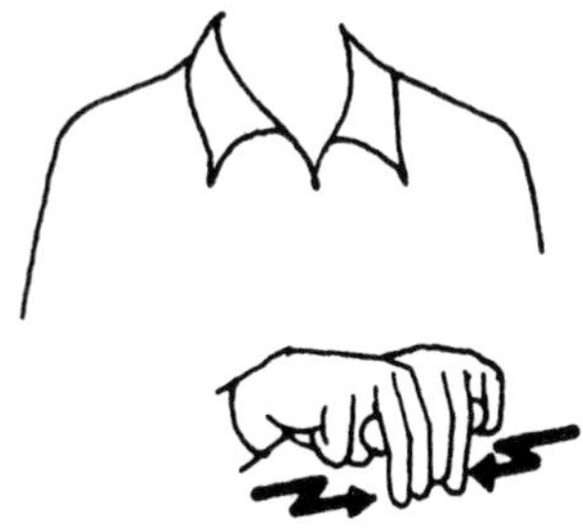

**normal**
Tap together index fingers of N shape hands.

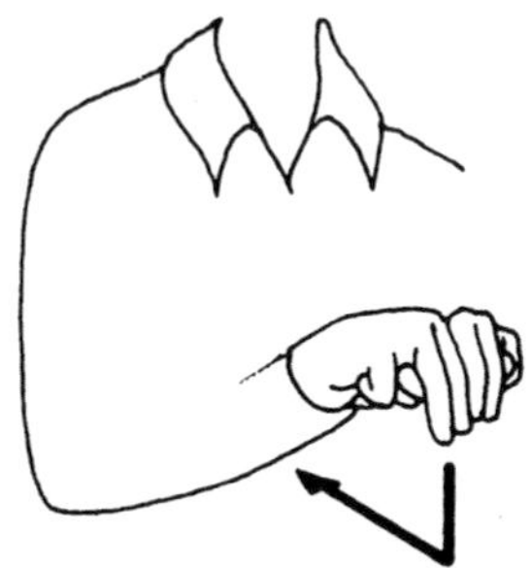

**abnormal**
N shape both hands, index fingers touching. Move right N down and away, i.e., "off the track".

**sampling**
Spread finger of LH. Pick at index, then middle finger of LH with thumb and index of RH.

**solution (liquid)**
Cupped shape LH, palm up. Stir right S, palm down, over LH.

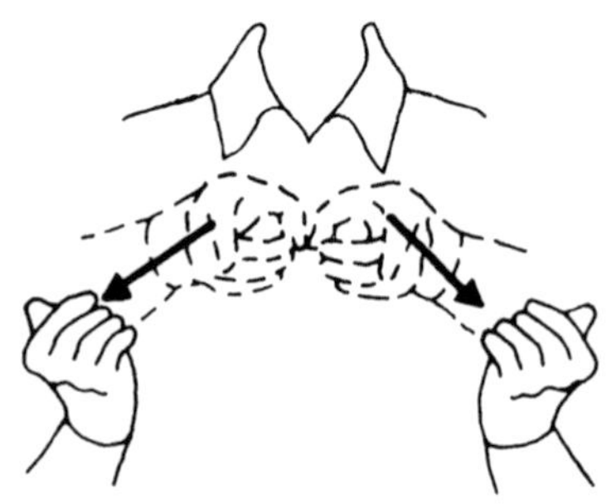

**dissolve**
D shape both hands, palms facing, tips touching. Draw down and apart ending in A shapes, knuckles out.

**distance**
A shape LH palm right. Place thumb and index tip of right D on fingers of left A, then move RH forward.

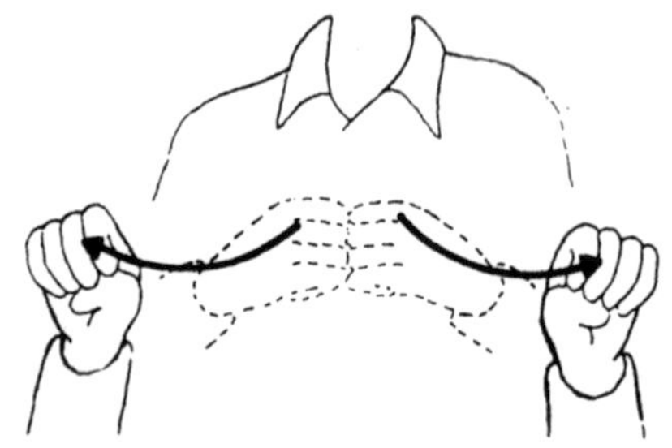

**extension**
E shape both hands, knuckles touching. Separate and turn out into correct E positions.

**modern**
LH open B palm up. Brush back of right M across left palm in scooping motion.

**develop**
Open B shape LH, tips up. Move fingertips of D shape RH up left palm.

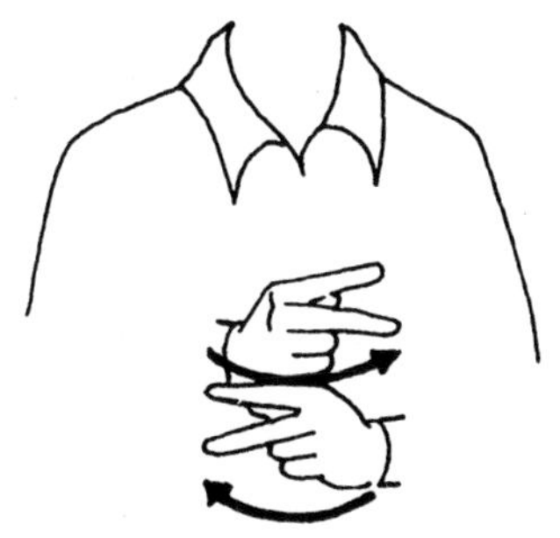

**produce**
P shape both hands, tips out, RH on top of LH. Quickly twist wrists in towards body, RH moving left, LH moving right.

**reproduce**
R shape both hands, palms in. Brush right wrist on inside of left wrist while moving hands in opposite directions. Repeat motion.

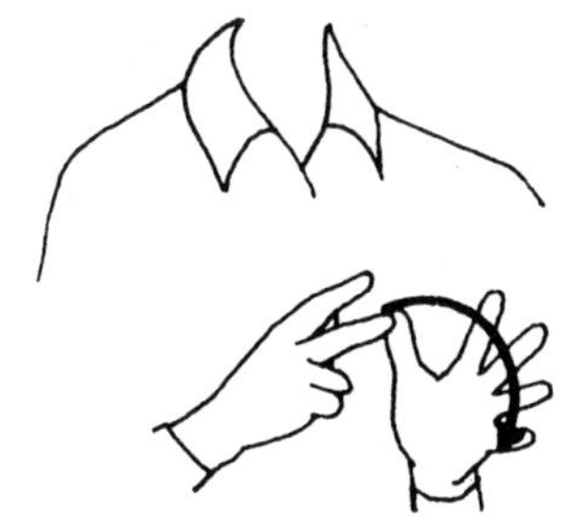

**population**
Sweep the tip of P shape over the open fingertips of LH.

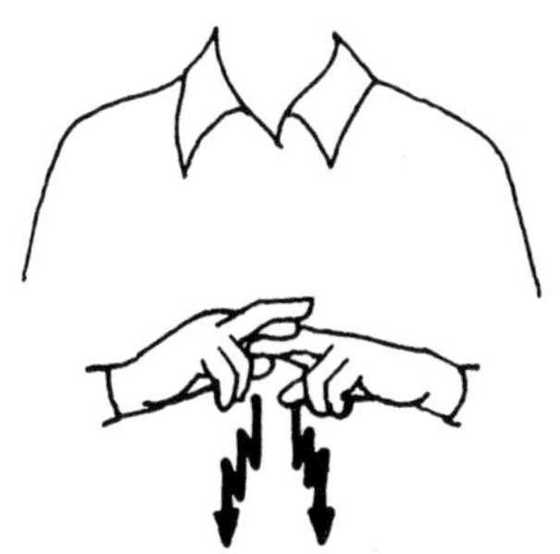

**reliable**
Place tips of right R on tips of left R. Gently bounce both hands up and down twice.

**sensitive**
Place middle fingertip of RH on chest. Then turn down and out sharply.

**chemistry**
C shape both hands. Alternately arc down as if pouring from vials.

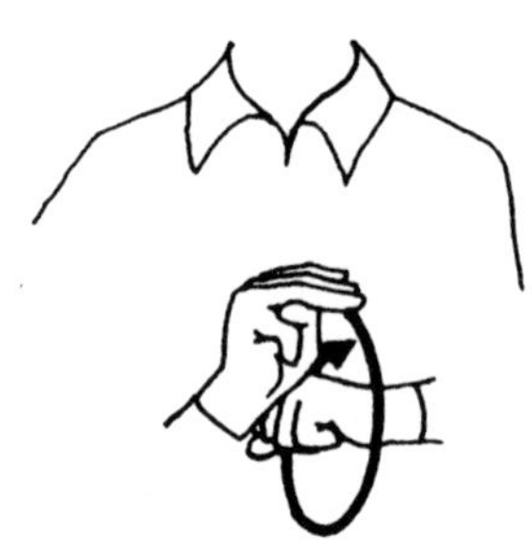

**molecule**
A shape LH, palm down. Revolve M shape RH forward around LH.

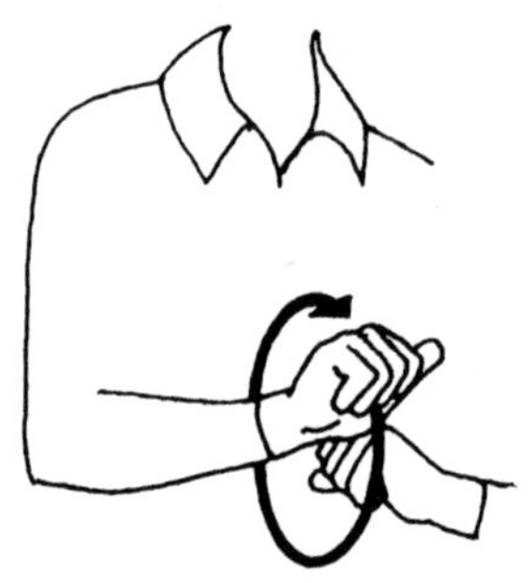

**atom**
A shape both hands, palms down. Revolve RH forward around LH.

**proton**
Place middle finger tip of right P in palm of LH.

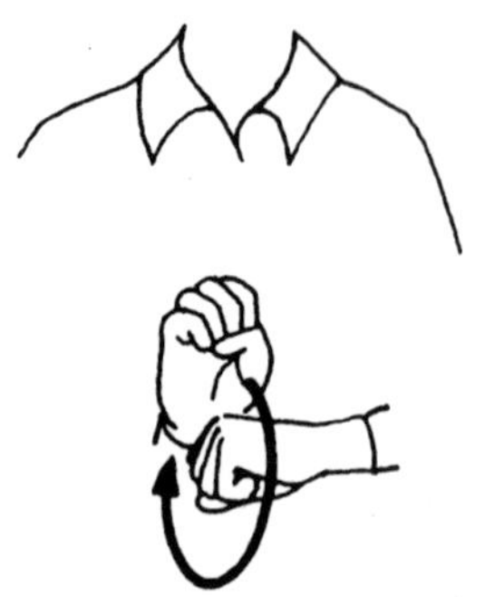

**electron**
A shape LH, palm down. Revolve E shape RH forward around LH.

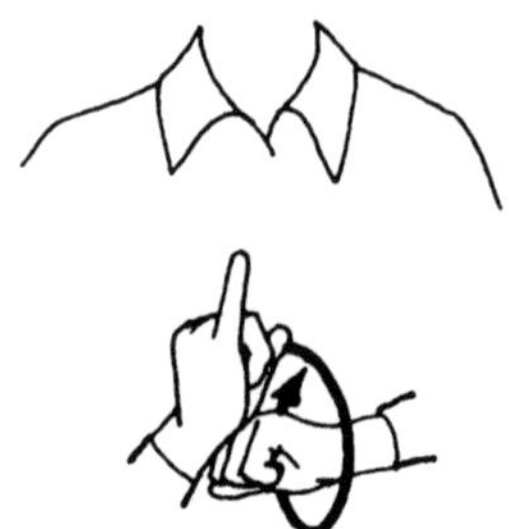

**ion**
A shape LH, palm down. Revolve I shape RH forward around LH.

**neutron**
Place tips of N shape RH in palm of LH.

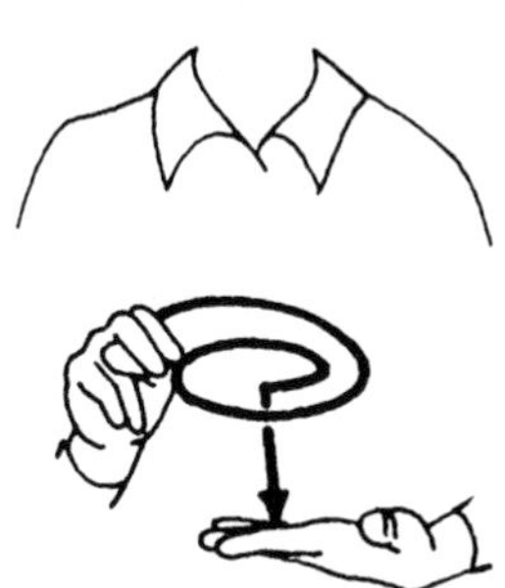

**nucleus**
Open B shape LH, palm up. Circle right N over LH, then drop tips into center of left palm.

**element**
Open B shape LH, palm down. Circle E shape RH under LH in counterclockwise direction.

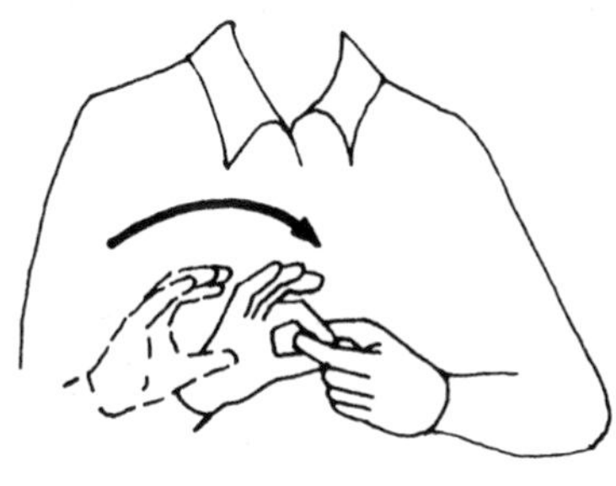

**compound**
Form a C shape with RH. Then lock together thumb and index fingers of both hands.

**science**
A shape both hands. Alternately arc thumbs down, as if pouring from vials.

**formula**
LH open B. Tap fingers, then base, of left palm with thumb and index of right F.

**volume**
V shape both hands, palms out, little fingers touching. Draw apart and circle forward, ending with palms in, little fingers touching.

**solid**
LH open B palm down. Hit little finger side of right bent V against back of LH.

**weight**
Fingerspell W-T.

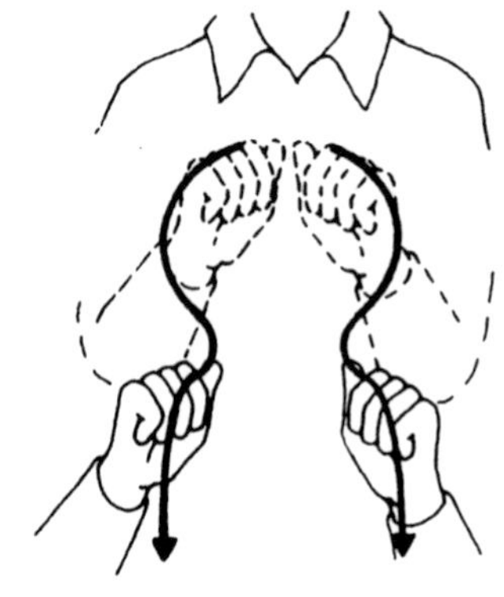

**shape**
A shape both hands. Curve downward, outlining shape of body.

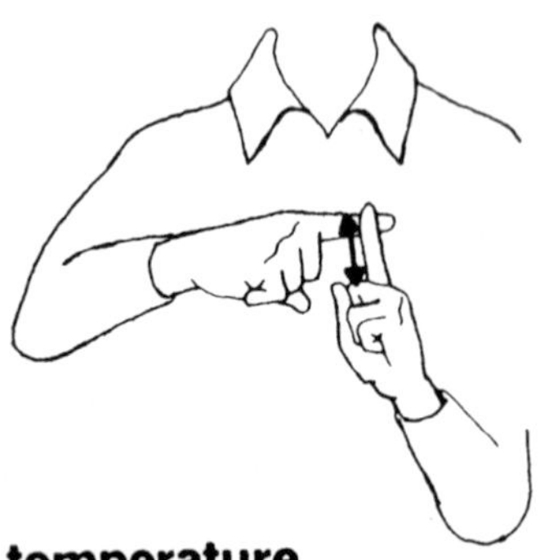

**temperature**
One shape both hands, left palm out, right palm down. Rub right index up and down back of left index.

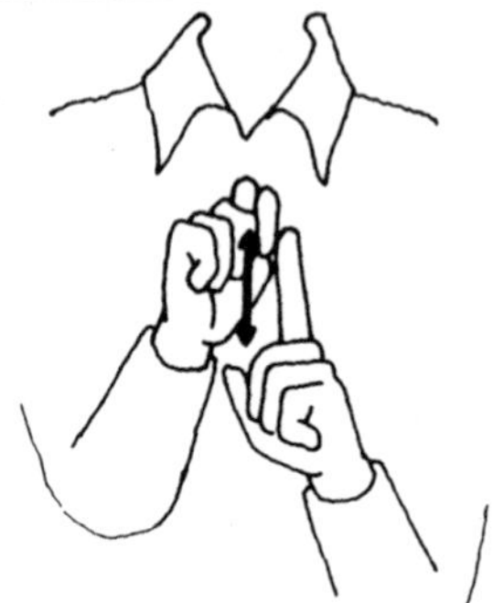

**thermometer**
One shape LH. T shape RH. Rub right T up and down left index.

**equipment**
E shape RH palm up. Bounce slightly out and to the right in short movements.

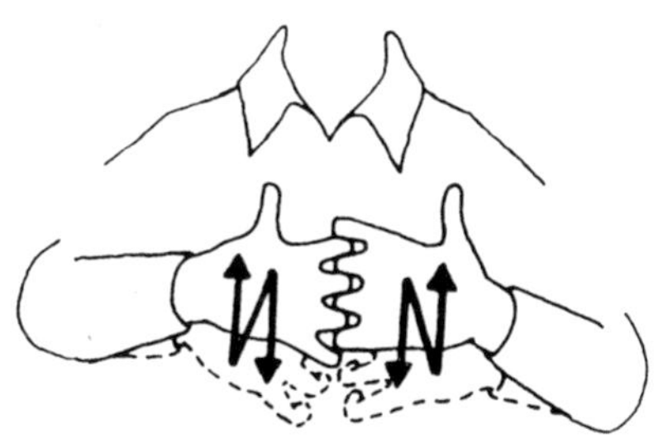

**machine**
Interlock fingers, palms in, and move up and down.

**instrument**
LH open B palm up, tips out. I shape RH palm up, tip left. Place tip on base of left palm and move forward in short jumps.

**microscope**
O shape both hands, palms in. Place left O by right eye and right O directly under it. Then twist right O to left, as if focusing microscope.

**magnet**
LH open B palm right, tips out. Five shape RH palm left. Close rapidly into flat O and "stick" to left palm.

**magnifying glass**
Mime holding a magnifying glass in front of face and "focusing" it by moving RH in and out.

**earth**
S shape LH palm down. Place right thumb and middle finger on back of left hand near wrist and rock back and forth.

**world**
W shape both hands, tips out. Place right W on top of left. Circle right W forward and under left W, returning to original position.

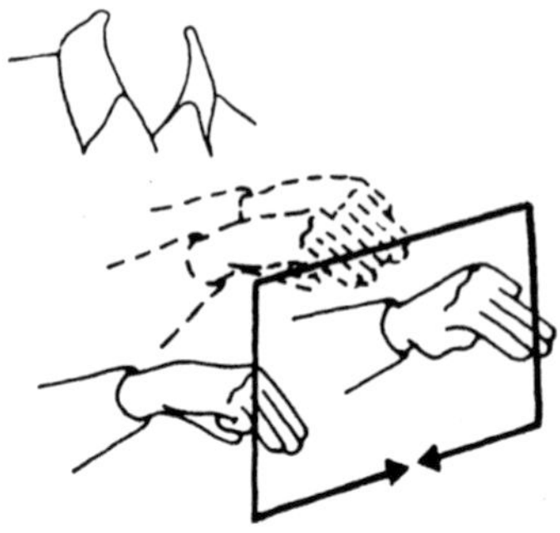

**map**
M shape both hands, palms down, tips out, index fingers touching. Move apart, down, and back together again.

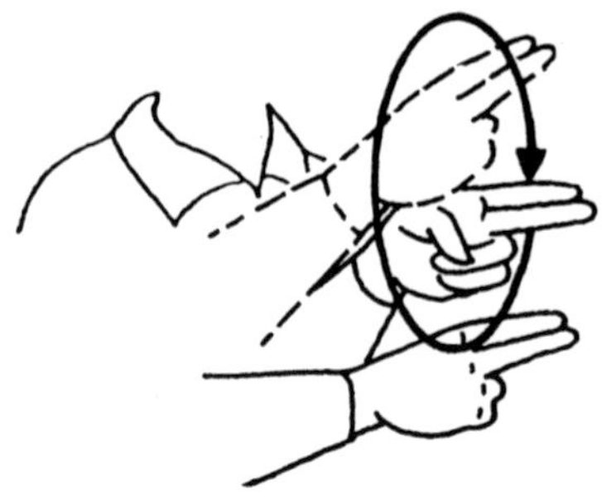

**universe**
U shape both hands, tips out, right on top of left. Circle right U forward and under left U, returning to original position.

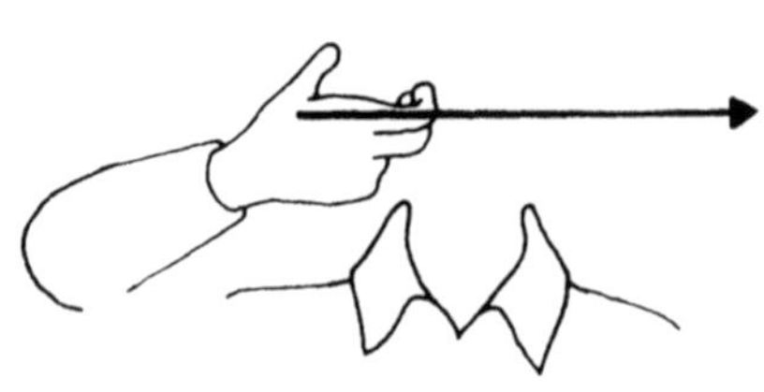

**spaceship**
H shape RH palm in, tips left, thumb extended. Bend finger and move swiftly to the left.

**rocket**
S shape LH palm and knuckles down. Place base of right R on back of left S then raise up suddenly.

# PRACTICE SENTENCES

Repeat each of the following phrases or sentences several times. Start forming each sign at the same time you begin to speak its corresponding word.

After you can sign, and simultaneously say, each phrase or sentence comfortably, pair each incomplete phrase with every appropriate sign in this chapter.

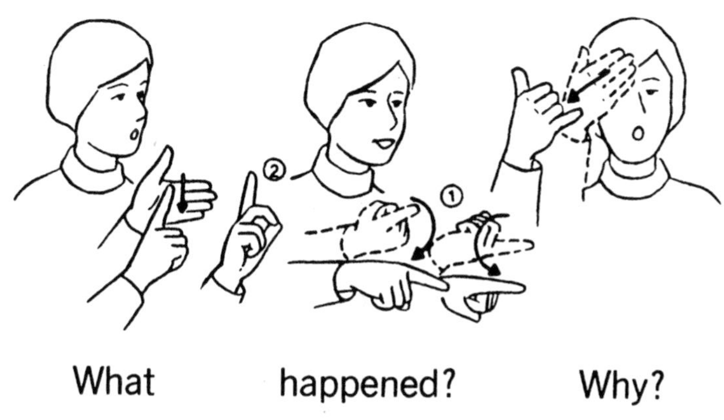

What happened? Why?

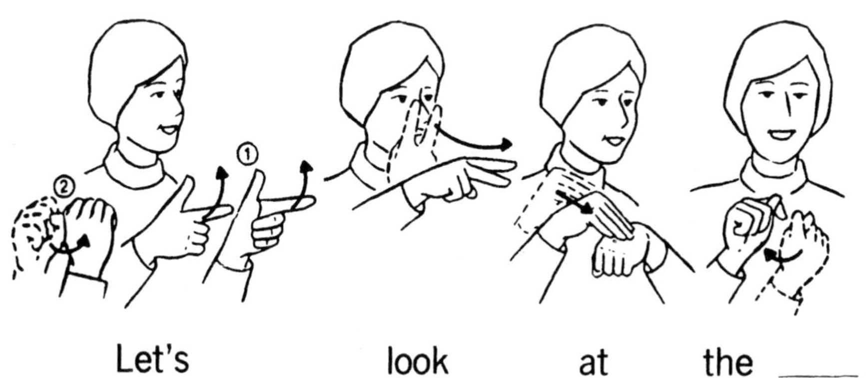

Let's look at the ____.

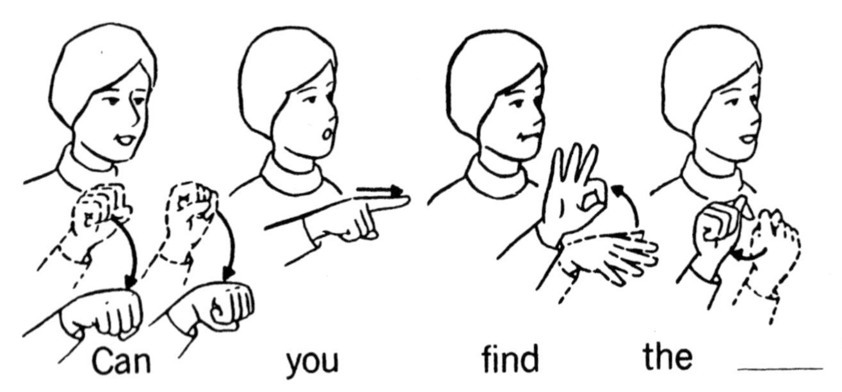

Can you find the ____ ?

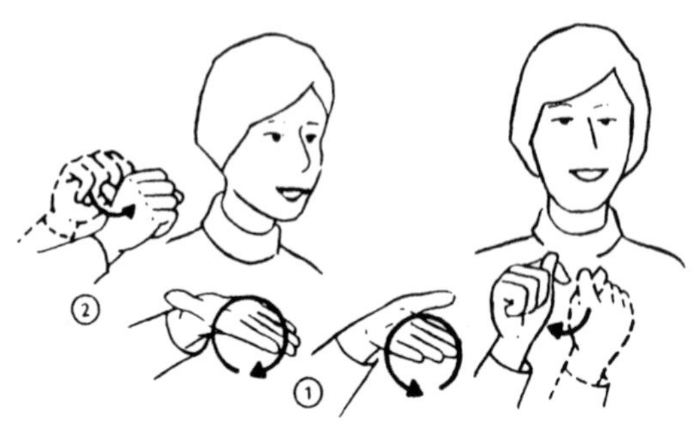

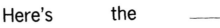

Here's the ____ .

What does this mean?

# 7.
# HUMANITIES

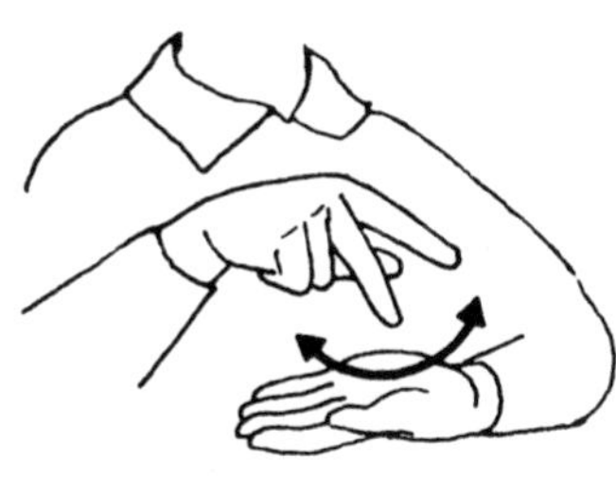

**poem**
LH open B palm up. Swing middle fingertip of right P, palm down, back and forth over left palm.

**rhyme**
LH open B palm up, tips slanted right. Swing tips of right R above left palm and forearm in rhythmic motion.

**riddle**
Draw question mark in air with tips of right R.

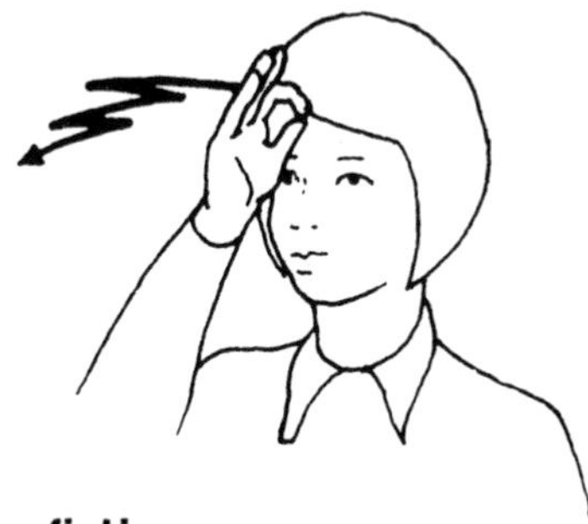

**fiction**
Place thumb and index tip of F shape RH on forehead. Then bounce right F forward several times.

**grammar**
G shape both hands, tips facing. Wiggle while moving apart.

**paragraph**
LH open B palm right, tips up. Place fingertips of cupped RH in left palm, indicating size of a paragraph.

**dictionary**
LH open B palm up, tips out. Brush thumb and index tips of right D inward on left palm (as if turning pages).

**encyclopedia**
LH open B palm up, tips out. Brush base of right E inward on left palm twice.

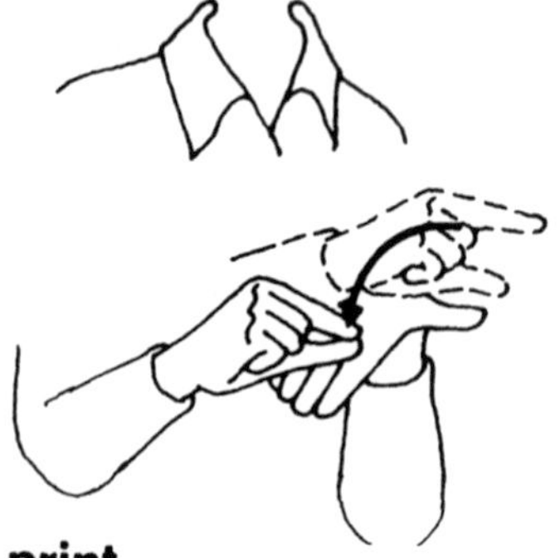

**print**
G shape RH. Hold over left palm then draw back and snap tips together in palm.

**quote**
Bent V shape both hands, palms out, held out from body. Twist inward, as if outlining quotation marks.

**topic**
Bent V shape both hands, palms out. Gently crook inward several times, suggesting quotation marks.

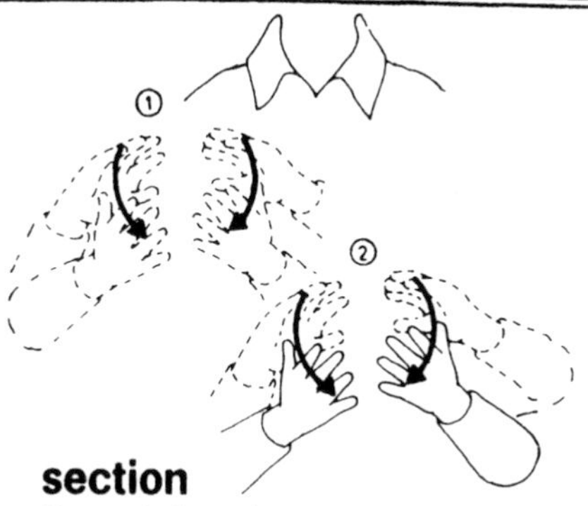


**section**
Cupped shape both hands, palms and tips facing. Twist down then move to left and repeat.

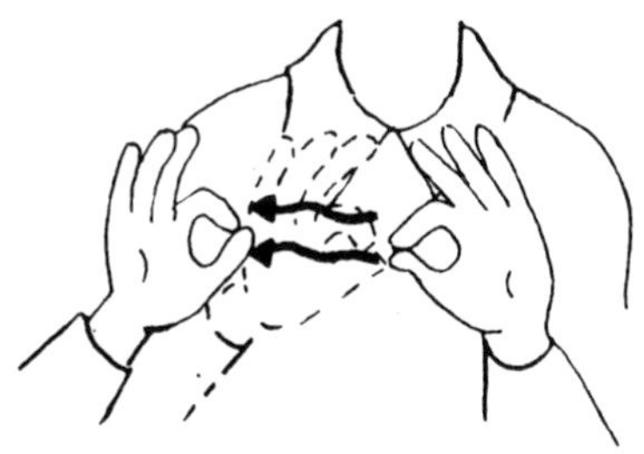

**caption**
F shape both hands, index fingers and thumbs touching. Wiggle right F to right (away from LH).

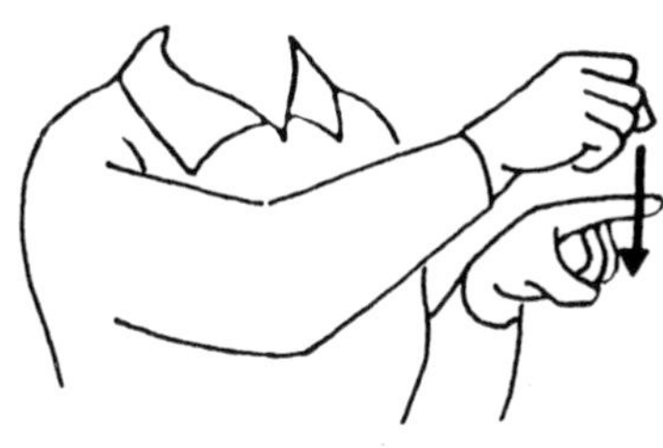

**syllable**
One shape LH palm down, tip out. Brush right S, palm left, down side of left index.

**verb**
V shape RH palm in, tips left. Slide across chin, moving from left to right.

**noun**
H shape LH palm right, tips out. N shape RH palm left. Tap index of left H twice with base of right N.

**metaphor**
M shape RH, cupped shape LH, palms facing. Twist hands in opposite directions, RH to the left, LH to the right.

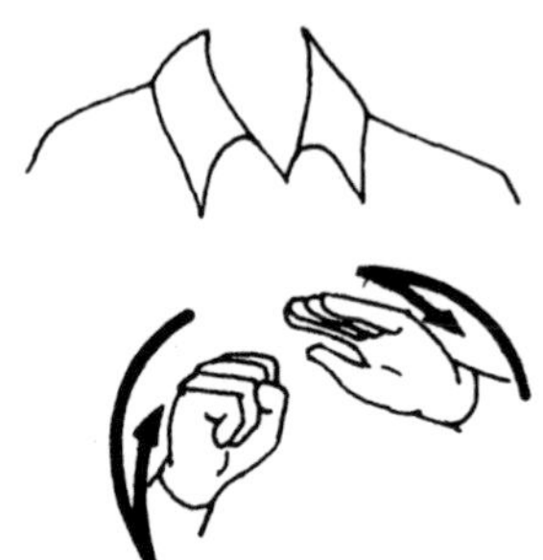

**simile**
S shape RH, cupped shape LH, palms facing. Twist hands in opposite directions, RH to the left, LH to the right.

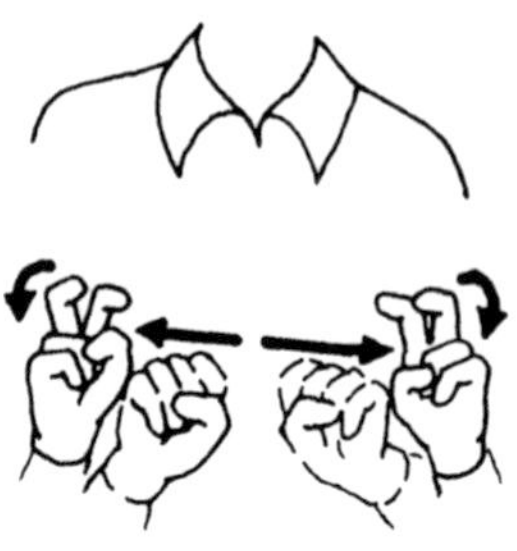

**slang**
S shape both hands, palms out. Move apart, changing to bent V's. Crook V's inward, suggesting quotation marks.

**clause**
C shape hands, palms out. Pull apart, changing to L shapes.

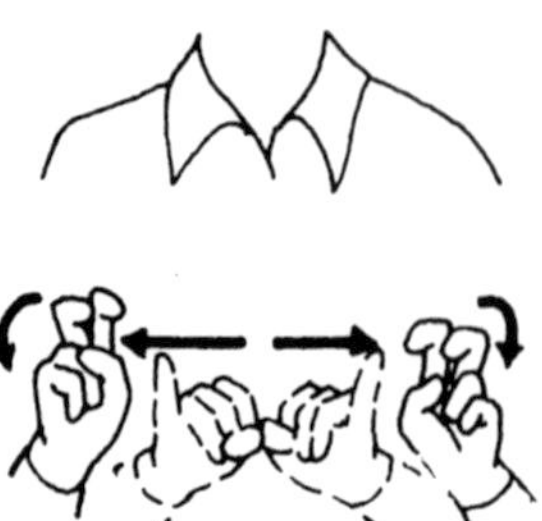

**idiom**
I shape both hands, palms out. Move apart, changing to bent V's. Crook V's inward, suggesting quotation marks.

**paraphrase**
P shape both hands, left palm up, right palm down. Place right wrist on top of left wrist, then twist to reverse position.

**drama**
D shape both hands. Alternately move back in circles, brushing down on chest.

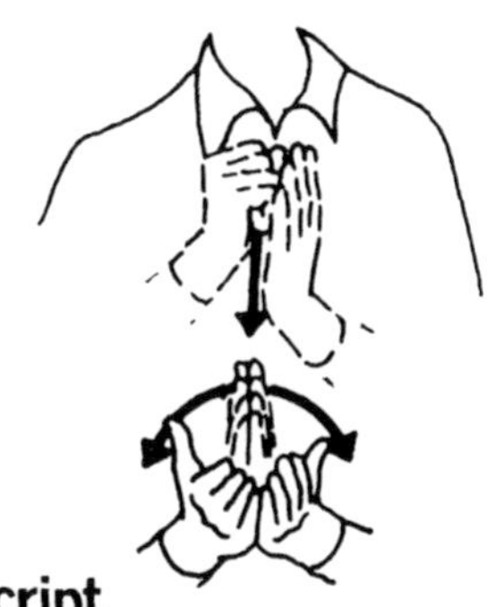

**script**
Move right S shape down left palm. Then place palms of hands together and spread apart, as if opening a book.

**role**
Open B shape LH, palm out. Tips of R shape RH circle, then touch, left palm.

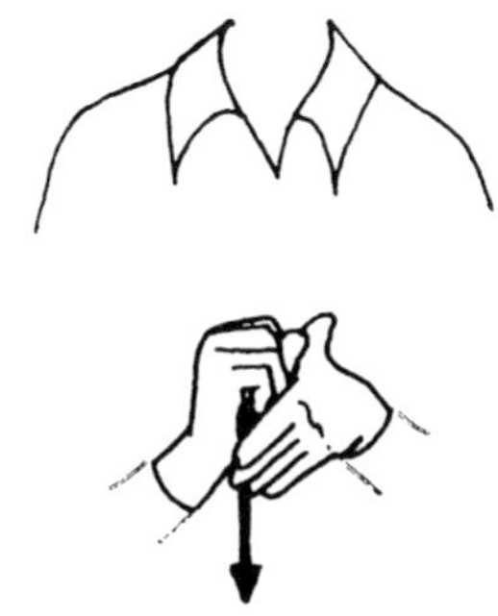

**scene**
Open B shape LH, palm in, tips right. Move right S shape down across left palm.

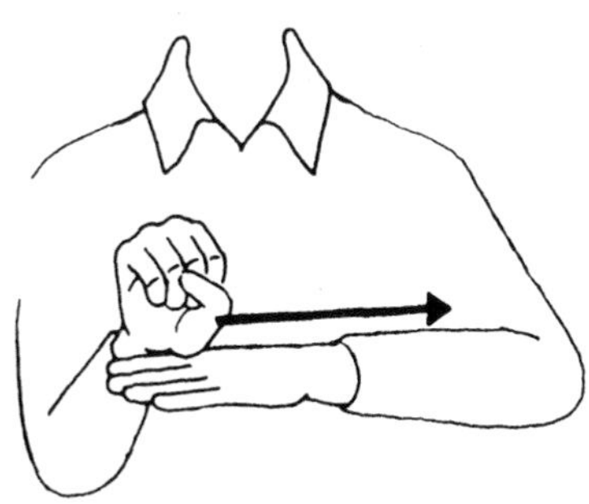

**stage**
LH open B palm down. Slide base of right S up left forearm, beginning at fingertips.

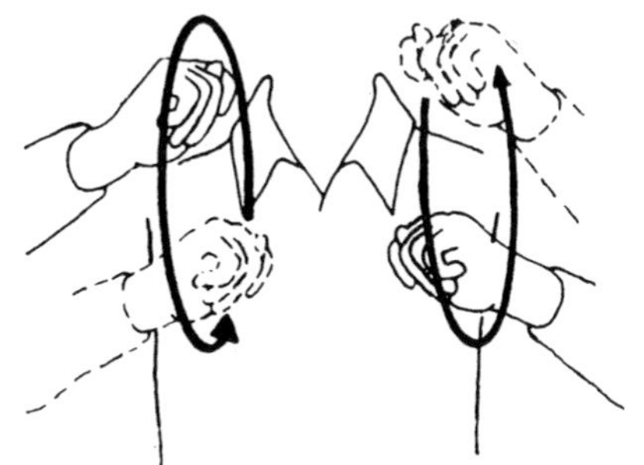

**theater**
T shape both hands. Alternately circle inward, brushing against chest.

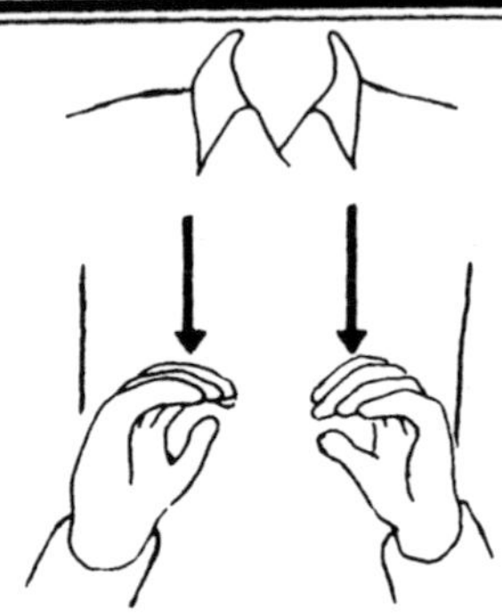

**costume**
C shape both hands, palms facing. Brush down chest.

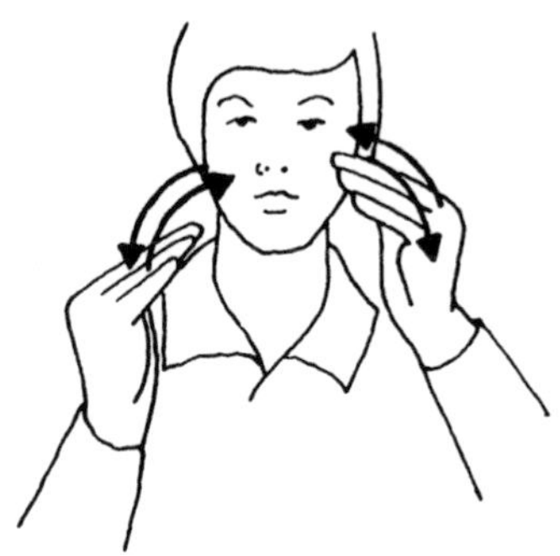

**makeup (cosmetics)**
Flat O both hands. Place tips on cheeks alternately.

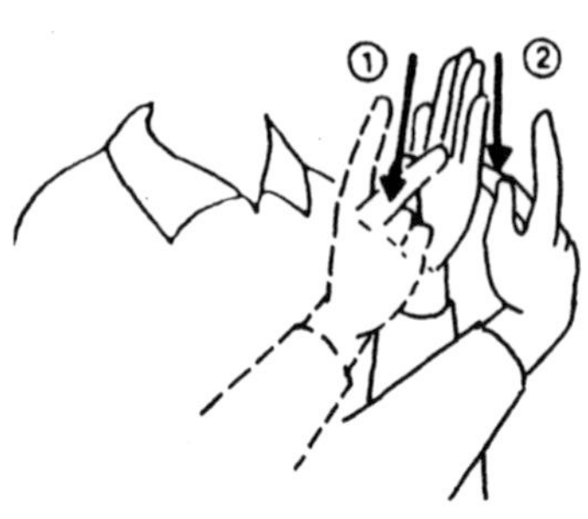


**program**
LH open B palm in, tips up, held away from body. Move middle fingertip of right P down left palm then down back of left hand.

**performer**
P shape both hands, palms out. Alternately move back in circles, brushing down chest. Follow with agent marker.

**comedy**
Place thumbs of C shape hands at sides of mouth and brush upwards to cheeks. Repeat motion.

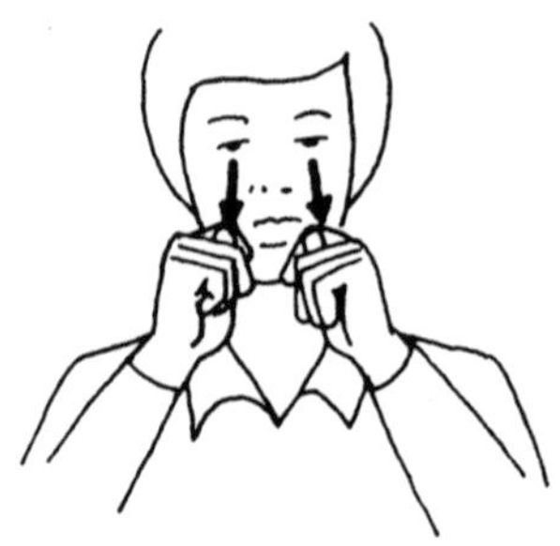

**tragedy**
Place T shapes under eyes and draw down as if tracing tears.

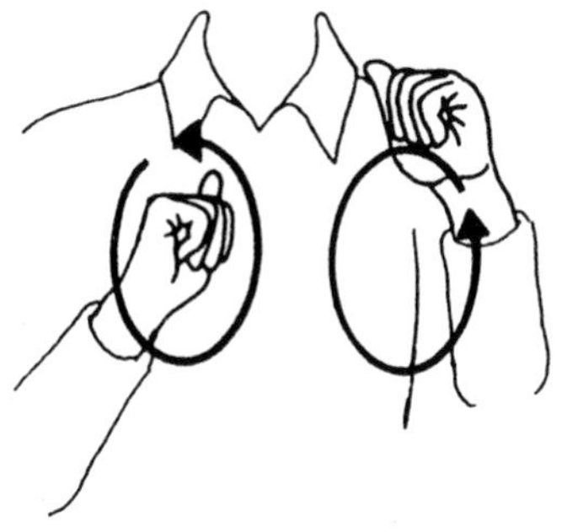

**act**
A shape both hands. Alternately move back in circles, brushing thumbs down chest.

**rehearse**
One shape LH palm right, tip out. Brush base of right R back and forth on left index.

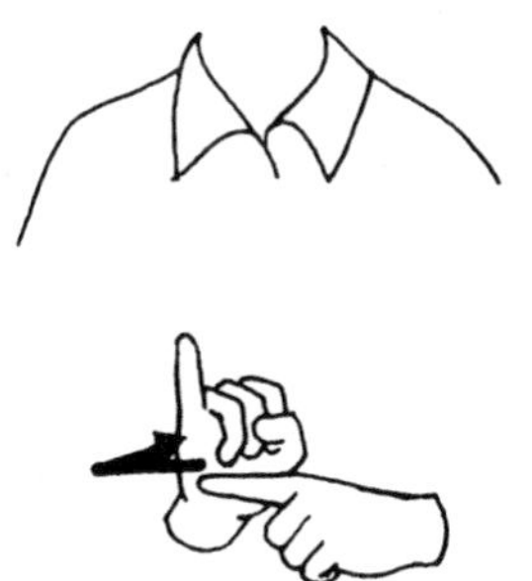

**improvise**
One shape LH, palm down, tip out. Brush base of I shape RH back and forth on left index finger.

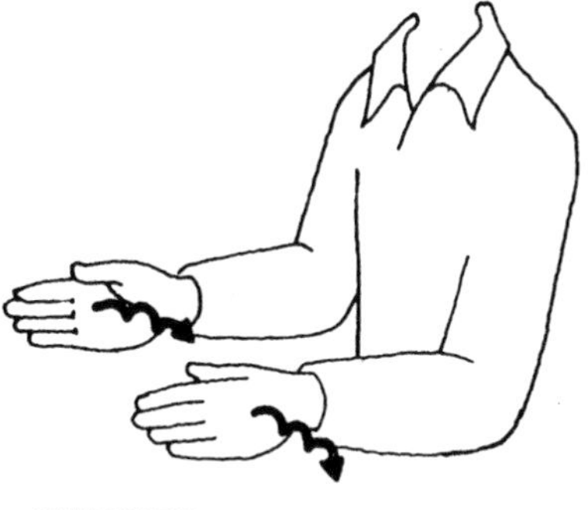

**arrange**
B shape both hands, palms facing, tips out. Move in short jumps to the left.

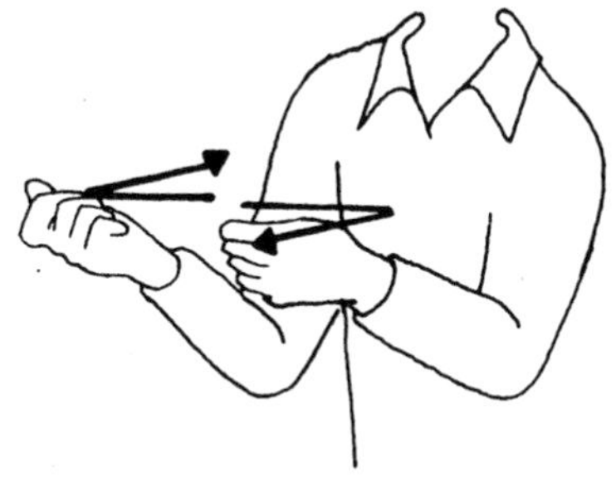

**manage**
"Loose" A shape both hands, palms up, thumbs out. Move back and forth alternately as if handling reins.

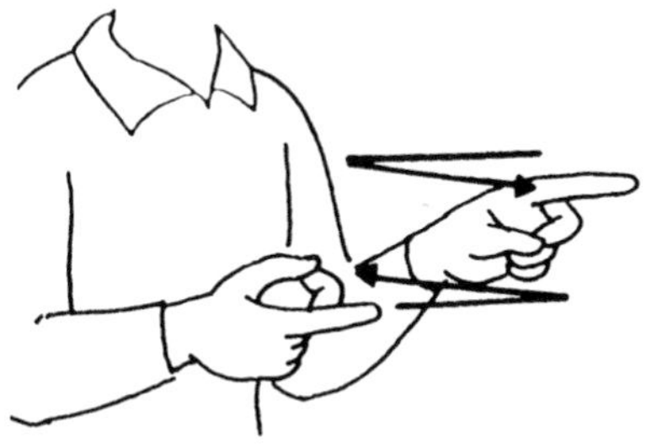

**direct**
D shape both hands, palms facing, index tips out. Move back and forth alternately as if handling reins.

**ballet**
Place tips of right V in left palm. Lift up into right R then repeat.

**performance**
P shape both hands, palms out. Alternately move back in circles, brushing down chest.

**episode**
E shape both hands, palms up. Twist toward each other, ending with palms down.

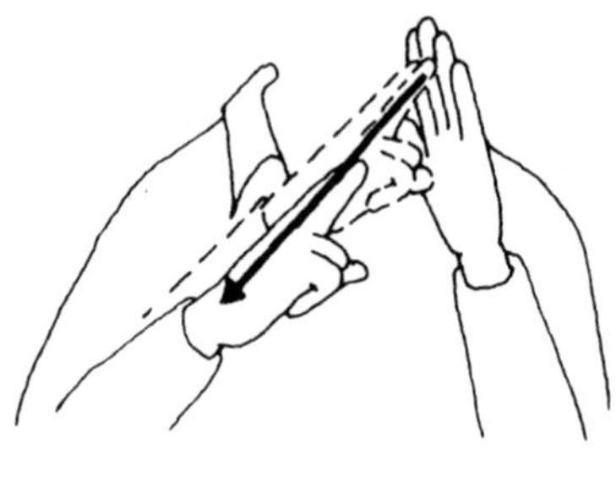

**easel**
LH open B palm right. Place tips of right H on left fingertips then draw away and down at angle.

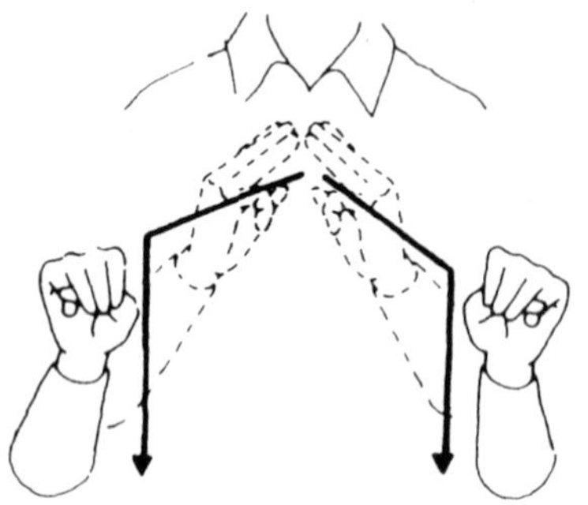

**museum**
M shape both hands, palms facing, tips touching. Draw apart and down, closing fingers over thumbs.

**exhibit**
LH open B palm out. Place thumb side of right E on left palm and move both hands out in a large circle.

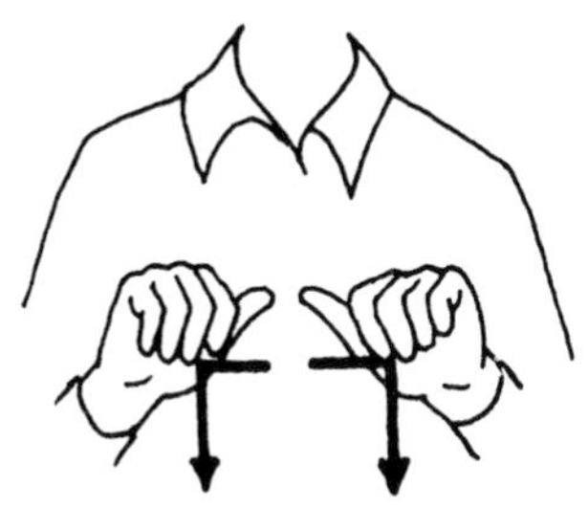

**architecture**
A shape both hands, palms out, thumbs touching. Move apart and down to form sides of house.

**byzantine**
Fingerspell B, then Z with RH.

**renaissance**
R shape RH, palm out. Move down in a wavy motion.

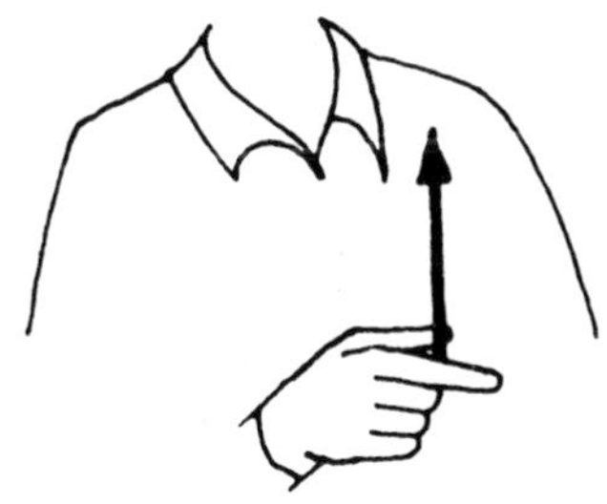

**Gothic**
G shape RH, palm facing left. Move upward.

**cathedral**
Place right C on back of left fist. Move right C upward to form a steeple.

**characteristic**
Open B shape LH, palm out. C shape RH circles, then taps against, left palm.

## PRACTICE SENTENCES

Repeat each of the following phrases or sentences several times. Start forming each sign at the same time you begin to speak its corresponding word.

After you can sign, and simultaneously say, each phrase or sentence comfortably, pair each incomplete phrase with every appropriate sign in this chapter.

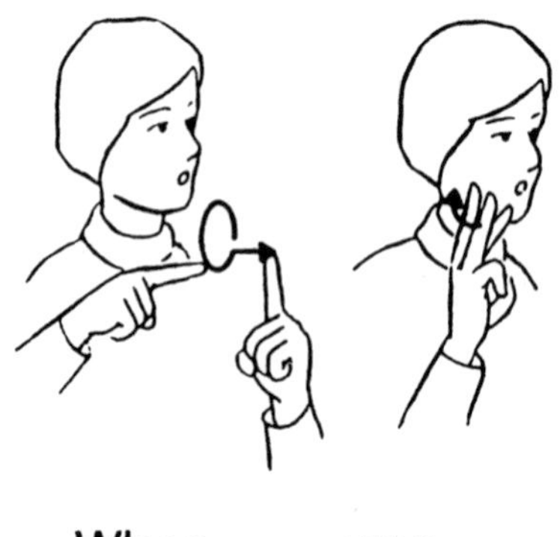

When was ____ ?

What shape is this?

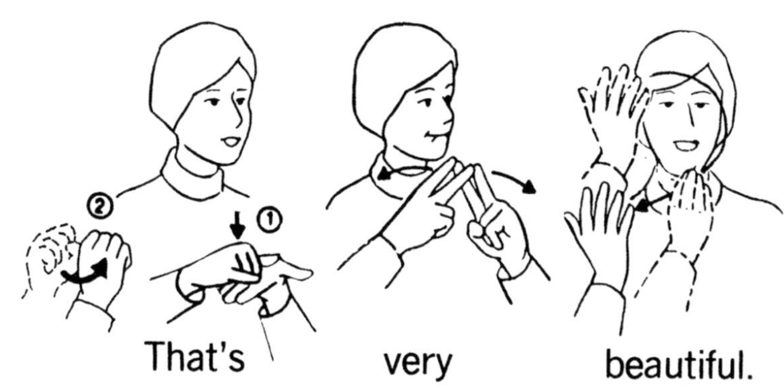


That's very beautiful.

Who can answer the question?

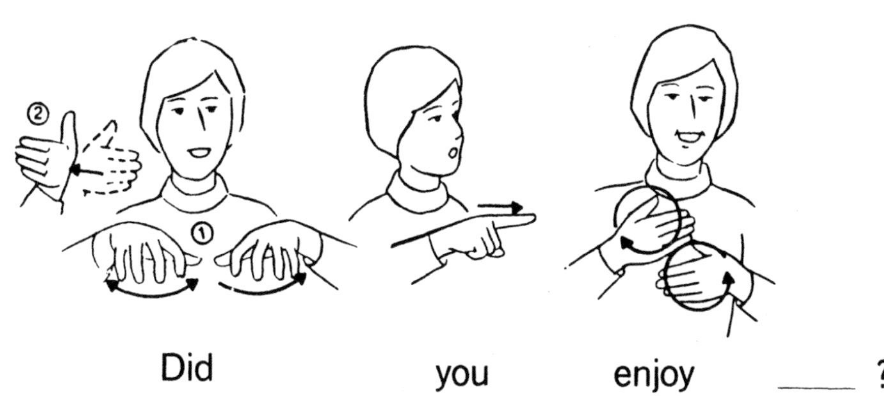


Did you enjoy ____ ?

# 8.
# SOCIAL SCIENCE

**Catholic**
Describe a cross in front of face with right U shape.

**Jewish**
Grab chin with fingers of RH then draw into flat O, indicating beard.

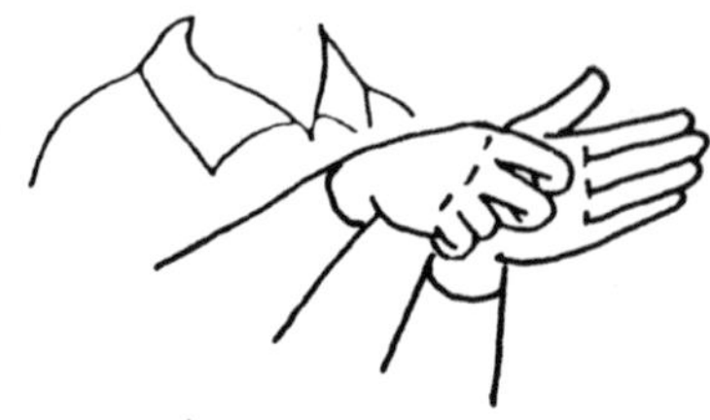

**Protestant**
LH open B palm right, tips out. Place knuckles of right bent V in left palm.

**history**
H shape RH palm left, tips out. Shake up and down.

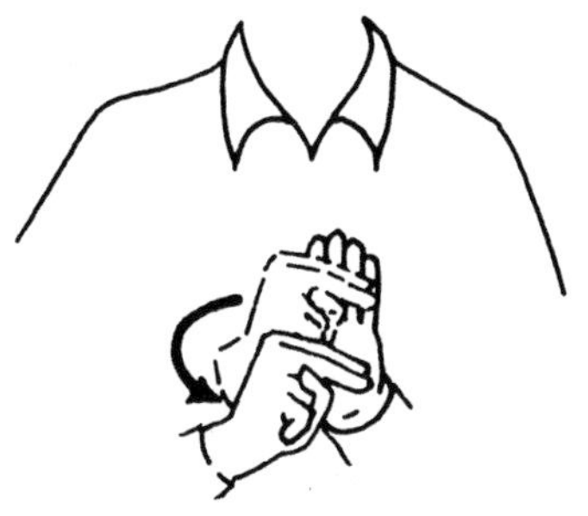

### norm
Open B shape LH, palm out. Place back of right N on fingertips, then on heel, of left palm.

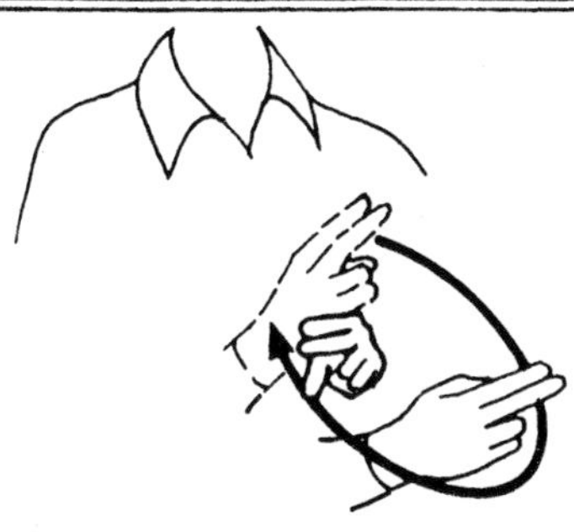

### universal
U shape both hands, right on top of left. Circle right U forward and under left U, returning to original position.

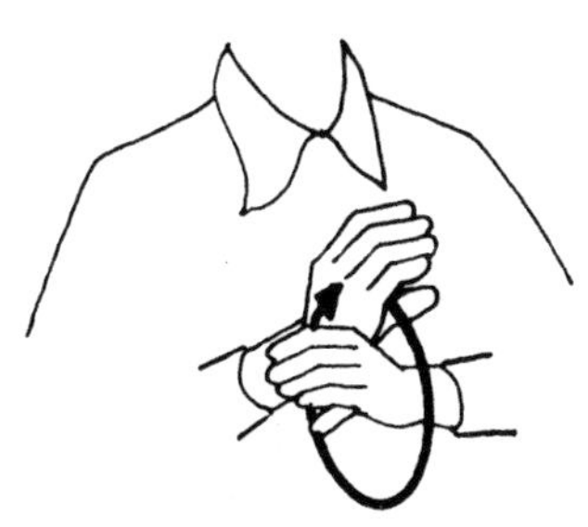

### civilization
C shape both hands, right on top of left. Circle right C forward and under left C, returning to original position.

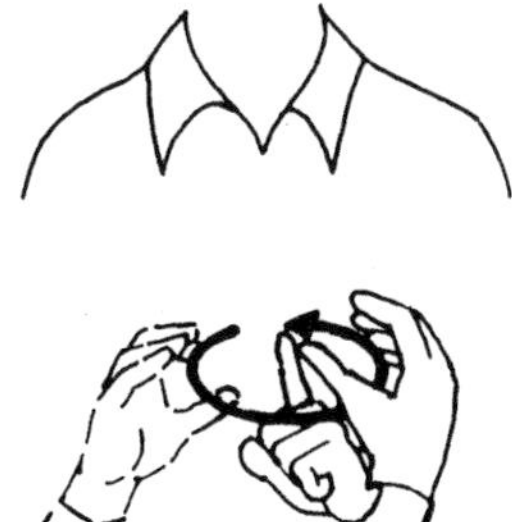

### culture
Circle right C shape counterclockwise around tip of left index finger.

### social
S shape both hands, thumbs touching. Draw apart and circle forward, ending with little fingers touching, palms in.

### environment
Circle right E counterclockwise around left index, tip up.

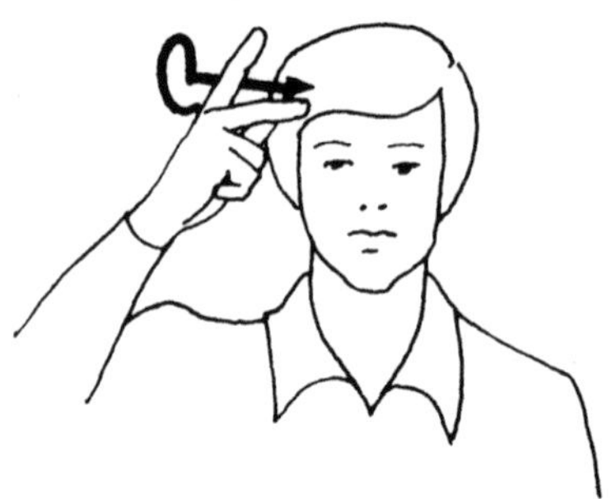

**politics**
Circle and touch right temple with middle finger of P shape RH.

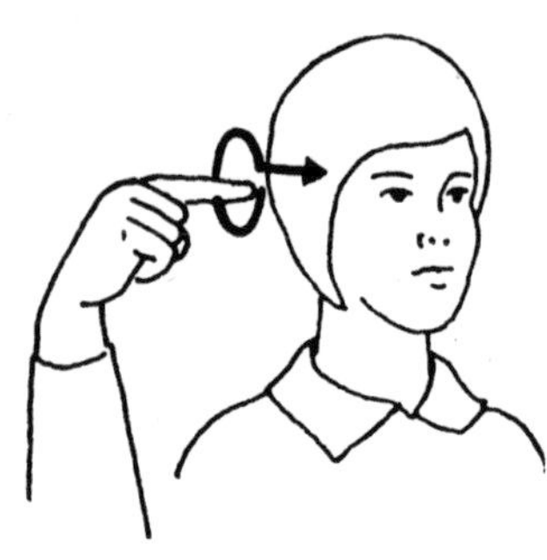

**government**
Circle and touch right temple with right index.

**capital**
Rest thumb of right C on right shoulder.

**Congress**
Place thumb of C shape RH on left breast. Sweep across to right breast.

**Senate**
Place S shape RH on left breast. Sweep across to right breast.

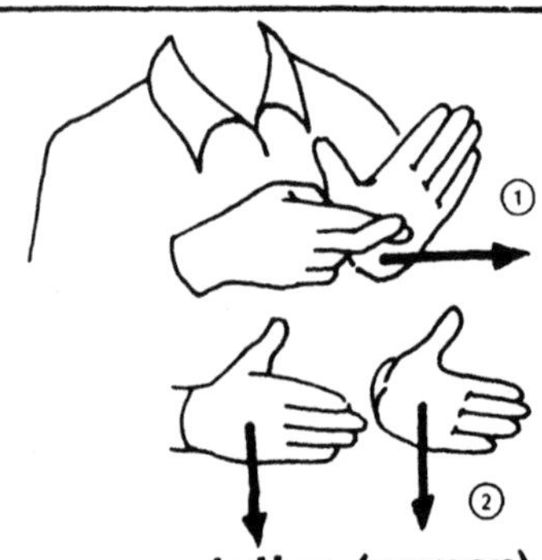


**representative (person)**
Open B shape LH, palm out. Place right R in middle of left palm and move both hands forward. Follow with agent marker.

**deficit**

Tap left palm twice with back of right flat O. Then push right V shape between index and middle fingers of LH, palm down.

**debit**

Form a D shape with right hand. Then tap left palm with index tip of right D.

**credit**

C shape both hands. Place right C on left C and draw both hands back towards body.

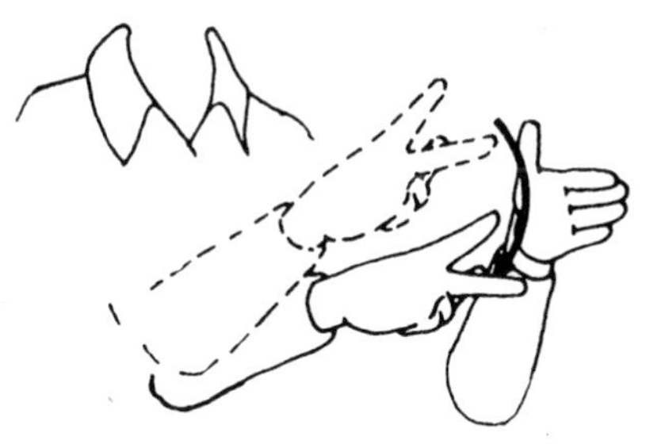

**price**

LH open B palm right, tips out. P shape RH palm and tips left. Strike middle fingertip of right P down across left palm.

**foreign**

Rub left elbow clockwise with thumb and index finger of F shape RH.

**neutralism**

N shape RH. Gently shake from left to right.

# PRACTICE SENTENCES

Repeat each of the following phrases or sentences several times. Start forming each sign at the same time you begin to speak its corresponding word.

After you can sign, and simultaneouosly say, each phrase or sentence comfortably, pair each incomplete phrase with every appropriate sign in this chapter.

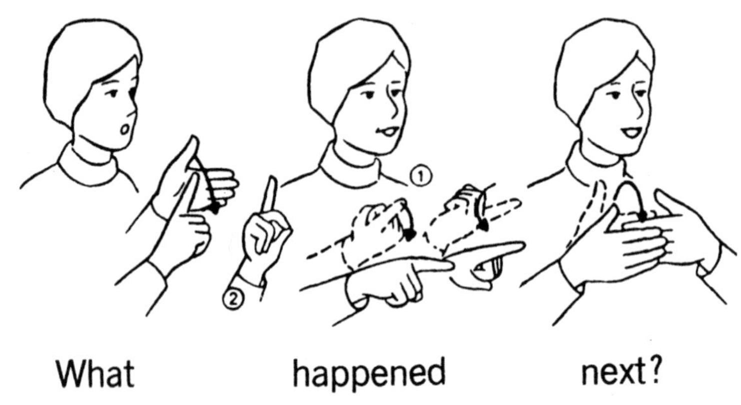

What happened next?

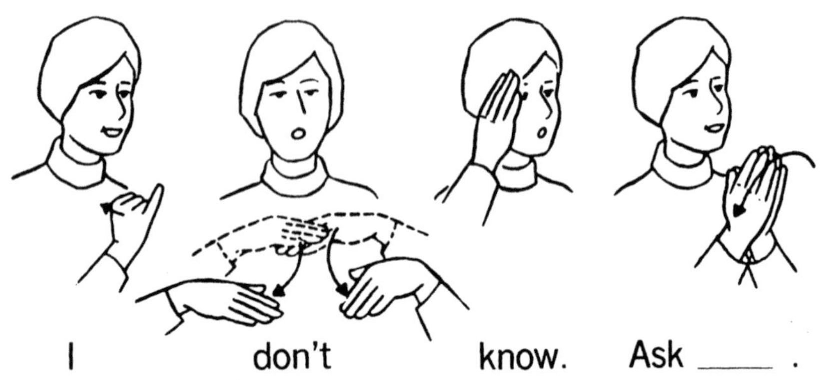

I don't know. Ask ____ .

Let's talk about ____.

Turn to the next page.

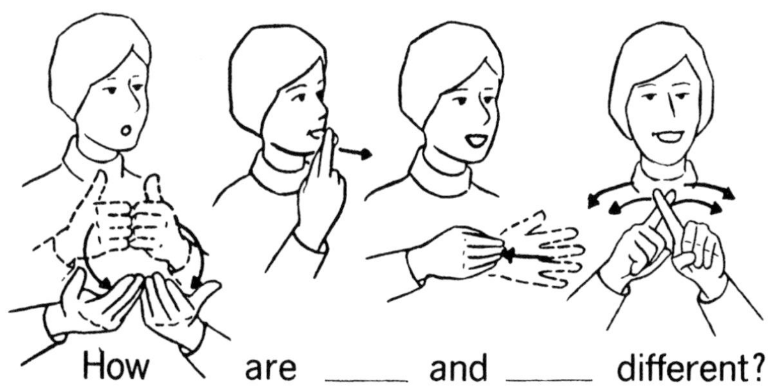

How are ____ and ____ different?

# 9.
# PLAY and SPORTS

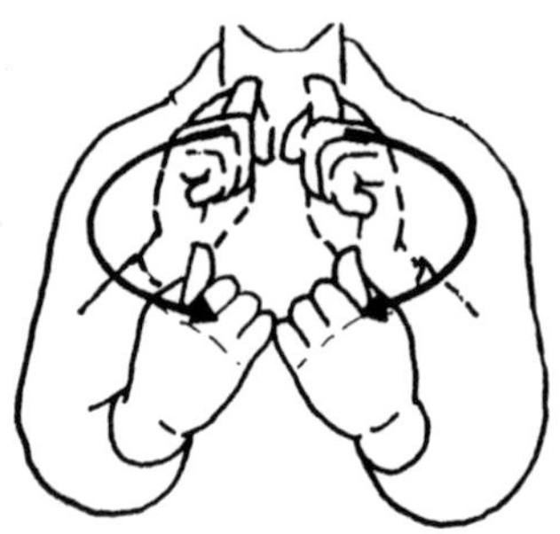

**team**
T shape both hands, palms out, held close together. Draw apart and around to front.

**sport**
S shape both hands, palms facing. Move back and forth alternately.

**exercise**
S shape both hands, arms held above shoulders. Push up and out.

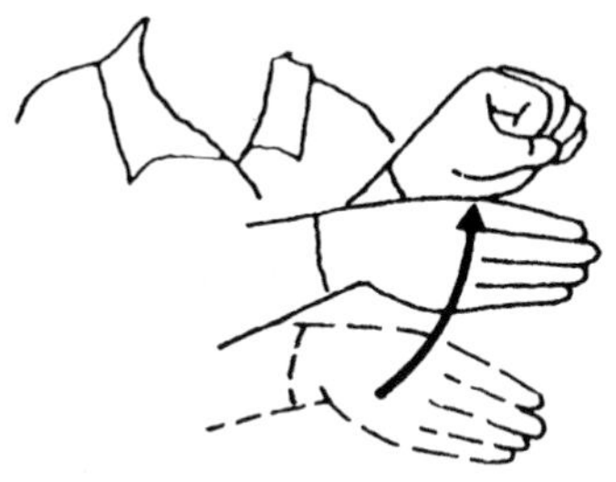

**soccer**
S shape LH palm down. Hit base of left wrist with index side of right B.

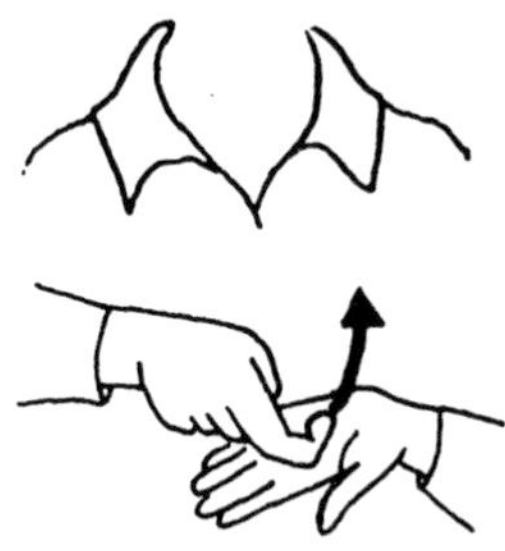

**hockey**
LH open B palm up. Swing right X against left palm then toward body.

**badminton**
Hold right A above right shoulder then arc forward. Repeat motion.

**track**
T shape both hands, palms facing. Move back and forth alternately.

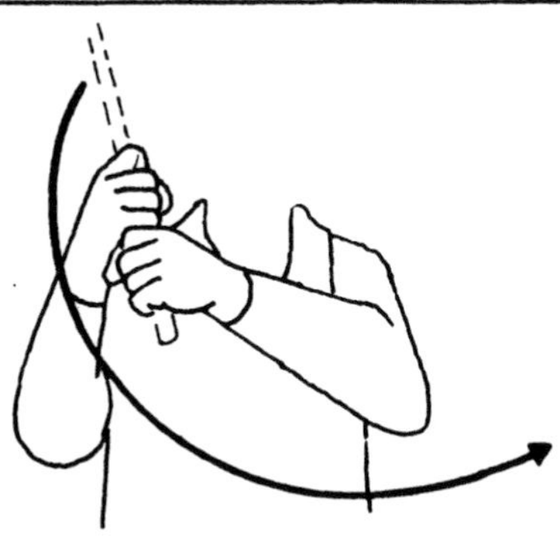

**golf**
Mime swinging golf club at ball.

**croquet**
Mime holding a croquet mallet and hitting ball through wicket.

**volleyball**
Open B both hands, palms out. Place at sides of head and push up and forward, as if hitting ball. Repeat motion.

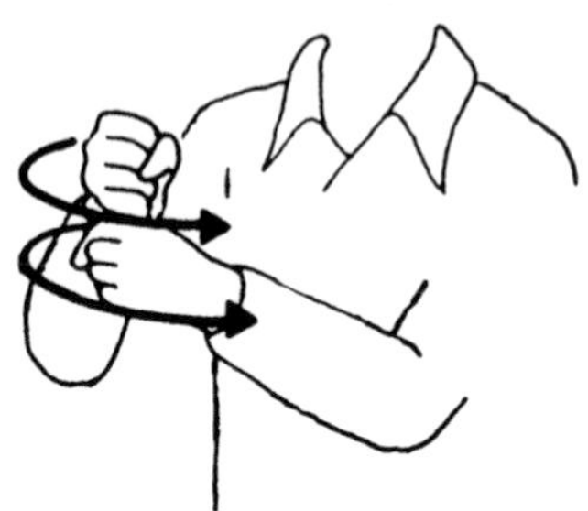

**baseball**
Mime grasping baseball bat with S shape hands and swinging at ball.

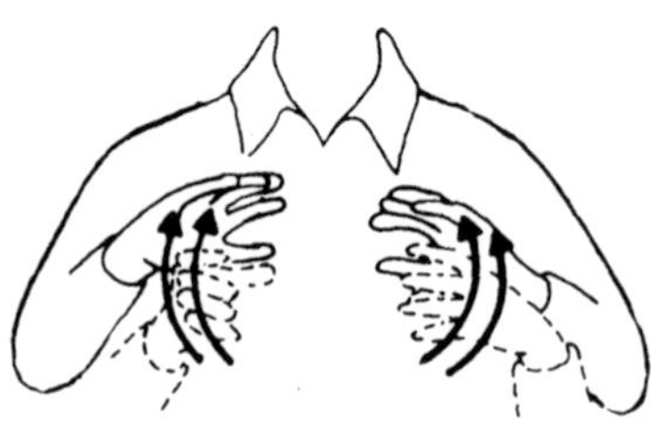

**basketball**
Mime holding ball then arc hands upward twice.

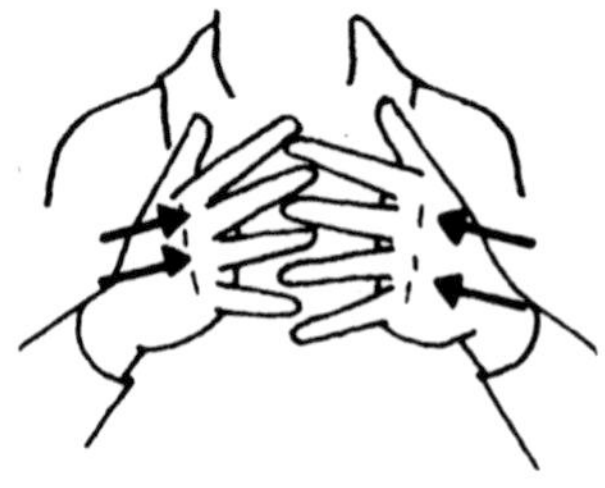

**football (game)**
Five shape both hands, palms in, tips facing. Mesh fingers together two or three times.

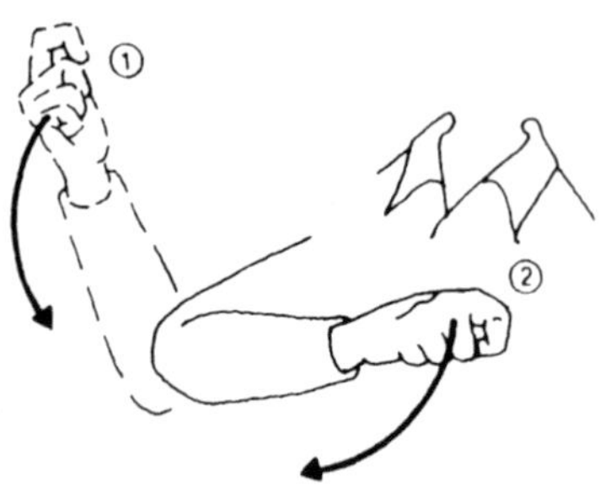


**tennis**
Mime swinging tennis racket.

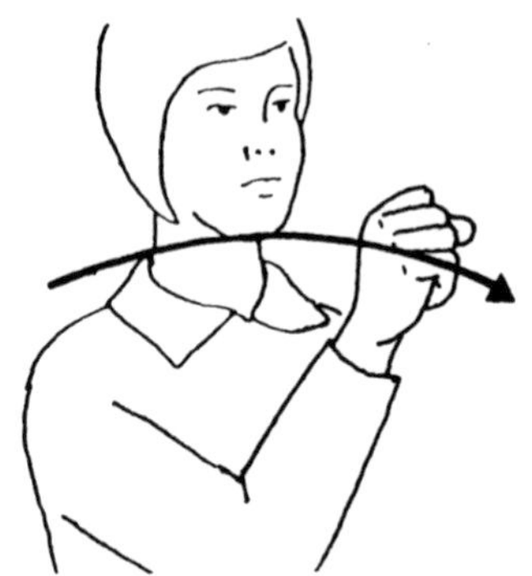

**racket (sports)**
Mime holding racket in front of right shoulder and batting forward.

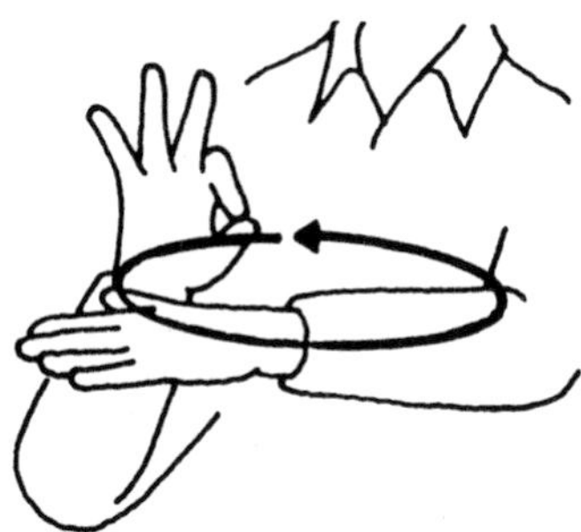

**field**
LH open B palm down, tips slightly right. Place right F on left wrist, circle counterclockwise over elbow, and return to original position.

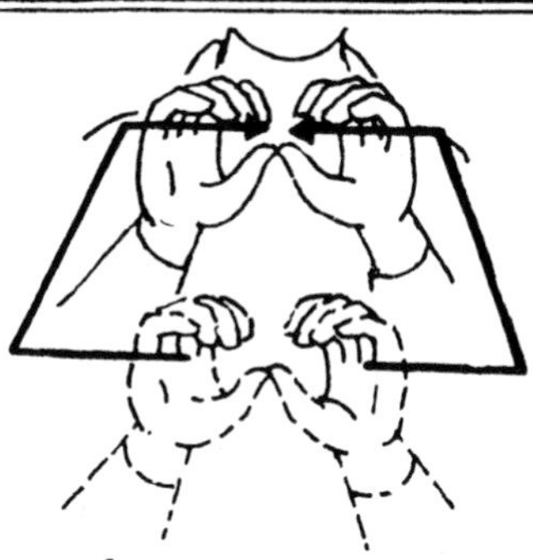

**court**
C shape both hands, thumbs touching. Draw apart, back, and then together, outlining a court.

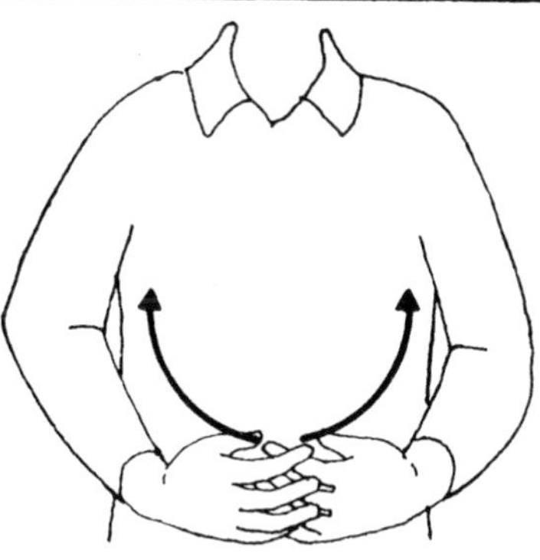

**net**
Open B both hands, palms up. Entwine fingers then pull apart and up.

**rule**
LH open B palm right. R shape RH palm left. Tap fingers, then base, of left hand with tips of right R.

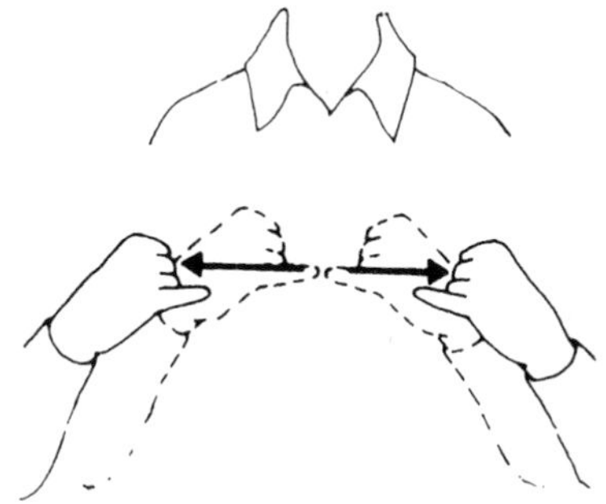

**line**
I shape both hands, palms in, tips touching. Draw apart in straight line.

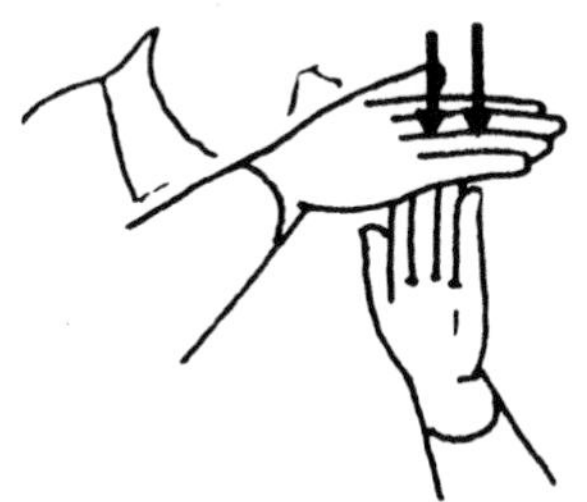

**time out**
Open B shape both hands, left palm right, right tip left. Tap tips of LH twice with palm of RH.

**sandbox**

S shape both hands, left S down, right S up. Place right S on back of left S and move in small circle counterclockwise. Open B both hands, palms facing, thumbs up. Turn LH right and RH left to form shape of box.

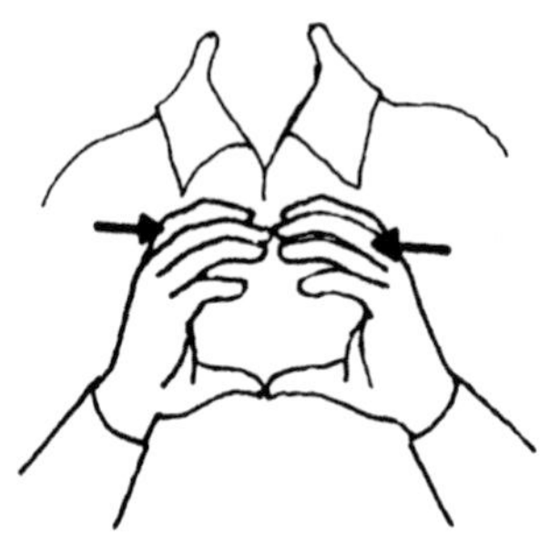

**ball**

Claw shape both hands, palms facing. Place tips together, outlining shape of ball.

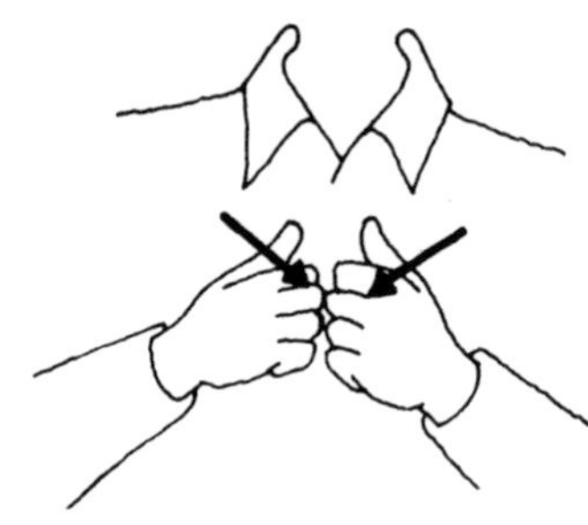

**game**

A shape both hands, palms in, thumbs up. Hit knuckles together once while moving hands down slightly.

**jungle gym**

J shape RH palm left. Place right elbow on back of LH, palm down, and twist RH back and forth. A shape both hands, knuckles facing. Hold above shoulders and move forward in circular movements. (Sometimes made with G shapes.)

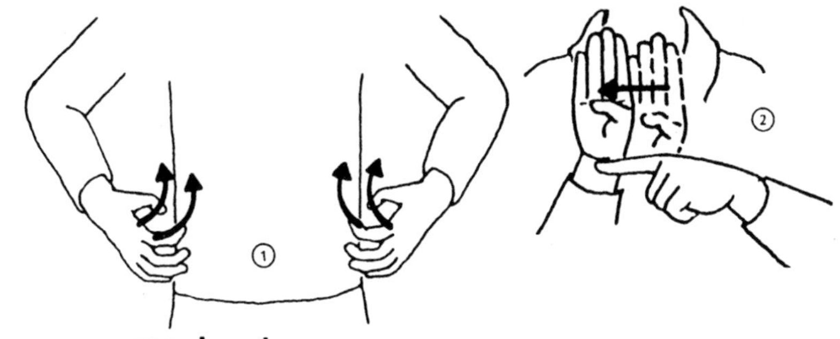

## monkey bar

Claw shape both hands. Scratch sides of body with tips. Slide base of right B forward on left index.

## merry-go-round

Bent V shape both hands, palms down. Circle down and up alternately.

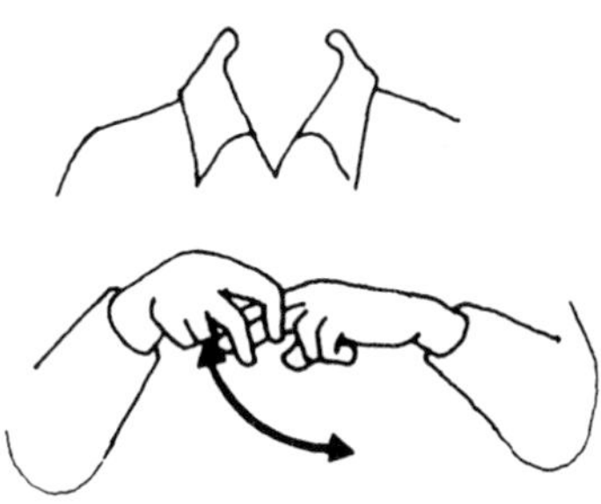

## swing

Hook right V over left H, palms down. Swing both hands back and forth.

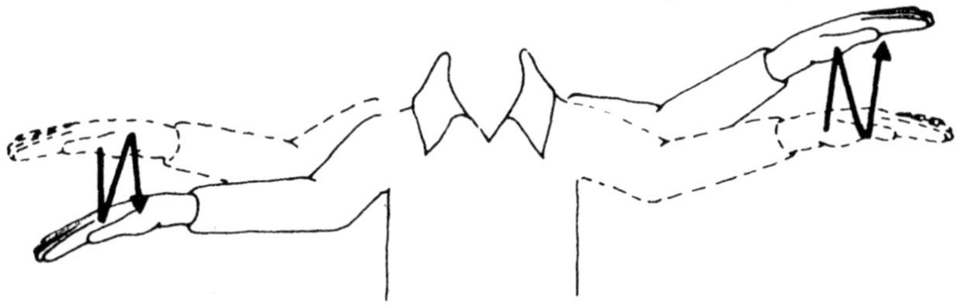

## seesaw

Extend arms from body. Move up and down alternately.

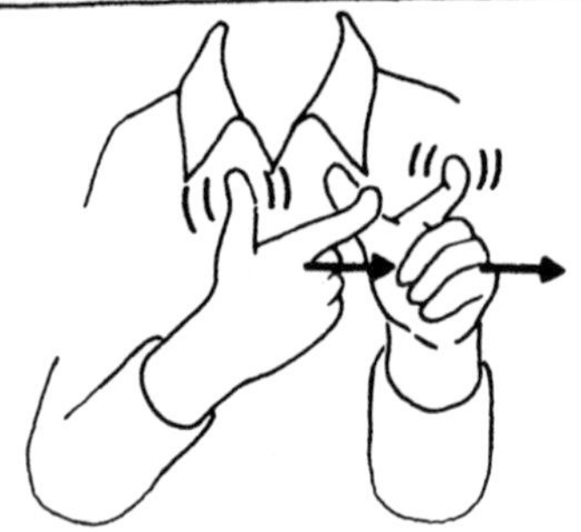

**run**
L shape both hands, index tips out, LH a little ahead of right. Hook right index finger around left thumb. Wiggle L shape fingers while moving both hands forward.

**jump**
LH open B palm up, tips out. Place tips of right V in left palm and pull up quickly, changing into bent V shape. Repeat motion.

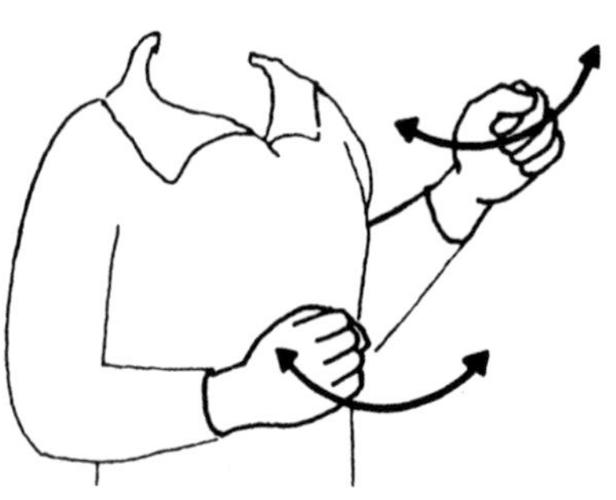

**jog**
S shape both hands, palms facing. Alternately swing back and forth.

**ride**
C shape LH palm right. Hook fingers of right H on left thumb and move both hands forward.

**climb**
RH bent V palm out. Move up in short circular movements.

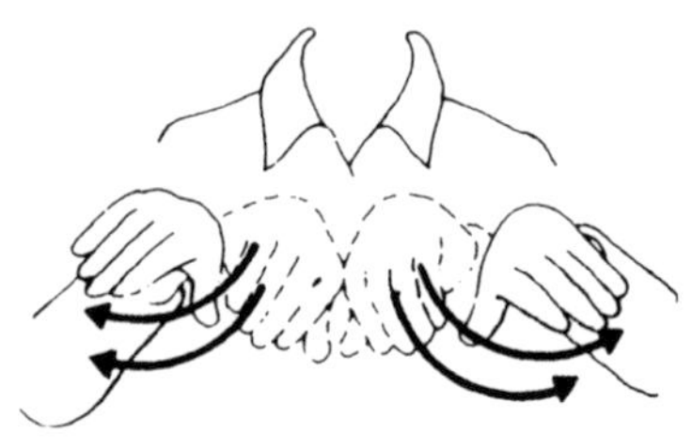

**swim**
Hands together palms down. Move forward and out (miming breaststroke).

**play**

Y shape both hands, palms in. Simultaneously twist back and forth.

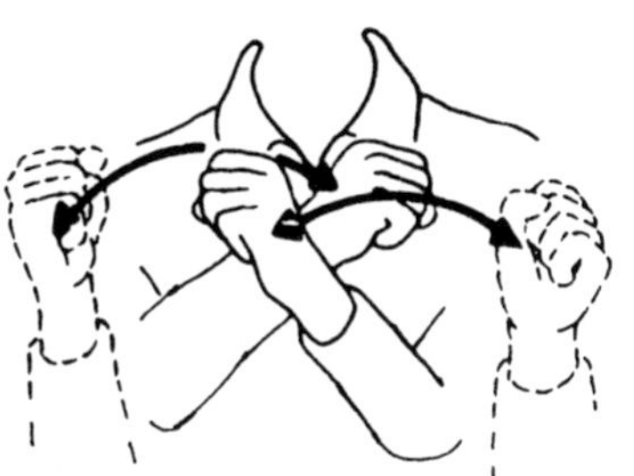

**fight**

S shape both hands, knuckles facing. Cross hands in front of body once or twice.

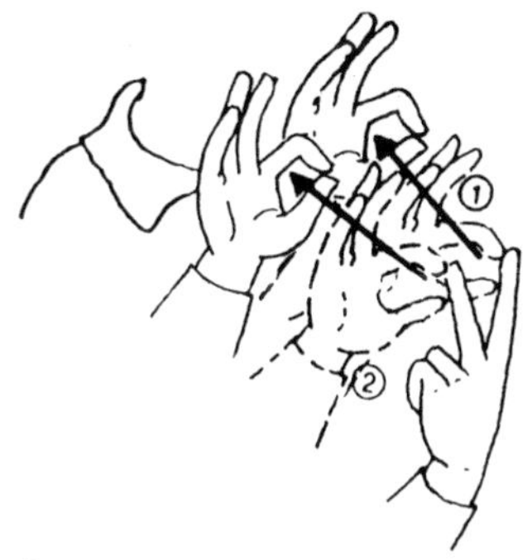

**choose**

V shape LH palm in. With right thumb and index, pick at left index and middle fingers, as if choosing something.

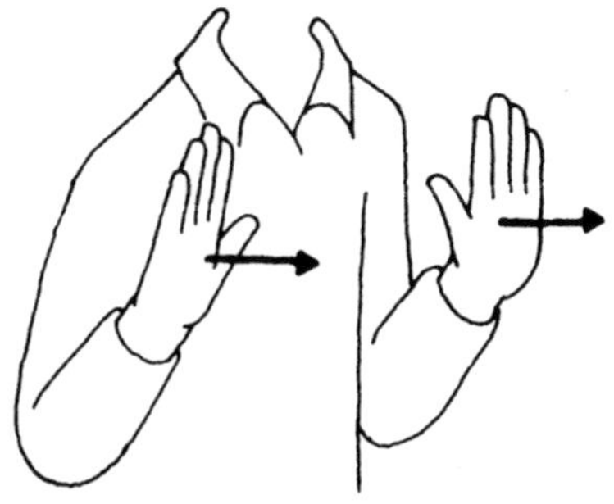

**push**

Open B both hands, palms out, tips up, left a little in front of right. Push out.

**yell**

Claw shape RH palm in. Place at mouth then move up and out sharply once or twice.

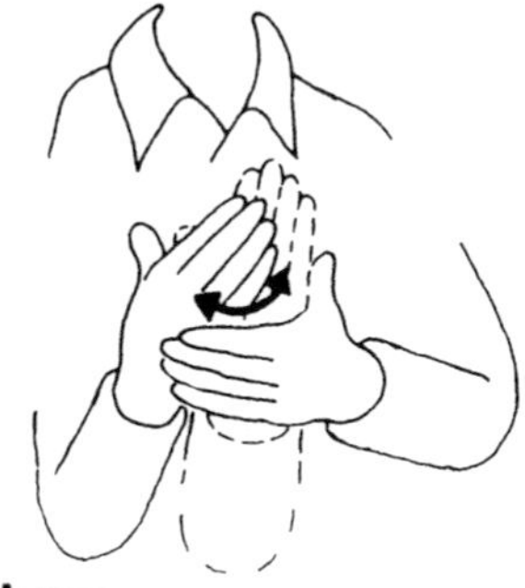

**share**

LH open B. Brush little finger side of right open B back and forth between left thumb and index finger.

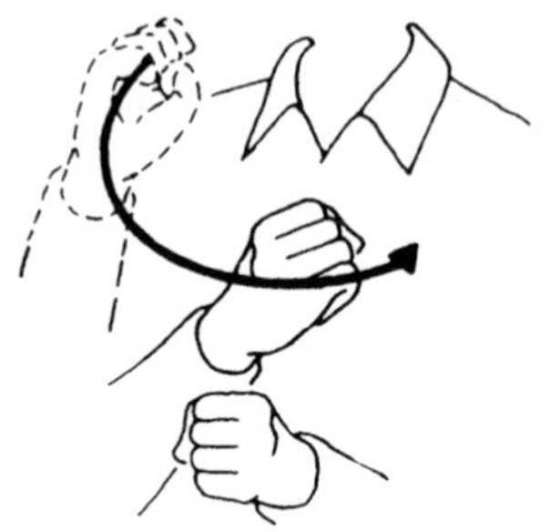

**win**
S shape LH knuckles right. Make sweeping pass with right C over left S closing C into S shape.

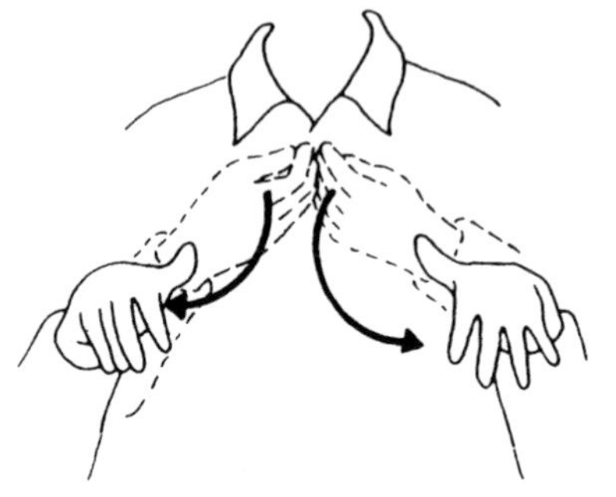

**lose**
Flat O shape both hands, backs of fingers touching. Drop into 5 shapes, palms down.

**defeat**
S shape LH palm down. Drop right D over left wrist.

**score**
LH open B palm right. Bounce tips of RH down left palm.

**improve**
LH open B palm down. Bounce little finger side of right open B up left forearm.

**cheat**
LH open B palm right, tips out. Straddle with index and middle finger of RH then move RH up and down.

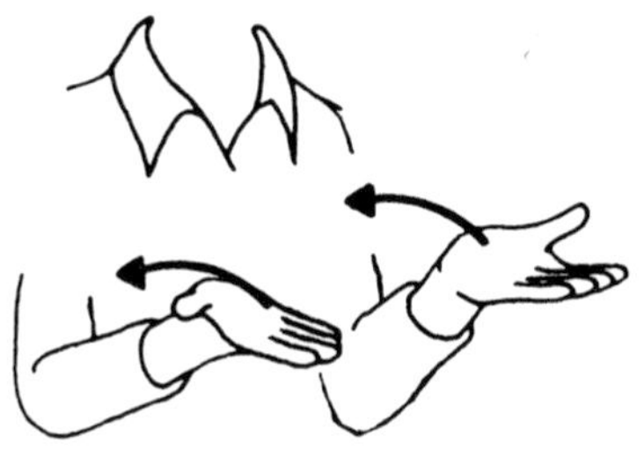

**bring**
Open B both hands, palms up, one slightly behind the other. Move toward body as if carrying something.

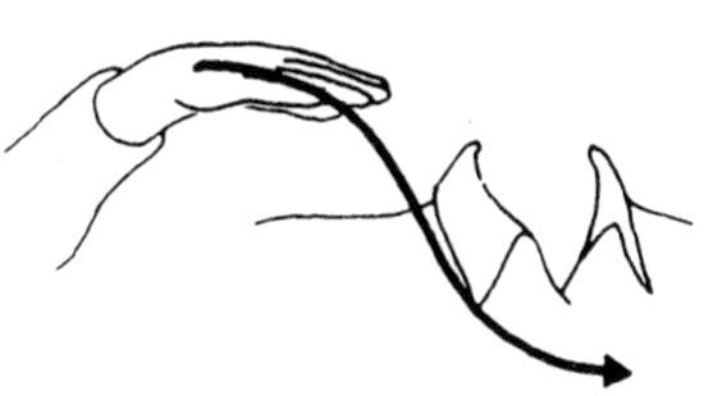

**slide**
B shape RH palm down held at shoulder. Bring down in sweeping movement.

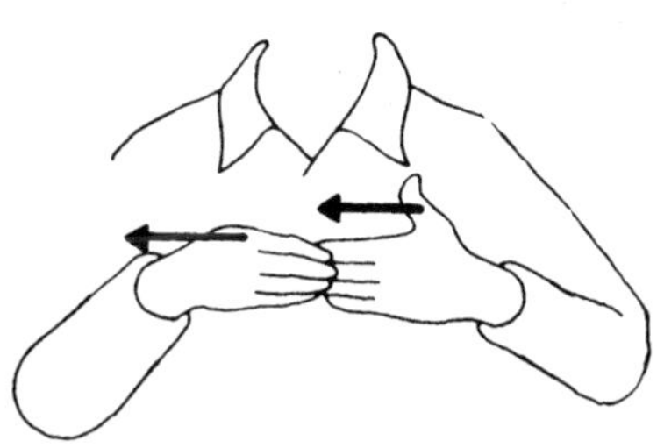

**lead**
LH open B palm in, tips right. Grasp with fingers and thumb of RH and pull to right.

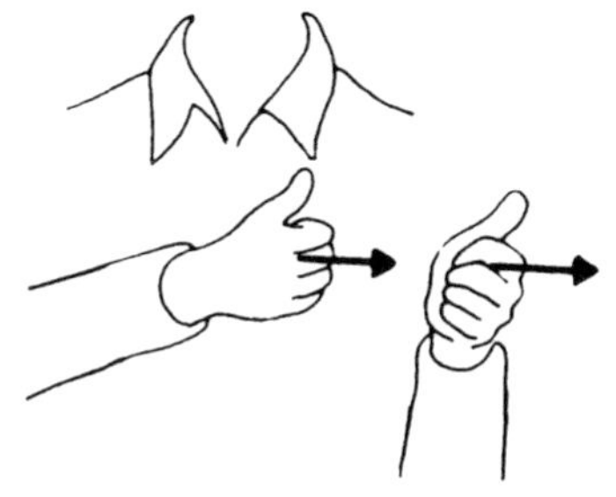

**follow**
A shape both hands, thumbs up, right behind left. Move both forward simultaneously.

**hobby**
S shape LH palm down. H shape RH palm in. Brush base of right H back and forth on back of left wrist.

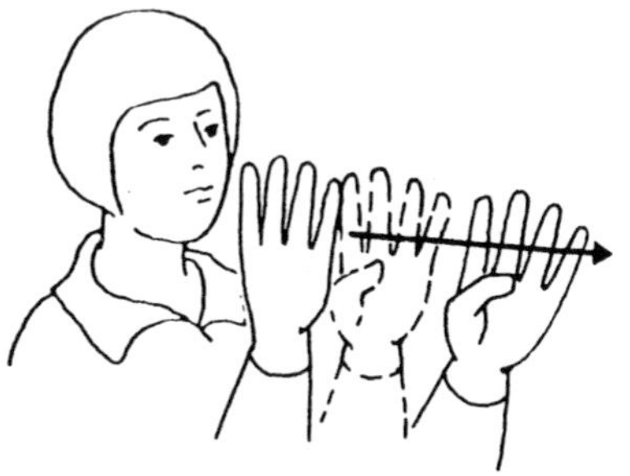

**line up**
Four shape both hands, left palm right, right palm left. Place right hand behind left then move LH forward.

# PRACTICE SENTENCES

Repeat each of the following phrases or sentences several times. Start forming each sign at the same time you begin to speak its corresponding word.

After you can sign, and simultaneously say, each phrase or sentence comfortably, pair each incomplete phrase with every appropriate sign in this chapter.

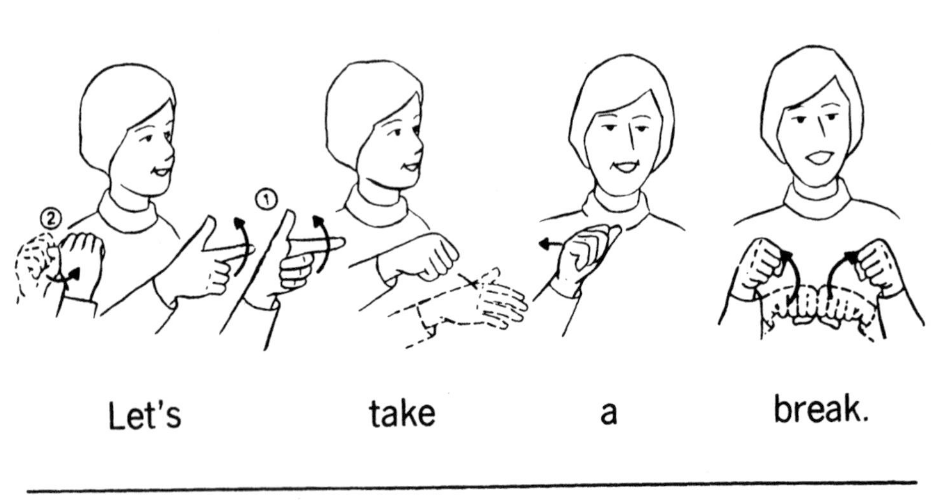


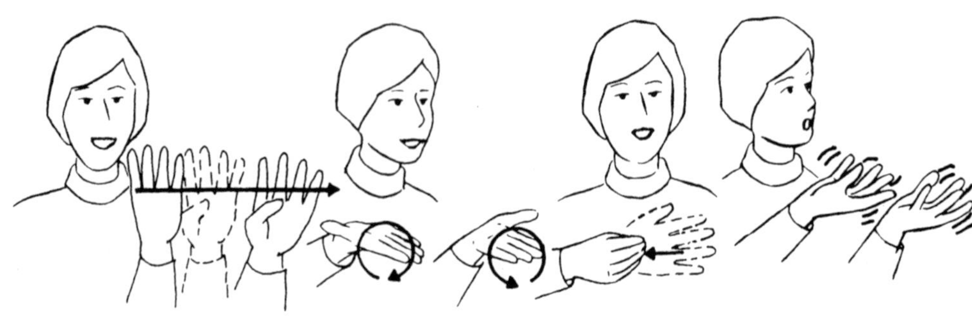

Line up here and wait.

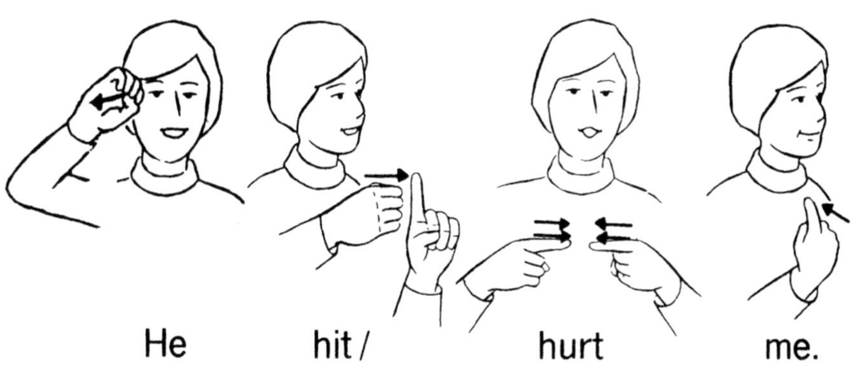

He hit / hurt me.

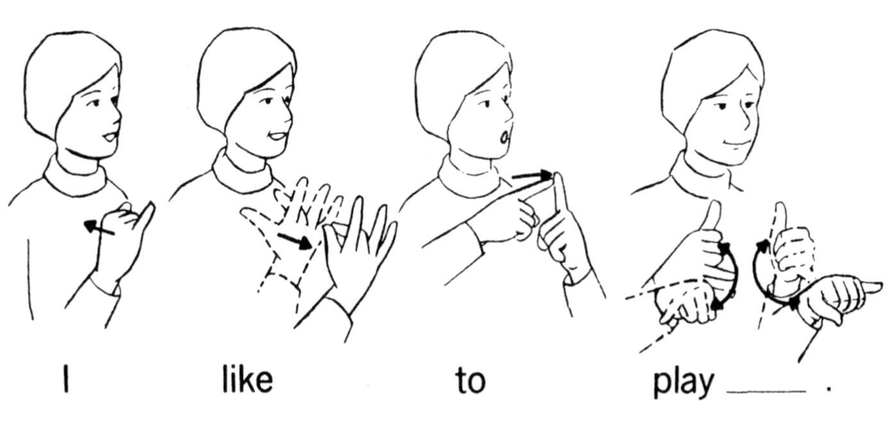

I like to play ____ .

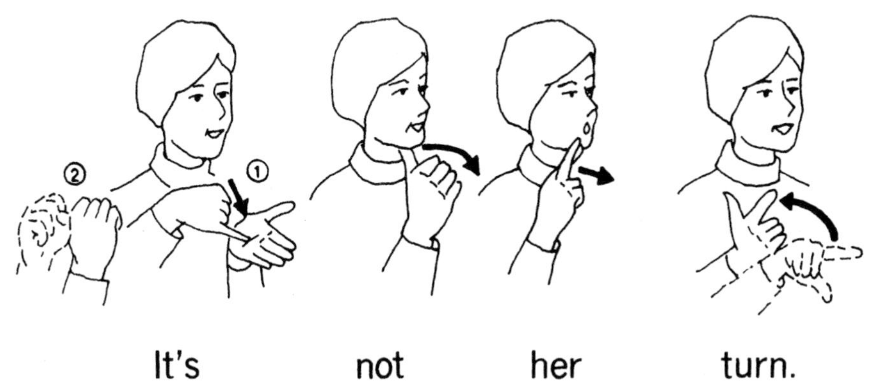

It's not her turn.

Please be quiet.

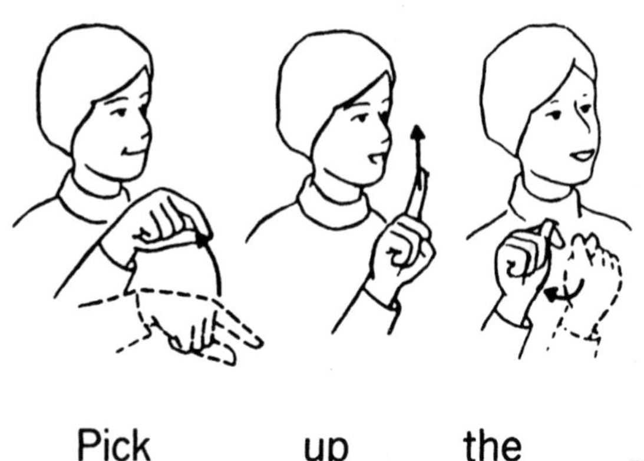
Pick up the ____ .

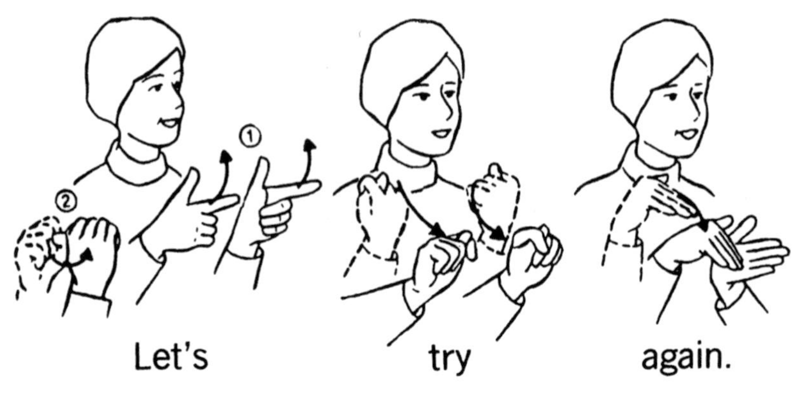

Let's try again.

# 10.
# FEELINGS

**feeling (noun)**
Place tip of right middle finger on left side of chest then stroke upward twice.

**hate**
Eight shape both hands, palms facing, tips out, left slightly in front of right. Flick middle fingers from thumbs.

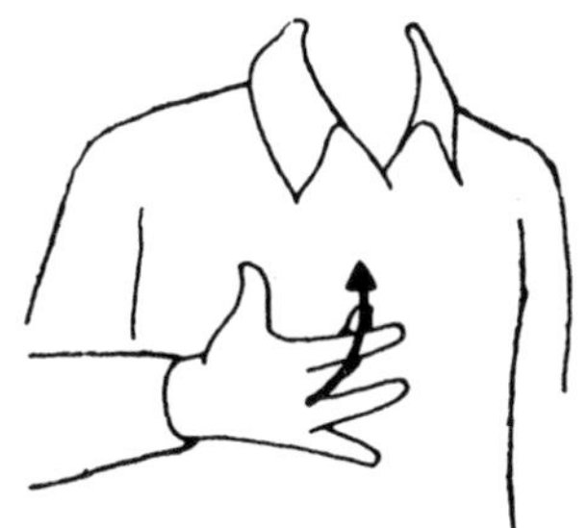

**feel**
Strike right middle finger upward on chest.

**love**
S shape both hands. Cross wrists and place over heart.

**nice**
B shape LH palm and tips slanted right. Slide right N forward on left index finger.

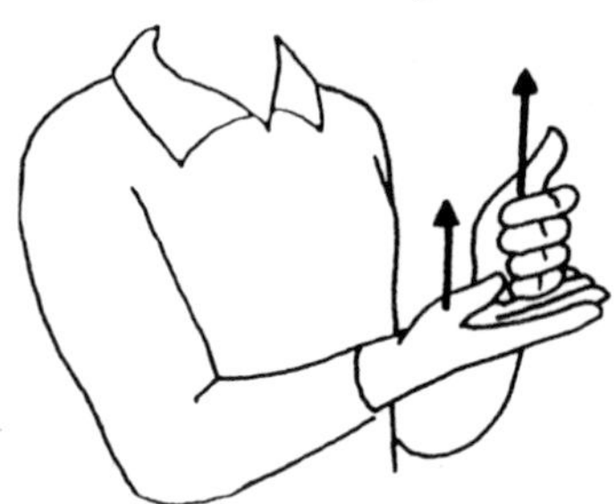

**help**
Place little finger side of left A, thumb up, in right palm. Raise right palm up.

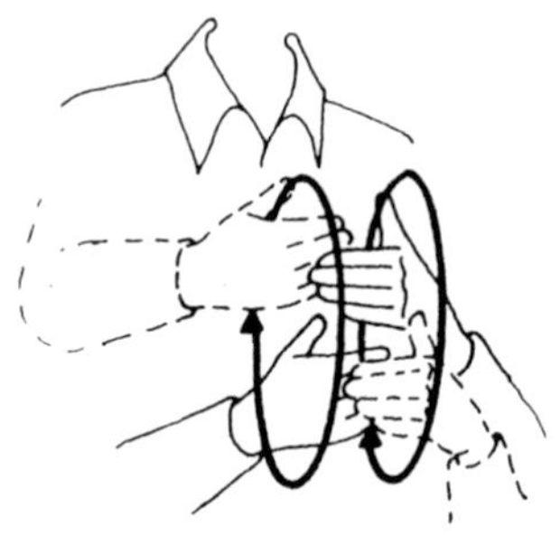

**kind (virtue)**
Open B both hands, palms in, left tips right, right tips left. Circle around one another moving out from the heart.

**interest (concern)**
Place open tips of middle fingers and thumbs on chest, RH above LH. Move out slightly, closing into 8 shape.

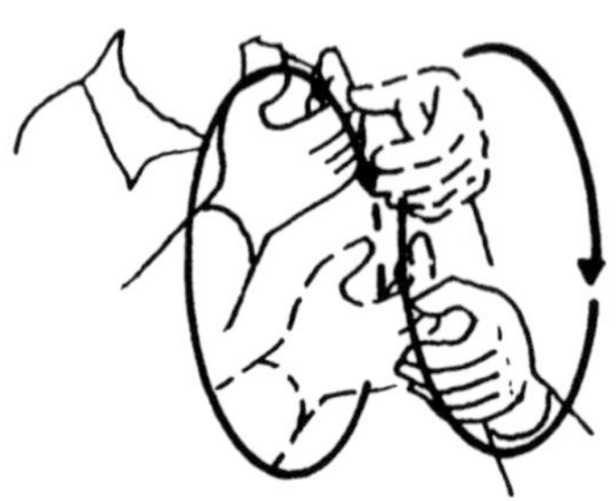

**considerate**
C shape both hands, left tips right, right tips left. Circle around one another.

**polite**
RH open B palm left. Tap chest with thumb twice.

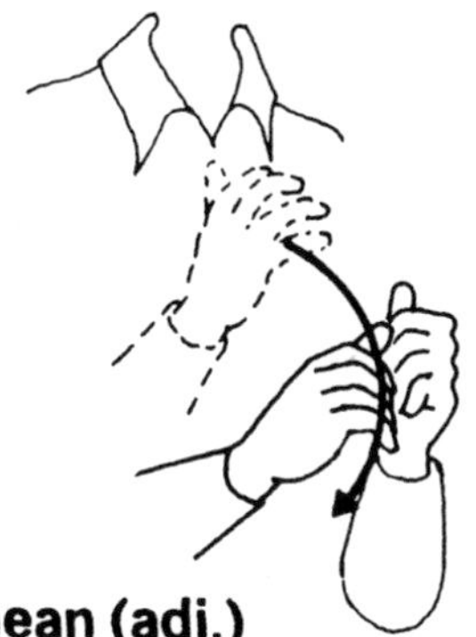

**mean (adj.)**
A shape LH thumb up. Claw shape RH thumb extended. Brush right knuckles down left knuckles.

**mood**
Brush tips of right M up against chest.

**angry**
Claw shape RH tips on chest. Draw up and out in forceful manner.

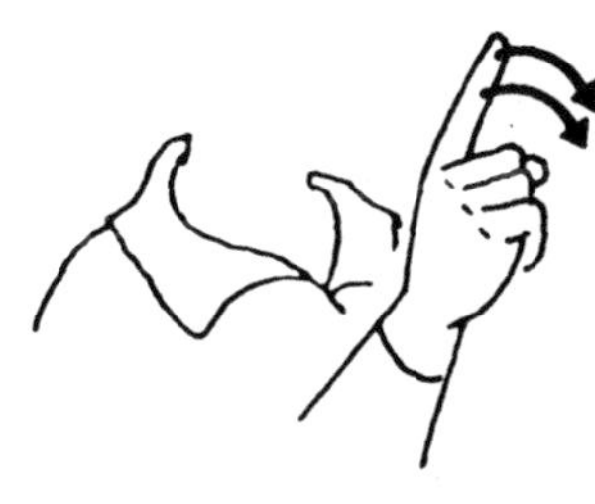

**scold**
Shake right index finger up and down vigorously.

**complain**
Claw shape both hands, palms in, RH above LH. Strike chest twice with tips.

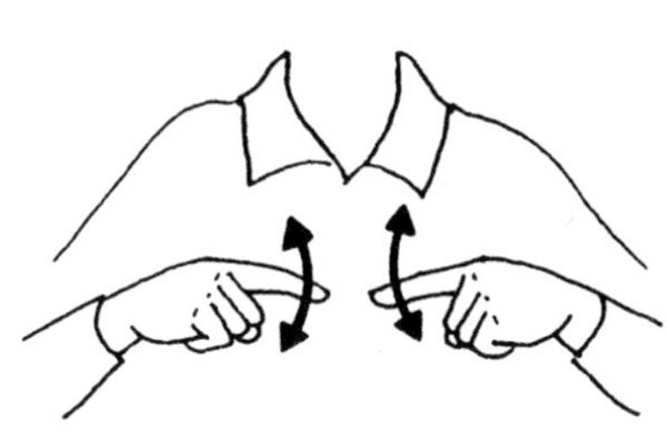

**argue**
One shape both hands, palms in, tips facing. Shake hands up and down simultaneously.

**like (verb)**
Place right middle finger and thumb on upper chest, then draw out and close fingers.

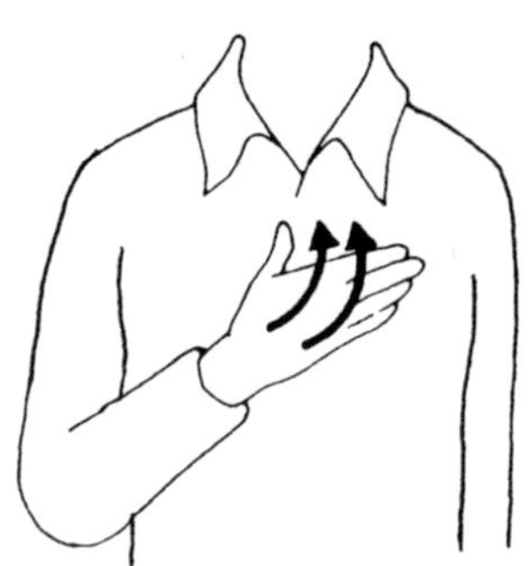

**happy**
RH open B palm in, tips left. Brush up chest twice with quick, short motion.

**enjoy**
Open B both hands, palms in, left tips right, right tips left. Place on chest. Circle RH clockwise and LH counterclockwise.

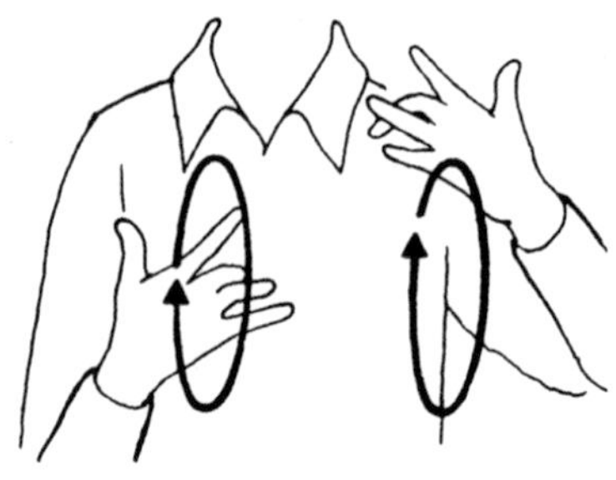

**excite**
Five shape both hands, palms in. Alternately brush tips of middle fingers upward on chest.

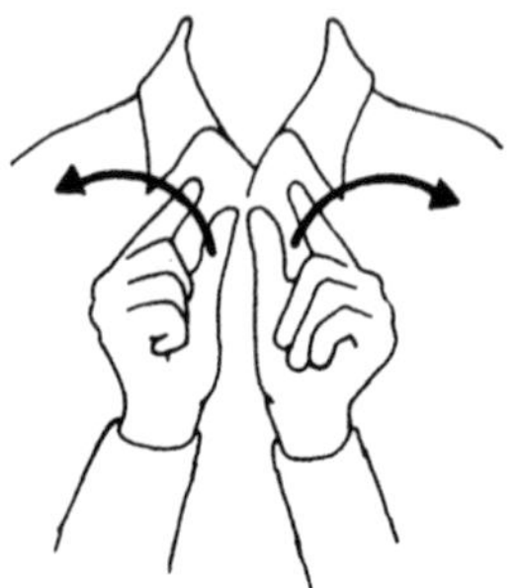

**great**
G shape both hands, palms and tips out. Arc hands apart.

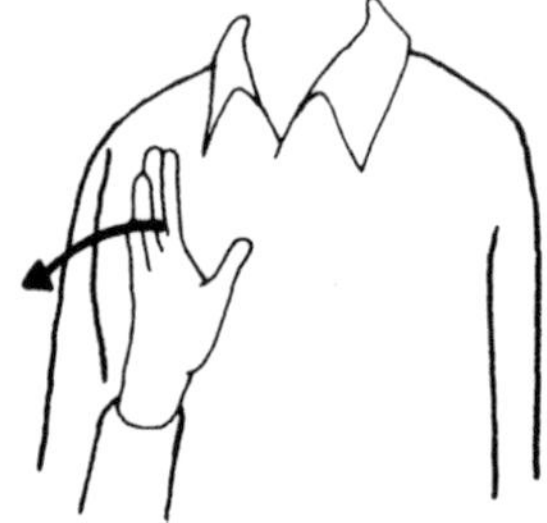

**fine**
Five shape RH palm left. Place thumb on chest and move slightly up and out.

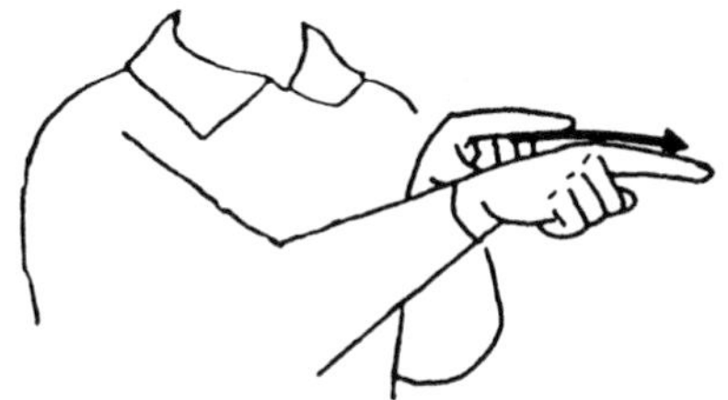

**rude**

One shape both hands, palms down, tips out. Move right index forward several times, striking against base of left index at each pass.

**selfish**

V shape both hands, palms down, tips out. Draw back into bent V shapes.

**discourage**

Place middle fingers on chest. Pull down.

**grouch**

Place right G on right side of mouth then draw down right side of chin.

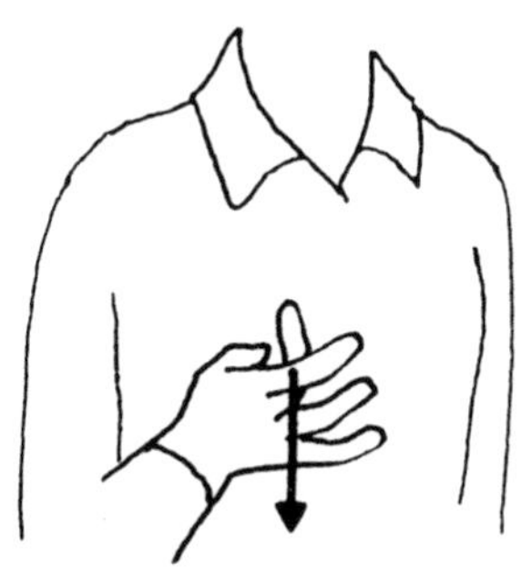

**depress**

Draw middle finger of RH down chest.

**disappoint**

Place tip of right index on chin.

**want**
Five shape both hands, palms up, fingers slightly curved. Draw back to body.

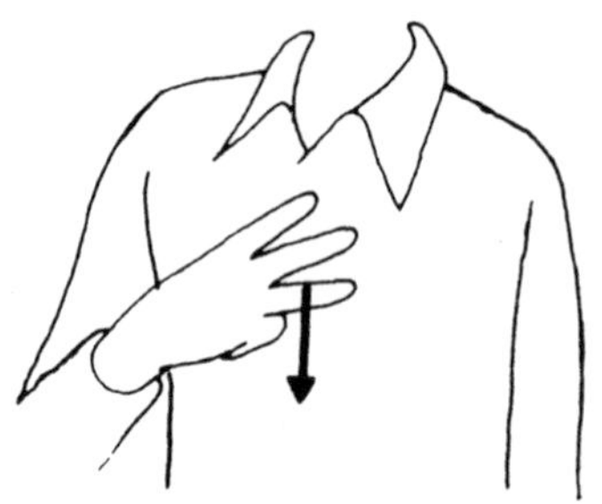

**wish**
W shape RH palm in. Place on chest and move down slightly.

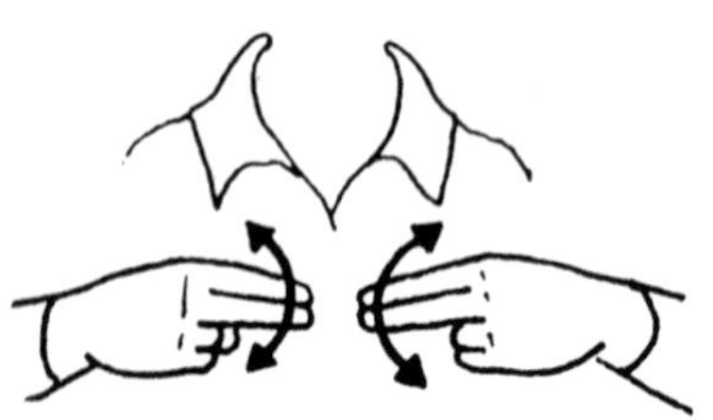

**hassle**
H shape both hands, palms in, tips facing. Simultaneously shake hands up and down.

**excuse**
LH open B palm up, tips out. Brush edge of left palm twice with tips of RH.

**embarrass**
Five shape both hands, palms facing. Move in circles alternately at sides of face.

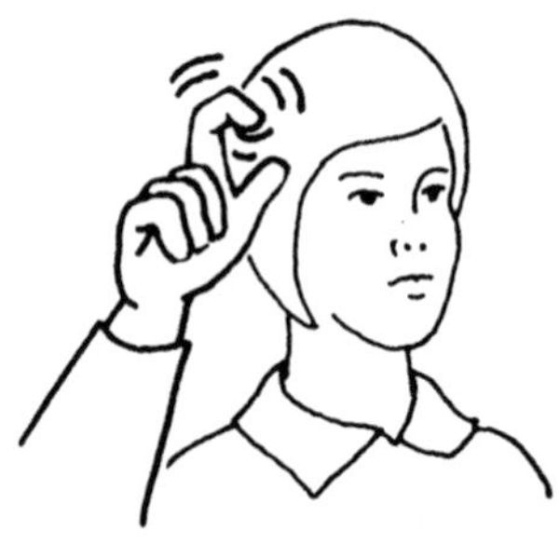

**mischief**
Place thumb of right L on right temple then crook and uncrook index several times.

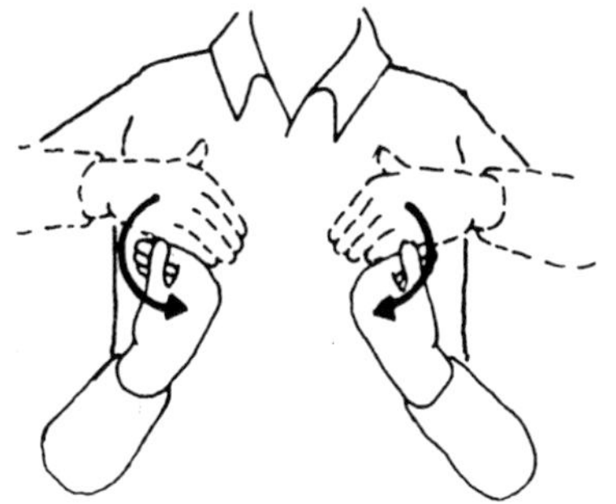

**tired**

Bent open B shape both hands, palms in. Place tips on chest then let hands drop, ending with little finger sides against chest.

**bore**

Place right index on right side of nose and twist to left.

**upset**

Place right C shape at chest with thumb against body. Twist down until palm is facing up.

**shy**

Place knuckles of right A on right cheek and twist forward while spreading fingers slightly.

**stupid**

Slap back of V shape RH against middle of forehead.

**silly**

Y shape RH. Shake in front of nose.

**worry**
W shape both hands, palms slanted out. Alternately circle inward in front of face.

**guilt**
Strike thumb side of right G against upper chest two or three times.

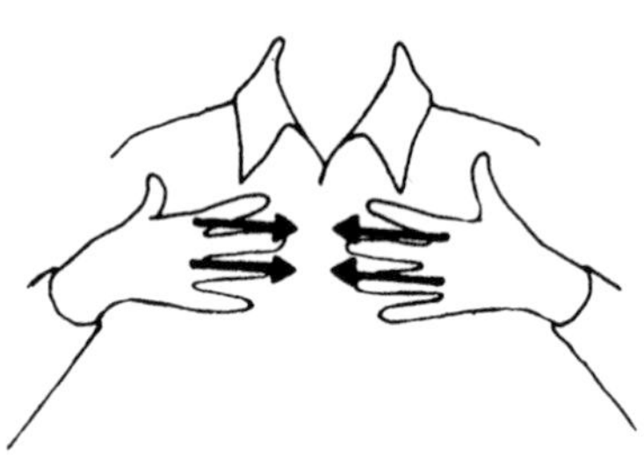

**afraid**
Open 5 both hands, palms in, tips facing. Move back and forth several times, as if shaking in fright.

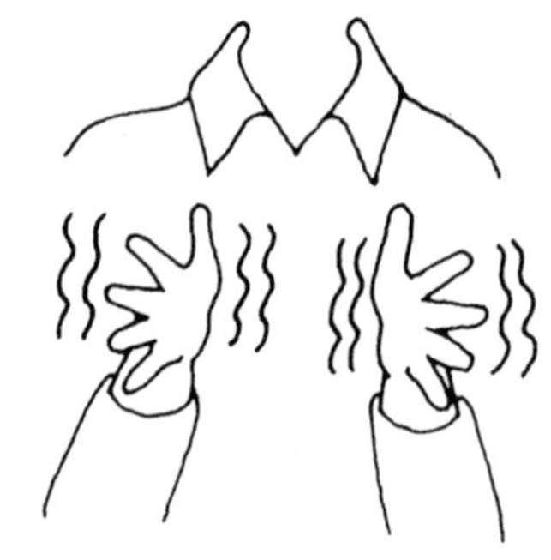

**nervous**
Five shape both hands, palms facing, tips out. Shake in nervous fashion.

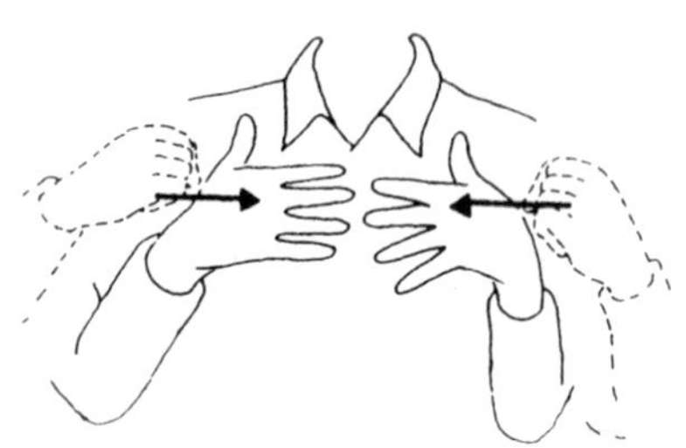

**scare**
S shape both hands, knuckles facing. Move toward one another sharply while opening into 5 shapes.

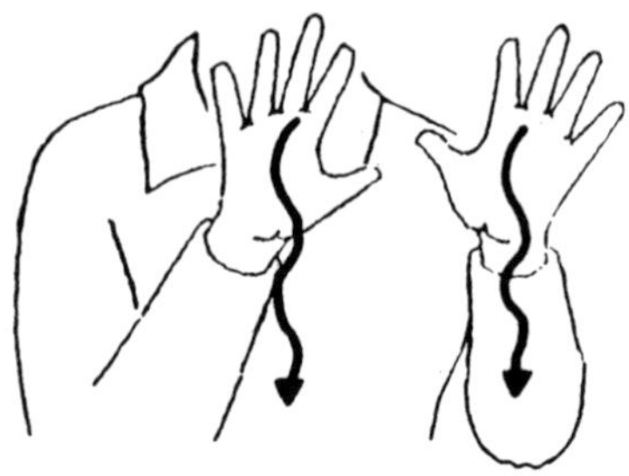

**fear**
Five shape both hands held to left of body. Shake hands while moving downward.

**responsible**
Tap left shoulder with tips of R shape hands, palms in.

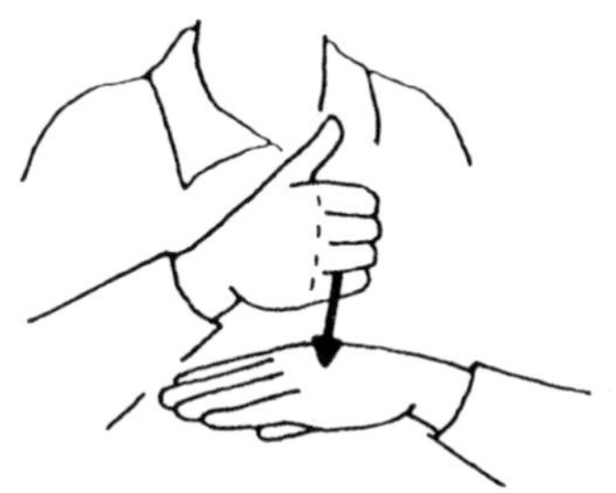

**fault**
LH open B palm down. Place little finger side of right A on back of LH.

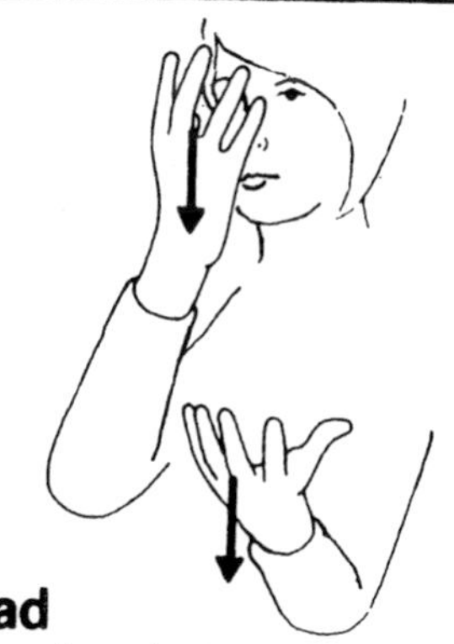

**sad**
Five shape both hands, palms in, fingers slightly curved, LH a little below RH. Hold in front of face and drop slowly.

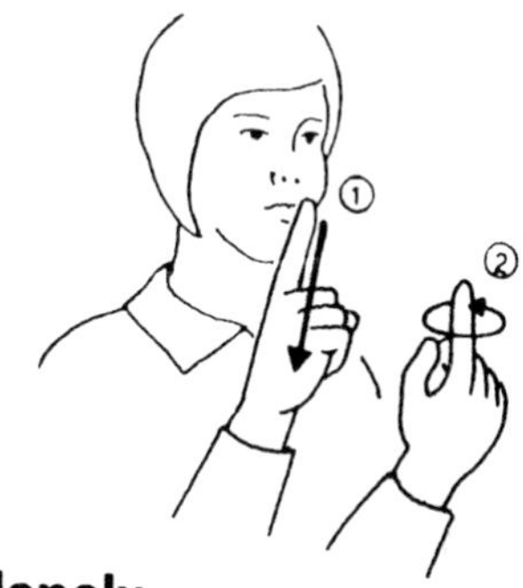


**lonely**
One shape RH palm left. Brush down lips. Then rotate right index, palm in, in circle counter-clockwise.

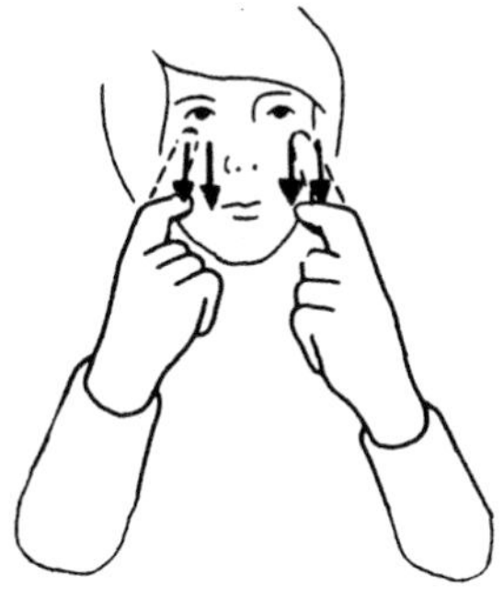

**cry**
Place index tips under eyes and draw down as if tracing tears.

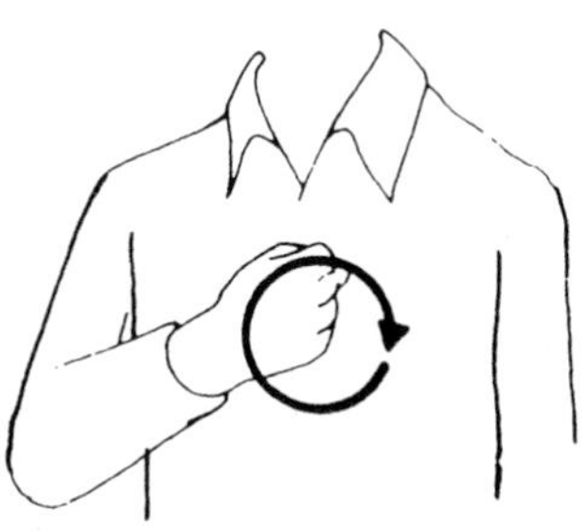

**sorry**
Circle right S on chest.

## PRACTICE SENTENCES

Repeat each of the following phrases or sentences several times. Start forming each sign at the same time you begin to speak its corresponding word.

After you can sign, and simultaneously say, each phrase or sentence comfortably, pair each incomplte phrase with every appropriate sign in this chapter.

Don't be so ____ .

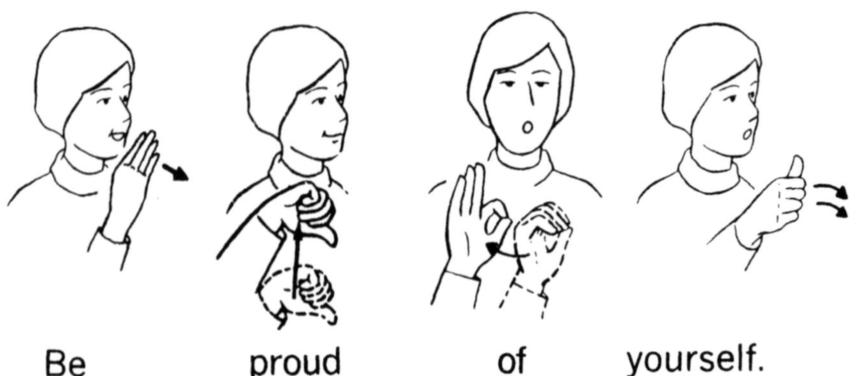

Be proud of yourself.

He / she feels ____ .

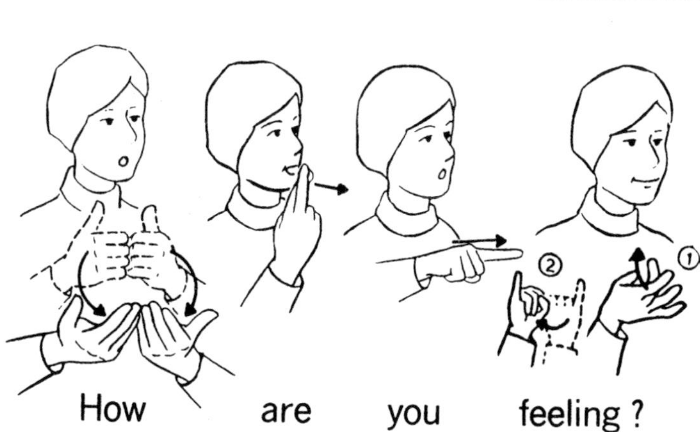

How are you feeling ?

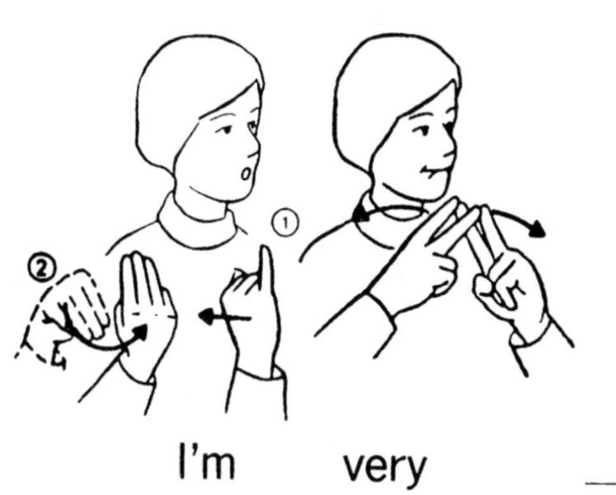

I'm very ____ .

# 11. FAMILY and LIFE EXPERIENCES

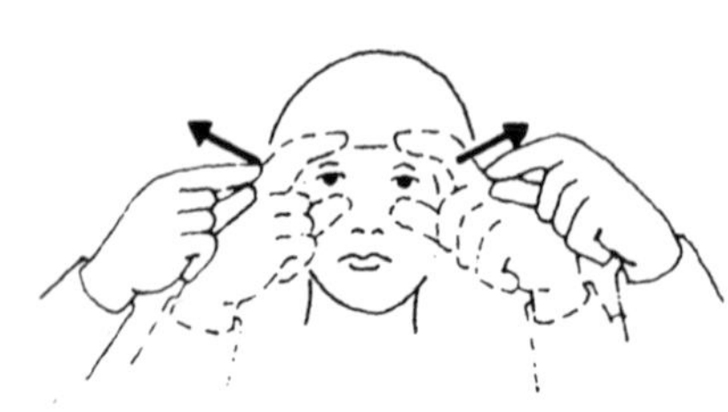

**glasses**
Place thumbs and index fingers at sides of eyes then draw back, closing fingers (as if outlining frame of glasses).

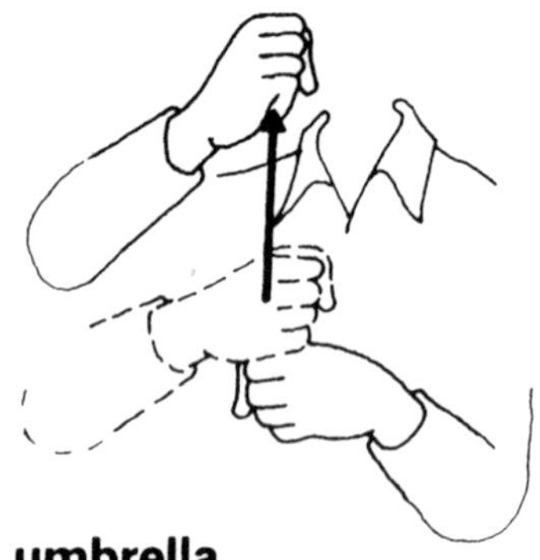

**umbrella**
Rest right S on left S and move RH up as if opening umbrella.

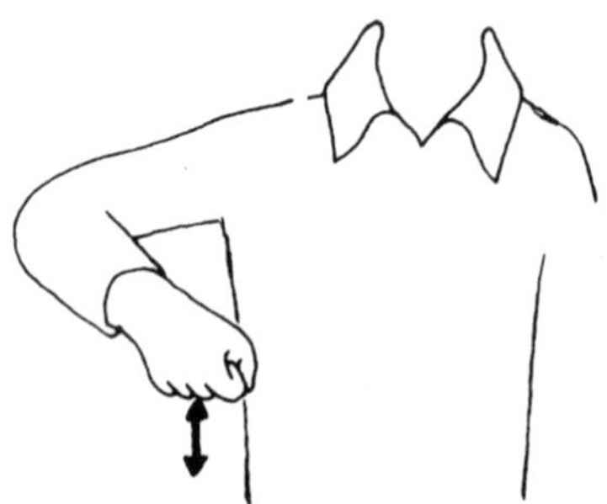

**suitcase**
Hold right arm down by side with fist clinched, as if carrying a heavy suitcase.

**hamper (basket)**
S shape LH palm down, arm extended. Place tips of right H against left wrist and arc down and up to elbow.

**change**
A shape both hands, left knuckles up, right knuckles down. Place right wrist on left wrist, then reverse positions.

**undress**
Place tips of claw shape hands on chest then pull apart. Lower hands slightly and repeat motion.

**unbutton**
Mime unbuttoning shirt or blouse with index fingers and thumbs.

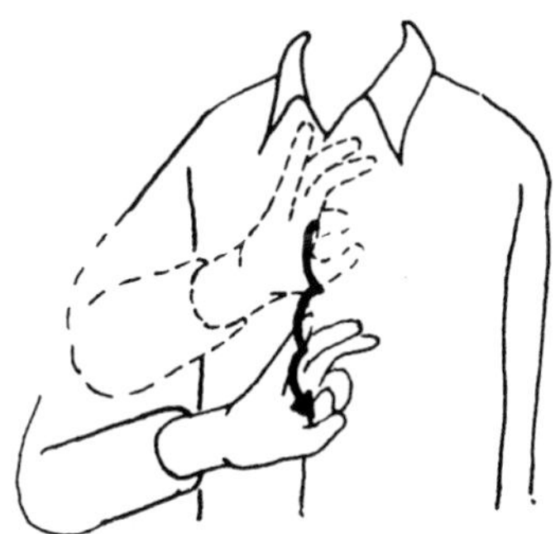

**button**
Curve index finger inside thumb. Tap three times on chest beginning at top.

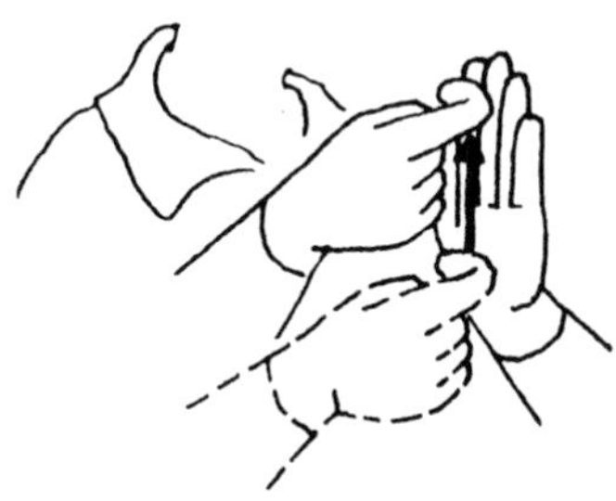

**zip**
LH open B palm right, tips up. Slide right X, palm in, up left palm.

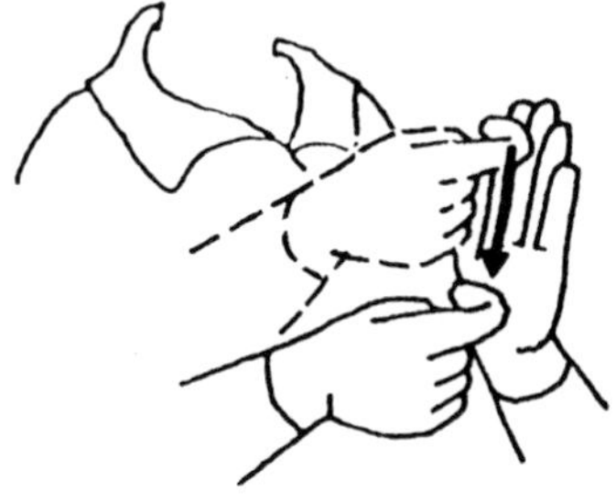

**unzip**
LH open B palm right, tips up. Slide knuckles of right X down left fingers and palm.

**pajamas**

Draw right fingers down over face ending in flat O. Form 5 shapes both hands, place on upper chest, then move down. (Sometimes fingerspelled P-J.)

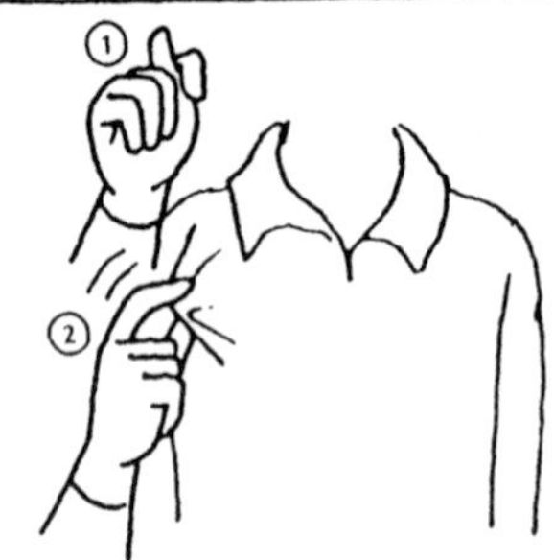

**tee shirt**

Form T with RH. Then grasp clothing on right upper chest with thumb and index finger of RH and tug slightly.

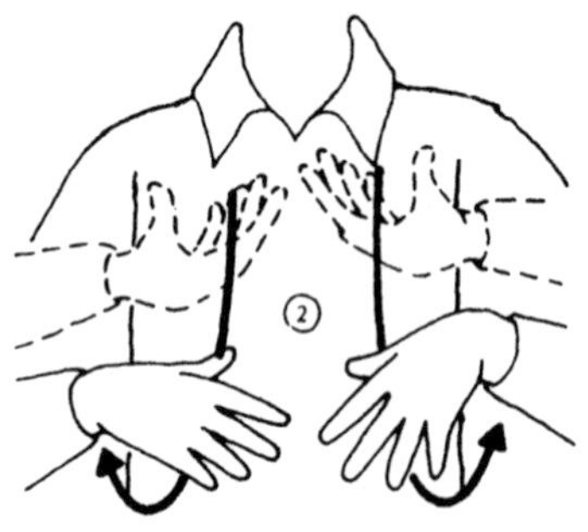

**nightgown**

Hold left arm in front of body, palm and tips slanted down. Place heel of right open B, tips down, on left wrist. Bent open B shape both hands, tips touching upper chest. Brush down and out, ending with palms down.

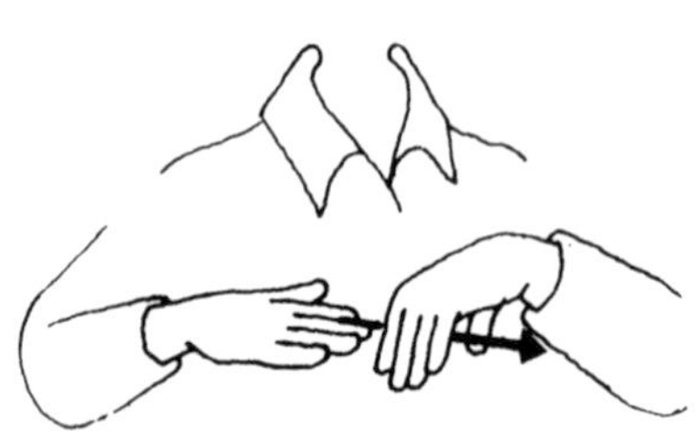

**slipper**

C shape LH palm down. RH open B palm down, tips left. Slide RH under left palm.

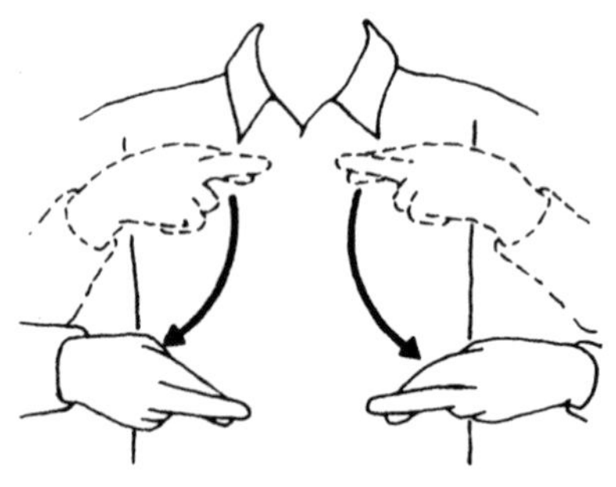

**robe**

R shape both hands, palms in, tips facing. Brush down chest.

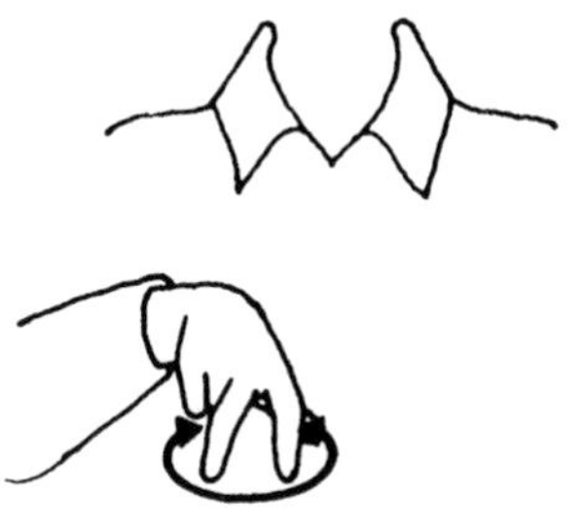

**faucet**
Mime turning faucet with thumb, index, and middle finger of RH.

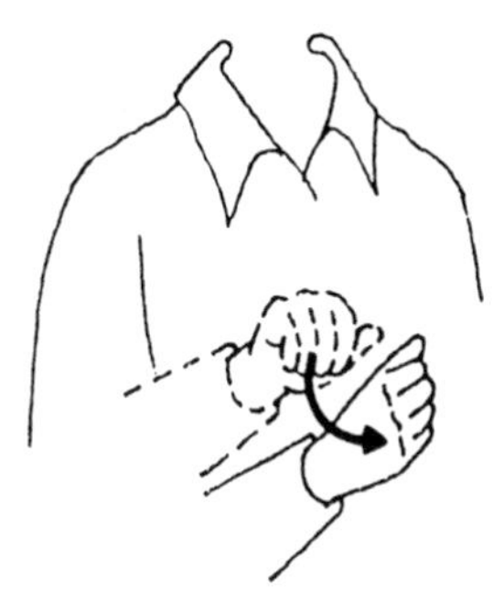

**flush**
Mime turning handle to flush toilet.

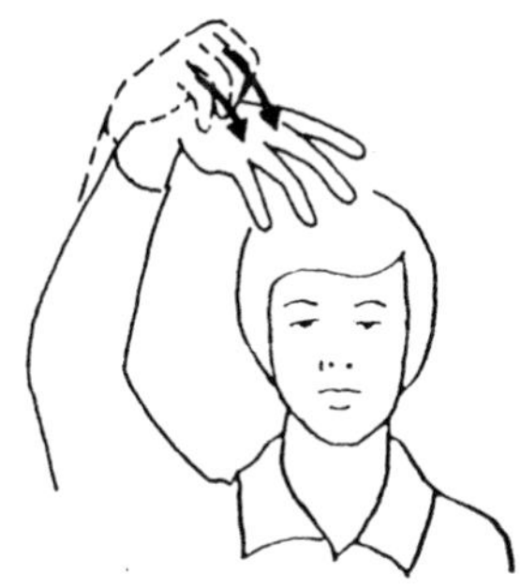

**shower**
S shape RH palm down. Hold above head and open into 5 shape. Repeat motion.

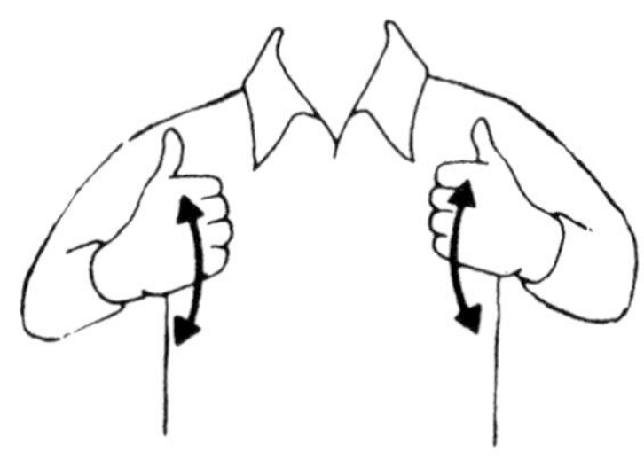

**bath**
A shape both hands, knuckles in, thumbs up. Make scrubbing motion on chest.

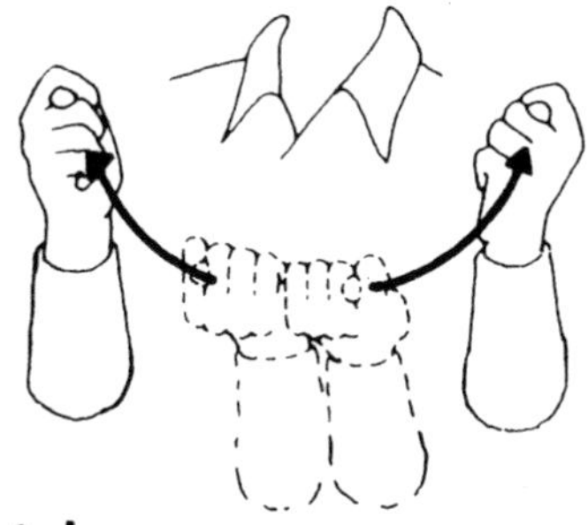

**tub**
T shape both hands, palms up, little fingers touching. Move apart and up, outlining shape of tub.

**sink**
C shape LH palm and tips right, little finger side down. S shape RH. Place right arm in left C and slowly wiggle down (sink out of sight).

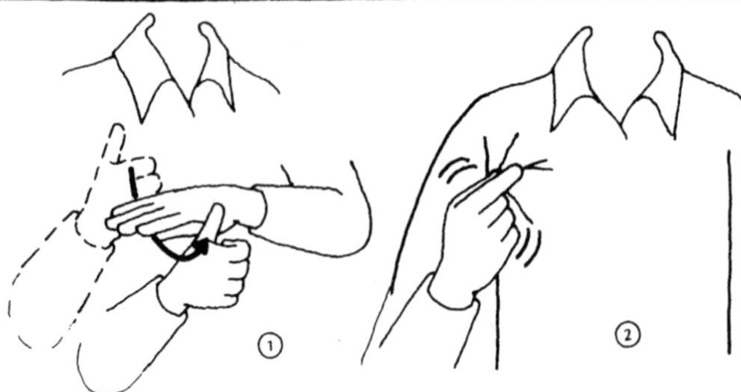


**undershirt**
LH open B palm down. Pass right A thumb extended, under left palm. Grasp clothing on right upper chest with RH thumb and index finger and tug slightly.

**underwear**
C shape LH palm in, tips on chest. RH open B palm in, tips down. Slide RH into left C.

**slip (clothing)**
One shape LH. C shape RH. Drop right C down around left index.

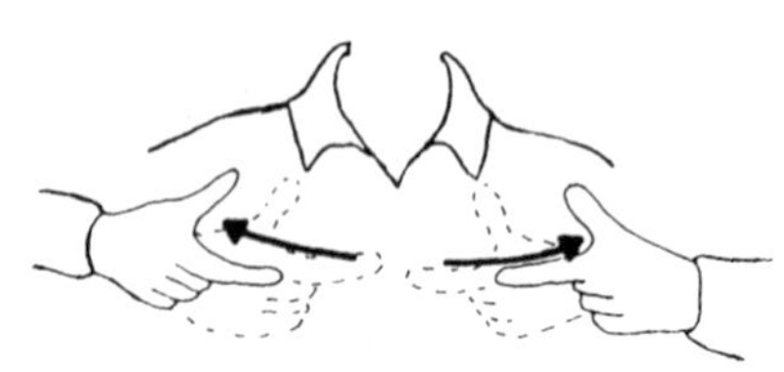

**bra**
L shape both hands, palms in, thumbs and index tips facing. Place on breast then draw apart, outlining bra.

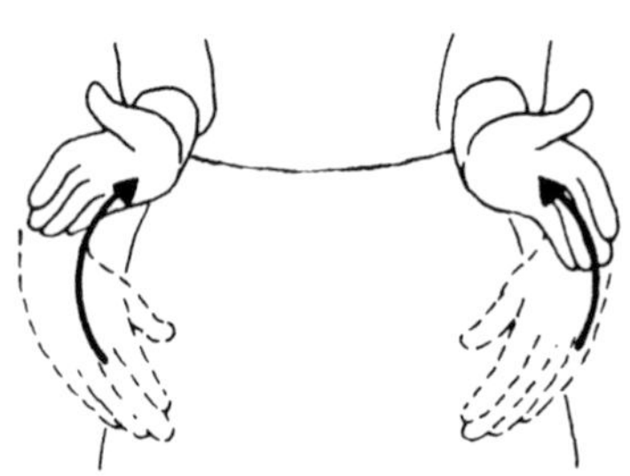

**panties**
Place tips of bent open B shapes on hip bones. Curve up slightly so that wrists rest on waist.

**boot**

B shape LH palm down, tips out. Place in right C which is held palm up, then slide right C up to left elbow.

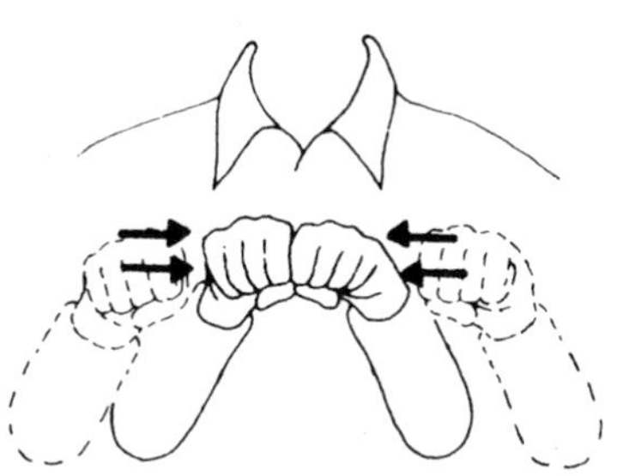

**shoe**

S shape both hands, palms down. Strike together several times.

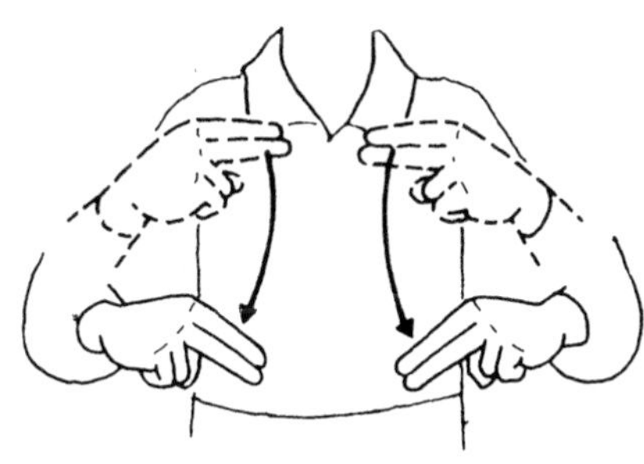

**uniform**

U shape both hands, palms in, tips facing. Place on upper chest then brush down.

**sock**

S shape RH palm down. Brush back and forth along side of left index held tip out, palm down.

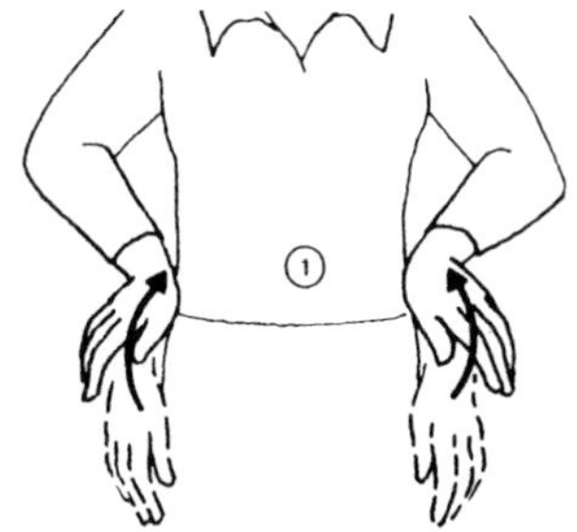


**panty hose**

Place tips of bent open B shapes on hip bones. Curve up slightly so that wrists rest on waist. Then form H shapes both hands, palms down. Alternately slide index fingers back and forth against each other.

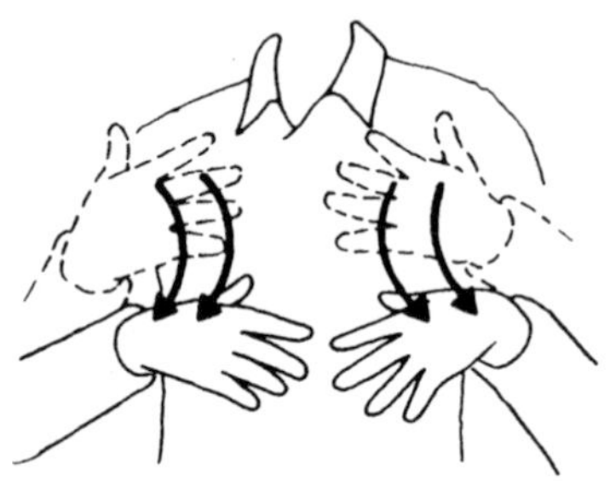

**clothes**
Brush open palms down chest twice.

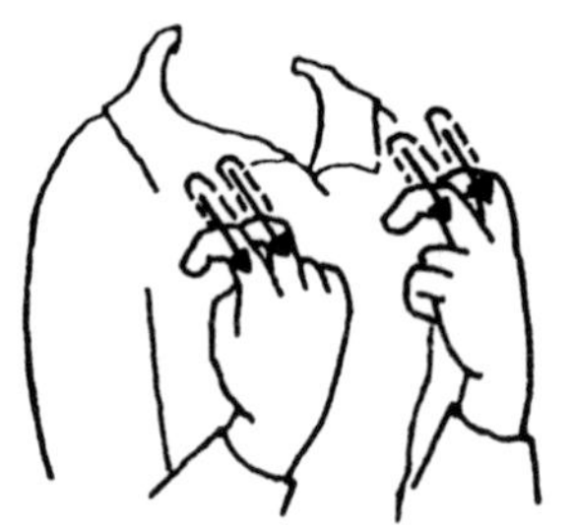

**jumper (clothing)**
Place tips of V shape hands on upper chest. Pull out into bent V shapes.

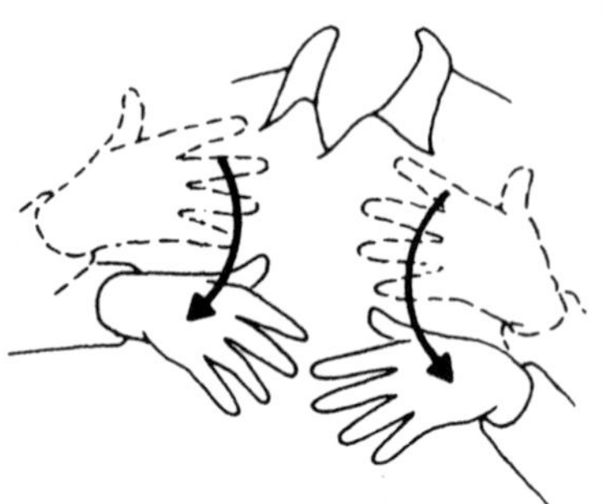

**dress**
Five shape both hands, palms in. Brush tips down chest while spreading hands apart slightly.

**blouse**
Bent B both hands, palms down, held at upper chest. Arc down, ending with palms up, little fingers against lower chest.

**coat**
A shape both hands. Trace shape of lapels with thumbs.

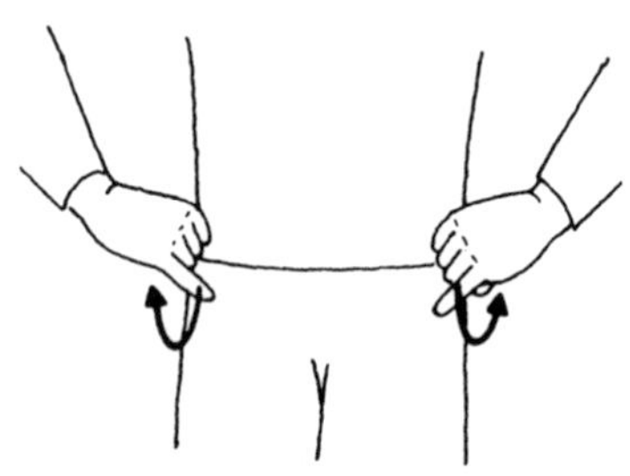

**jeans**
Place little fingers on hips and form J shapes.

**suit (clothes)**
Y shape both hands, palms in, thumbs up. Place on chest and brush down to waist.

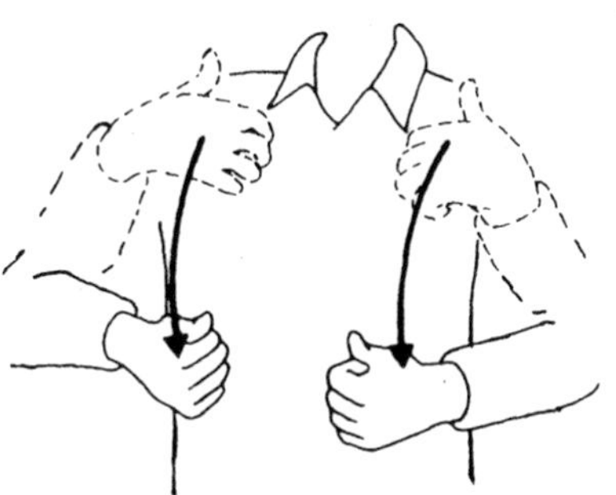

**sweater**
Claw shape both hands, palms in, tips in. Place on chest and move down, ending in A shapes.

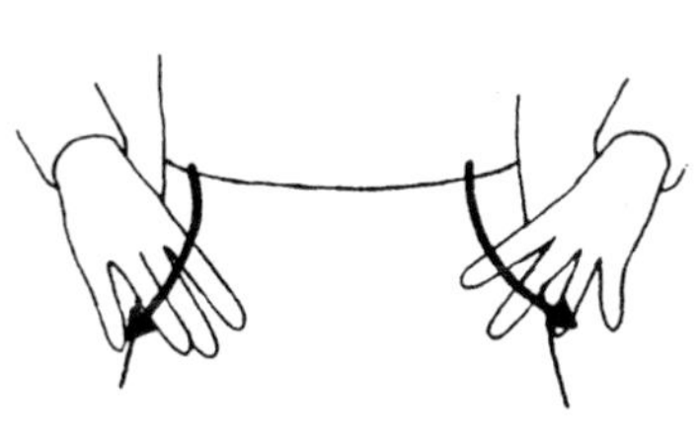

**skirt**
Five shape both hands, thumbs on waist. Brush down.

**shorts**
Open B both hands. Place fingertips on inside of thighs and move out, outlining bottom of shorts.

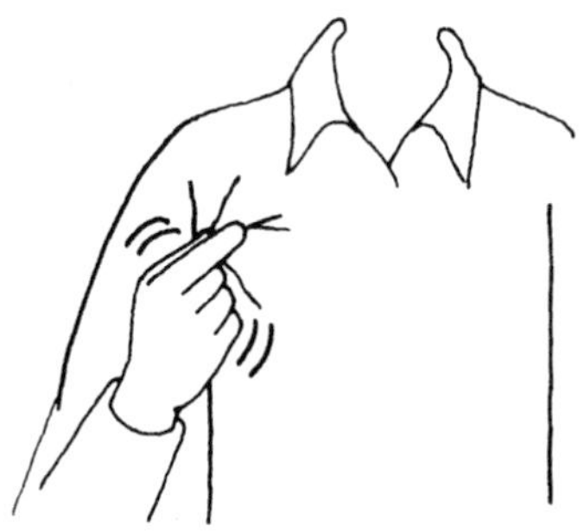

**shirt**
Grasp clothing on right upper chest with thumb and index finger of RH and tug slightly.

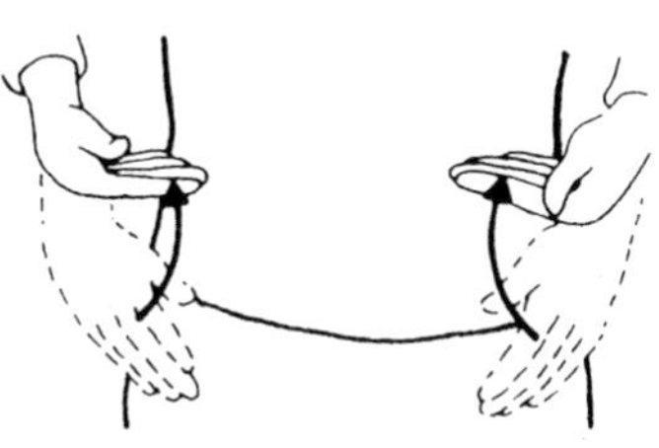

**pants**
Open B both hands. Place palms on hips and brush fingertips up toward waist.

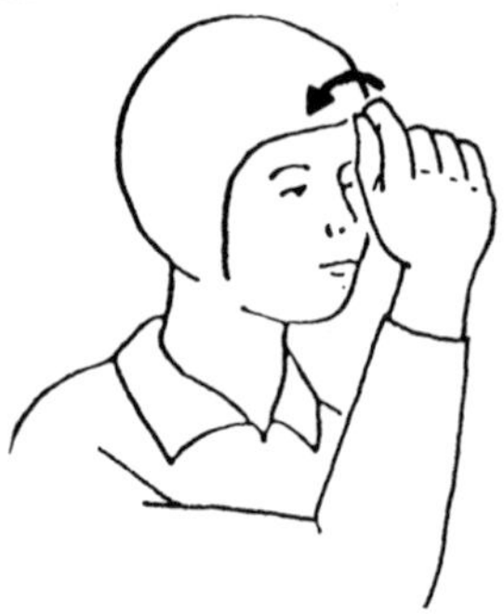

**cap**
Mime placing cap on head with thumb and index finger of RH holding brim.

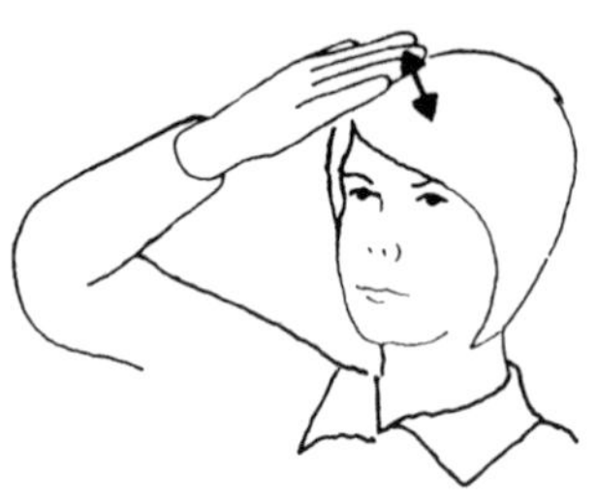

**hat**
Pat top of head with palm of RH.

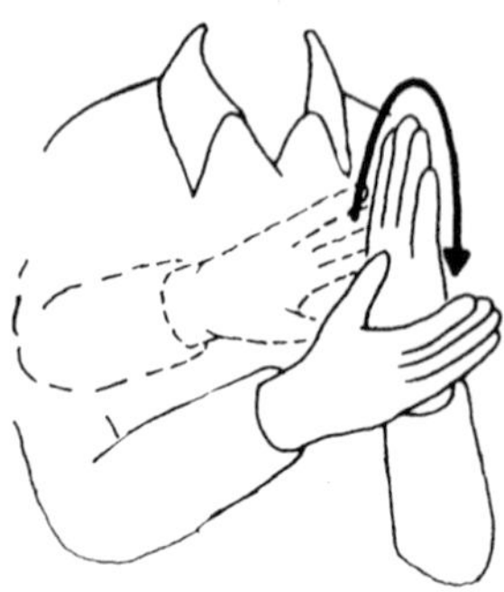

**mitten**
LH open B palm right, tips up. Outline with right fingers.

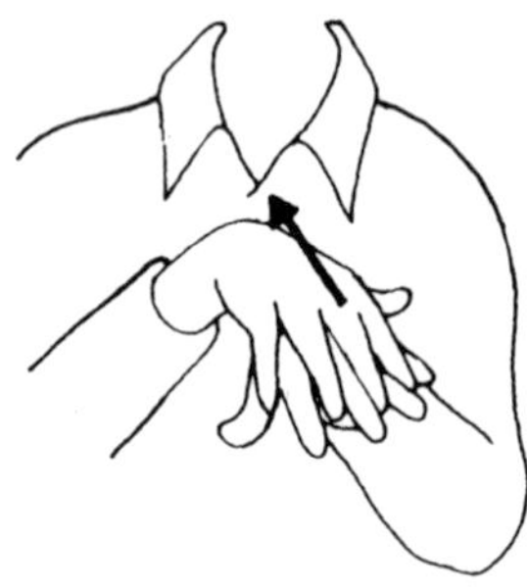

**glove**
Five shape both hands, palms down, tips out. Draw right fingers back over left fingers.

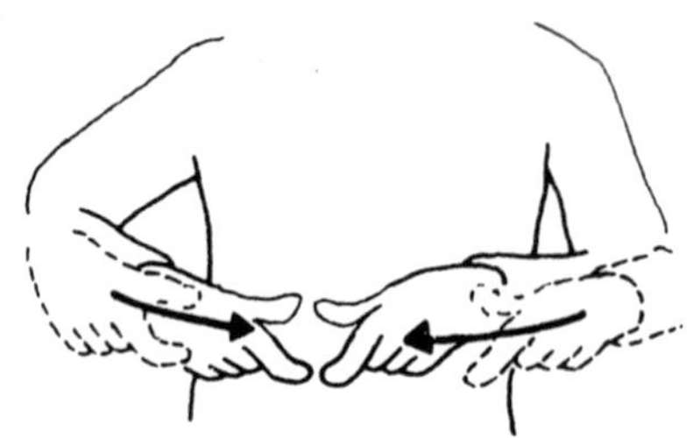

**belt**
Run index fingers and thumbs from each side of waist to middle of stomach (as if fastening buckle).

**wear**
A shape LH knuckles down. Circle right W over back of left A.

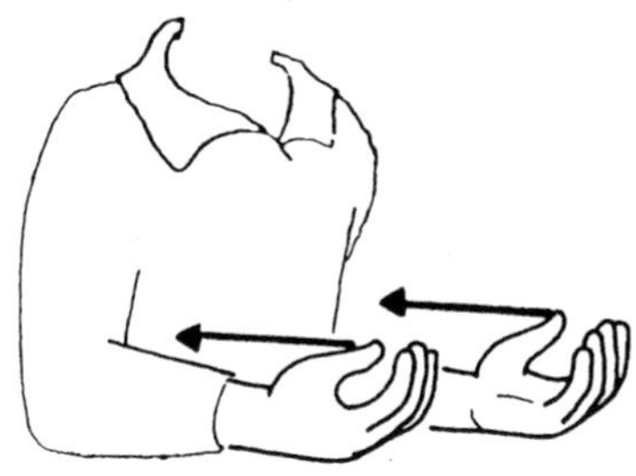

**drawer**

Hold cupped hands in front of body palms up, then draw back as if pulling drawer open.

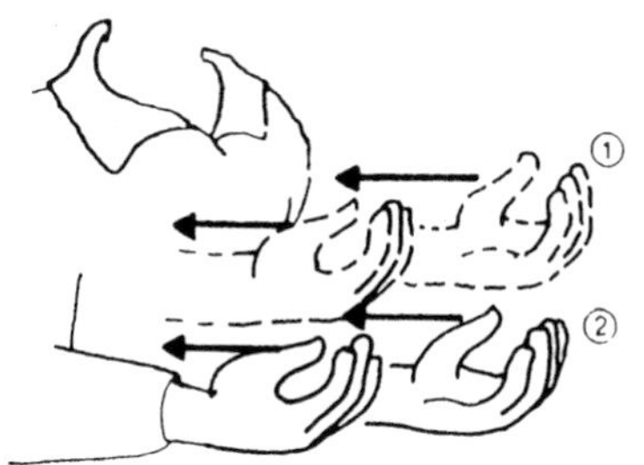


**dresser**

Hold cupped hands in front of body, palms up. Draw back as if pulling drawer open; lower hands and repeat motion.

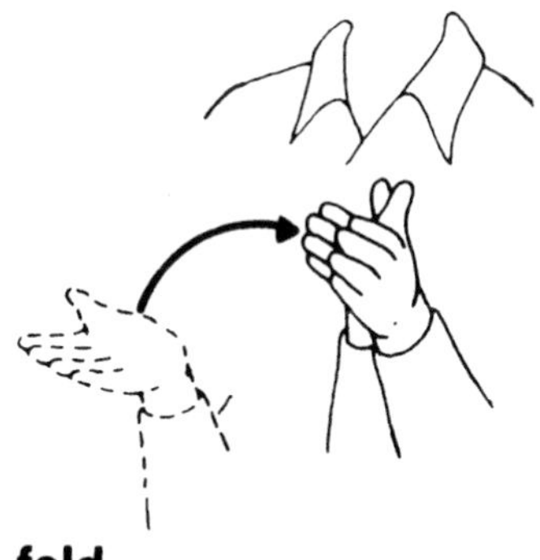

**fold**

Open B both hands, left palm right, tips out; right palm up, tips out. Bring right hand up and place against left.

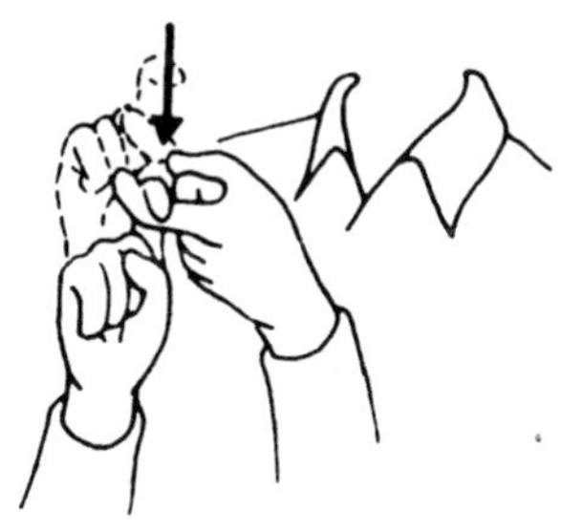

**hang**

X shape both hands. Hook right X over left X.

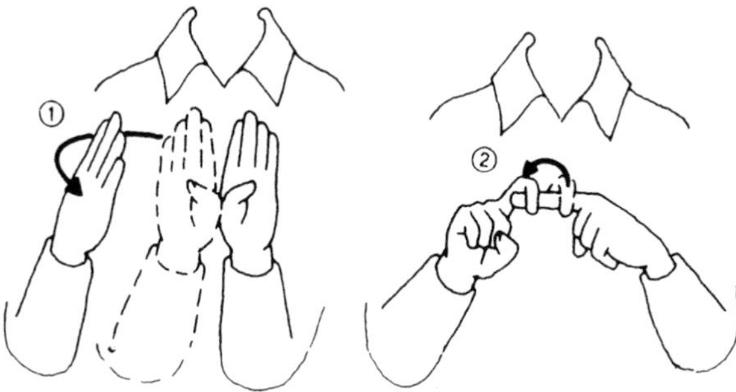


**closet**

B shape both hands, index fingers touching. Turn RH to right, then hook right index over base of left and move forward.

**hair**
Grab hair with right thumb and index finger.

**shampoo**
Claw shape both hands. Place tips on head and rub back and forth, as if shampooing hair.

**brush (hair)**
Brush knuckles of right A down hair twice.

**comb**
Brush open fingers through hair twice.

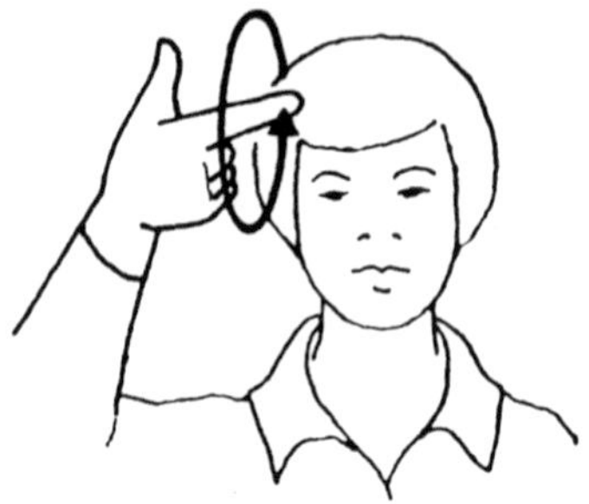

**hair dryer**
L shape RH palm in, knuckles left. Circle clockwise at right side of forehead.

**roller (hair)**
One shape both hands, tips facing. Circle around one another, as if rolling hair on curler.

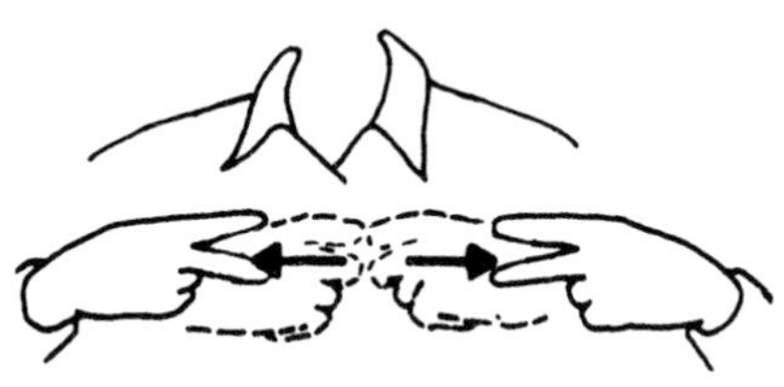

**bow**
Place knuckles of bent V shapes together, palms in. Draw apart into straight V shapes.

**ribbon**
H shape both hands, palms down, tips touching. Draw right H away from left in wavy motion.

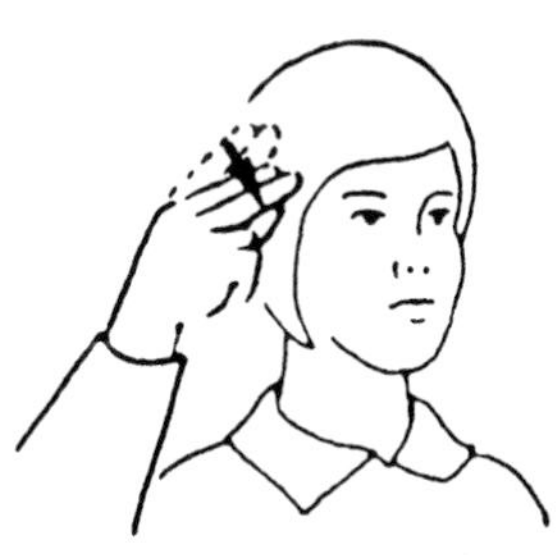

**clip (barette)**
Place right 3 shape on hair. Close fingers.

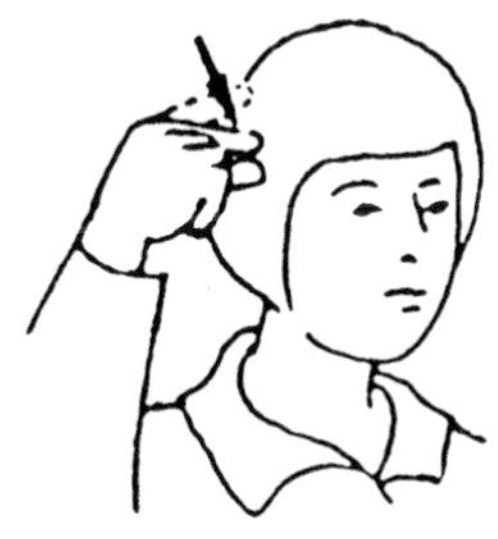

**bobby pin**
Place right thumb and index fingers on hair. Close fingers.

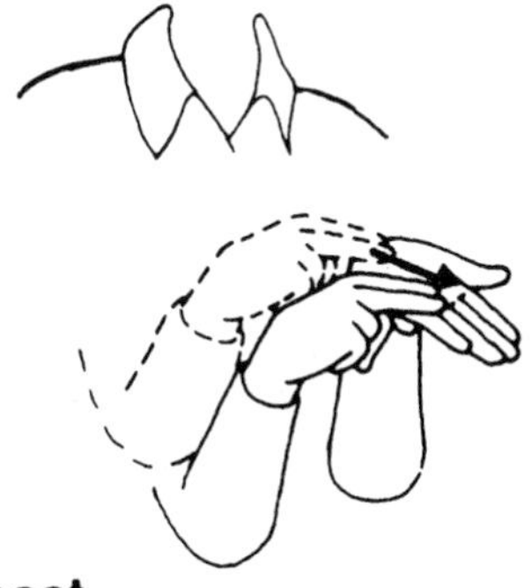

**neat**
LH open B palm up, tips out. Place tips of right N in left palm and slide forward.

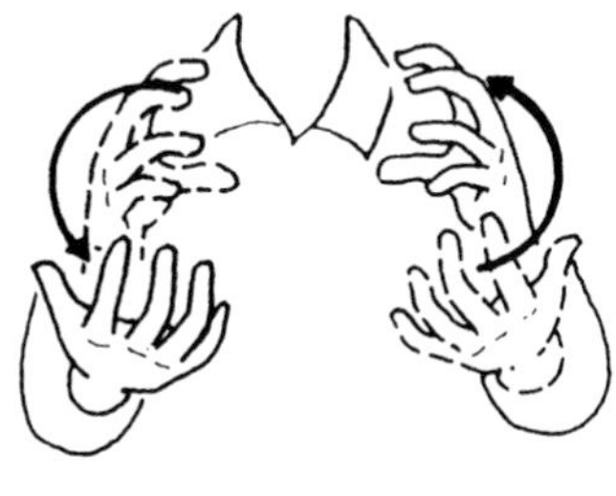

**mess**
Claw shape both hands, palms facing. Simultaneously twist LH inward and RH outward.

**towel**
Open B both hands, palms facing, tips up. Circle palms on cheeks.

**toothbrush**
Rub edge of right index finger back and forth over teeth.

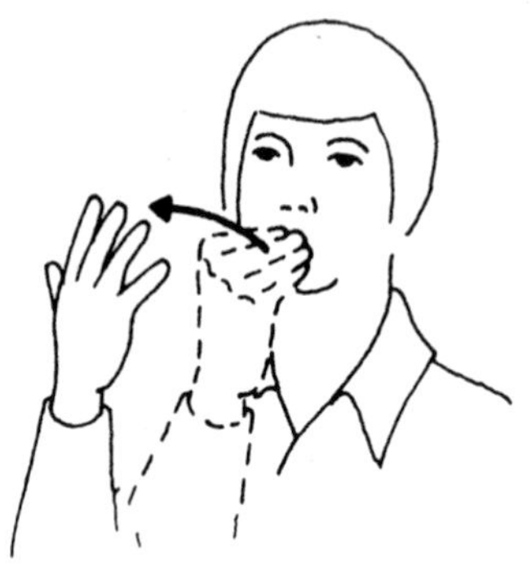

**warm**
Place tips of right O at mouth then open up fingers into 5 shape.

**hot**
Place tips of right claw on mouth. Twist wrist quickly so that palm faces down.

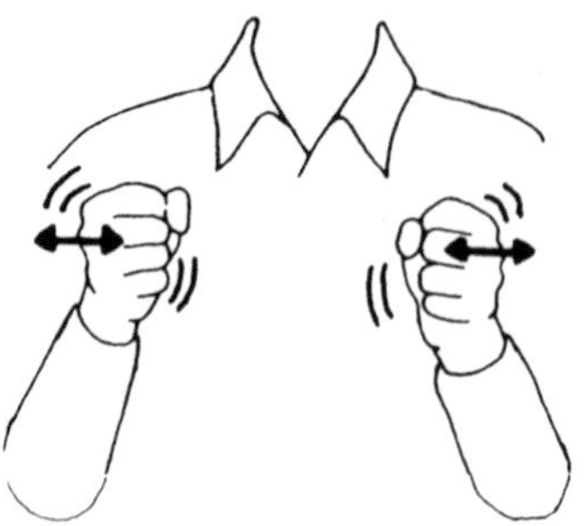

**cold (adj.)**
S shape both hands. Draw hands close to body and "shiver."

**cool**
Open B both hands, palms in, tips up and slanted toward one another. Hold above shoulders and wave fingers backward.

**wet**
Five shape both hands, palms in, fingers slightly curved. Place right index tip on mouth then drop both hands into flat O shapes.

**wipe**
LH open B palm up. Rotate right open B in left palm, as if wiping something.

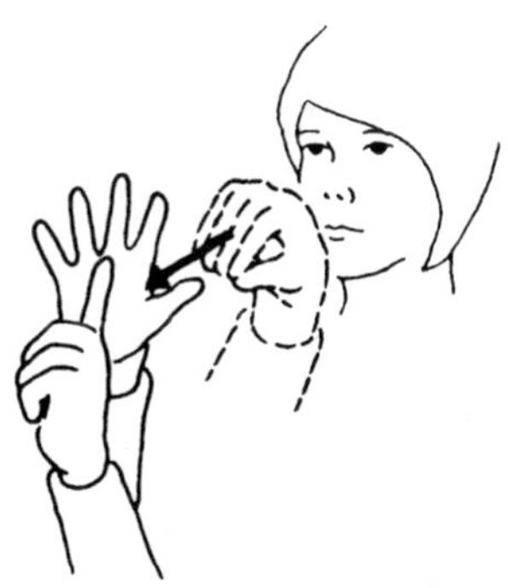

**blow**
Place right O on right edge of lips. Bring out into open 5 toward left index finger which is pointed up.

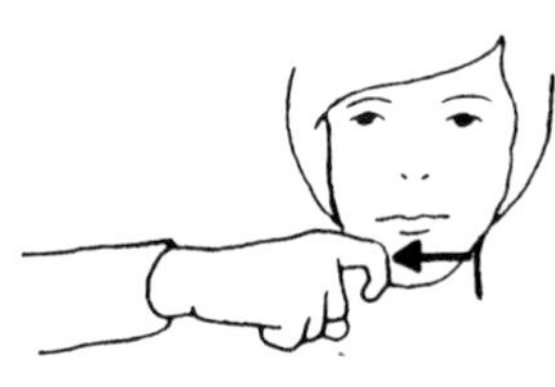

**dry**
Draw bent index finger from left to right across chin.

**wash**
Rub right S in circular motion on upturned left palm.

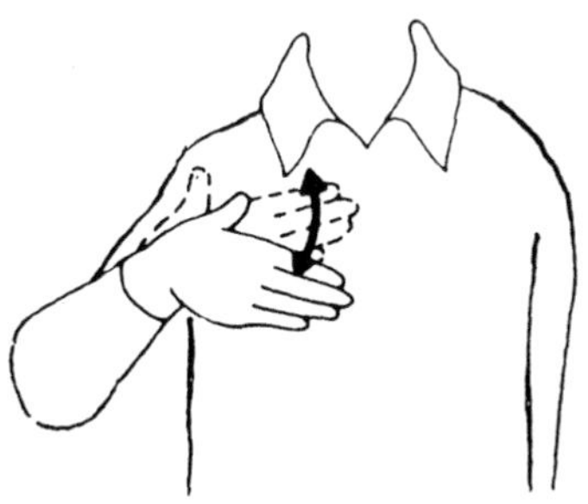

**cloth**
RH open B palm in, tips left. Rub up and down on upper right side of chest.

**soap**
Open B both hands, left palm up, tips out; right palm in, tips down. Draw right fingers backward across left palm ending in A shape.

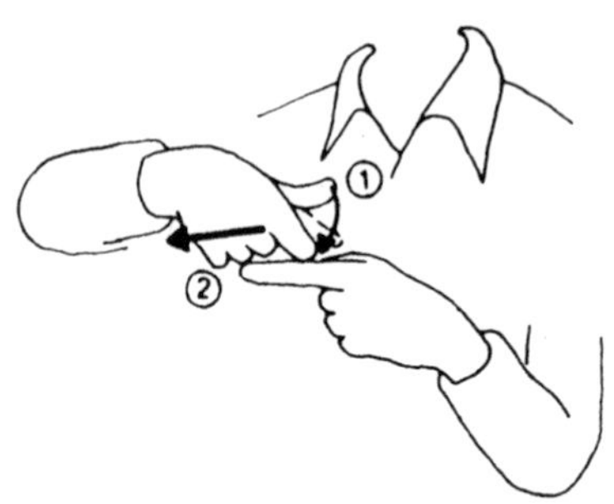

**toothpaste**
Mime spreading paste on toothbrush.

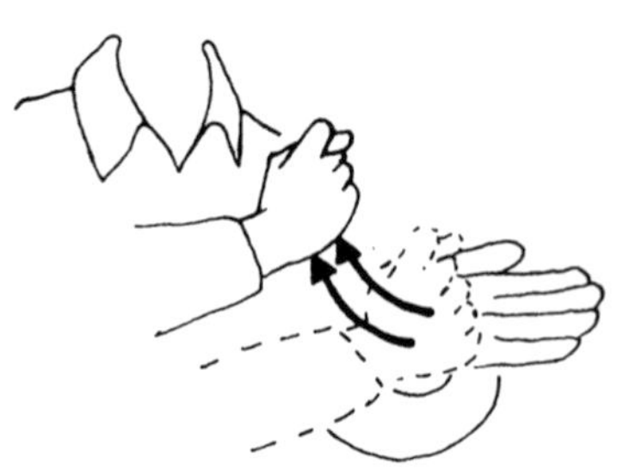

**tissue**
LH open B palm up, tips out. T shape RH palm down, knuckles left. Brush base of right T across base of left palm twice.

**lotion**
LH open B palm up, tips out. Dip thumb of right L into left palm (as if pouring).

**shave**
Y shape RH palm left. Draw thumb down right cheek, as if shaving.

**mirror**
RH open B palm in. Hold before face and twist slightly to the right. Repeat motion.

## PRACTICE SENTENCES

Repeat each of the following phrases or sentences several times. Start forming each sign at the same time you begin to speak its corresponding word.

After you can sign, and simultaneously say, each phrase or sentence comfortably, pair each incomplete phrase with every appropriate sign in this chapter.

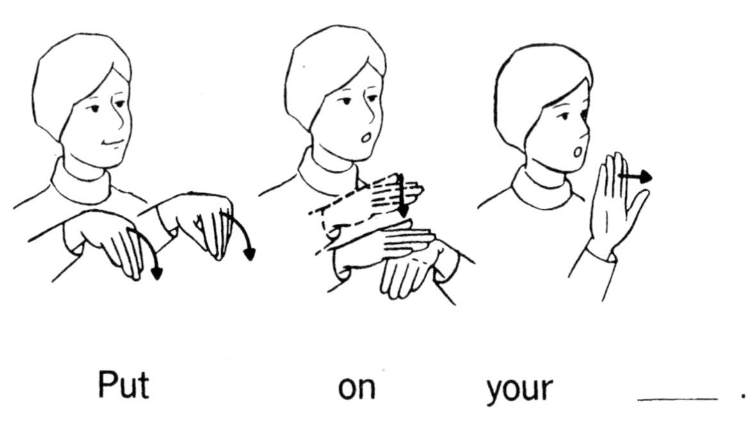

Put on your ____ .

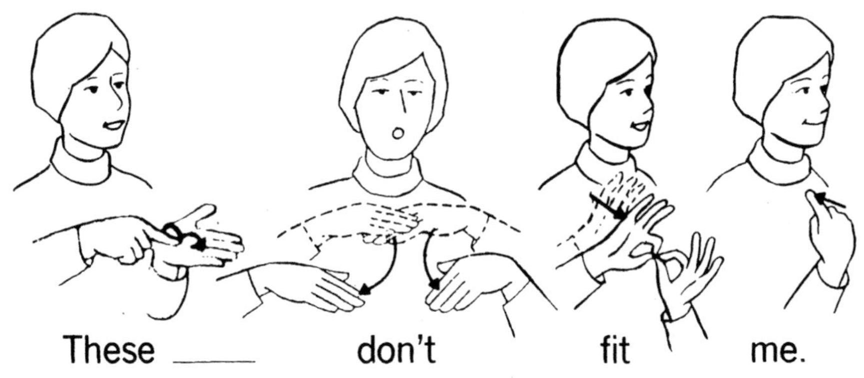

These ____ don't fit me.

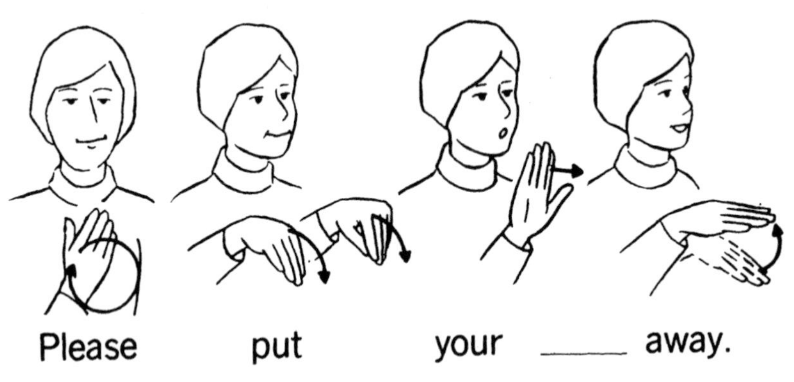
Please put your ____ away.

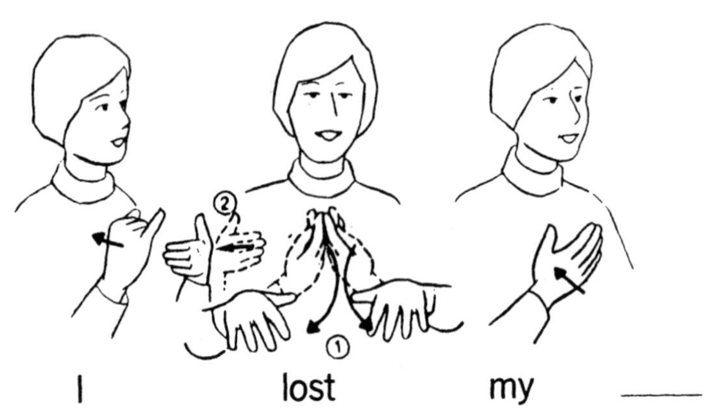
I lost my ____ .

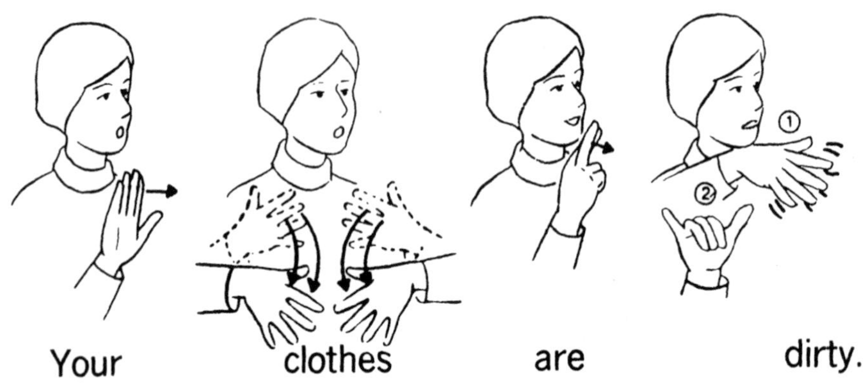
Your clothes are dirty.

# 12.
# HEALTH and SEXUALITY

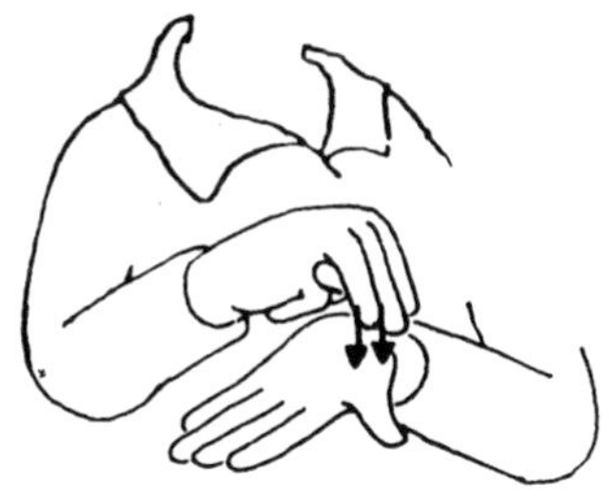

**doctor**
LH open B palm up, tips out. Tap left wrist with tips of right M.

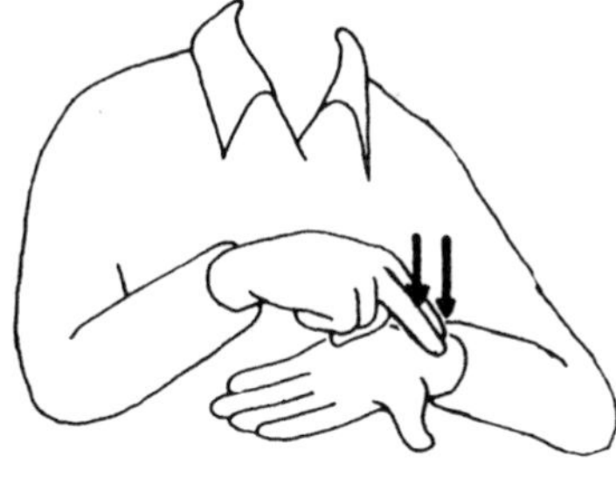

**nurse**
LH open B palm up. Tap left wrist twice with tips of right N.

**dentist**
Tap right side of mouth with middle finger and thumb of right D.

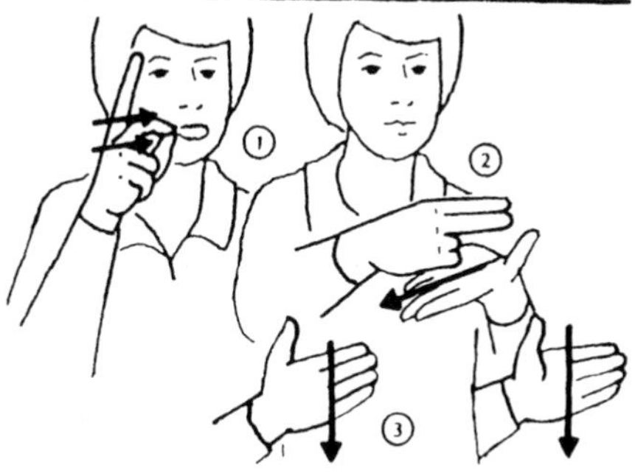


**dental hygienist**
Tap tips of right D twice at mouth. Now place base of right H on left palm and slide forward. Follow with agent marker.

**health**
H shape both hands, palms in, tips facing. Place tips on upper chest then move down to stomach.

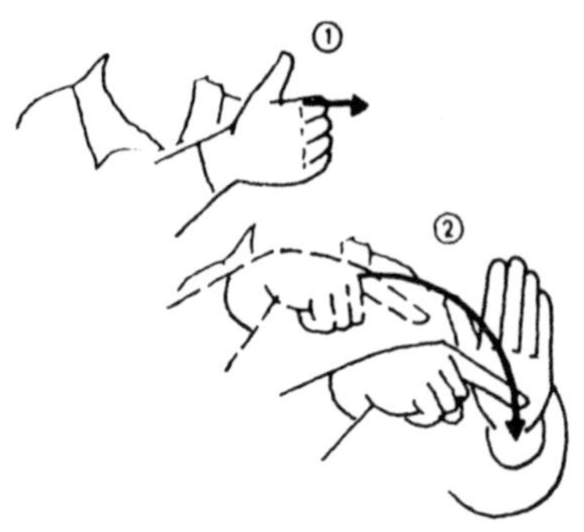


**suicide**
A shape RH palm left, thumb up. Move forward. Then strike index finger down across left palm.

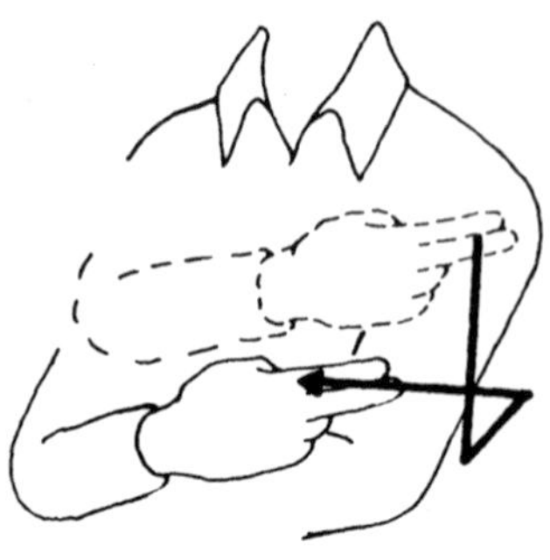

**hospital**
H shape RH. Make cross on upper left arm.

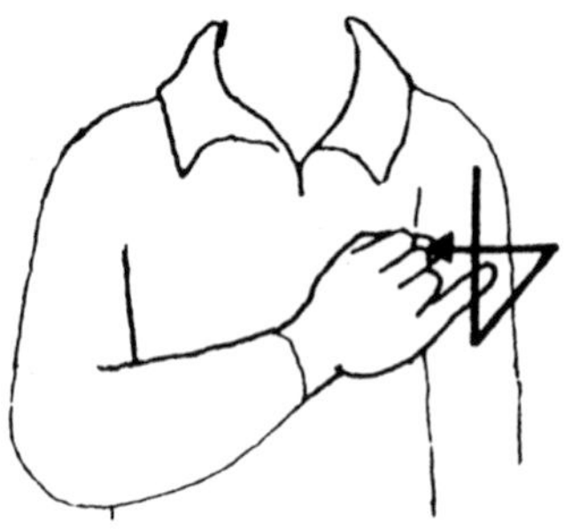

**infirmary**
I shape RH palm in, tips left. Outline cross on left upper arm.

**accident**
S shape both hands, knuckles facing. Strike knuckles together.

**operation**
LH open B palm out. Draw tip of right thumb down left palm.

**pulse**
Place fingers of right hand on upturned left wrist.

**stethoscope**
Three shape RH palm in. Place tips on chest and take a deep breath.

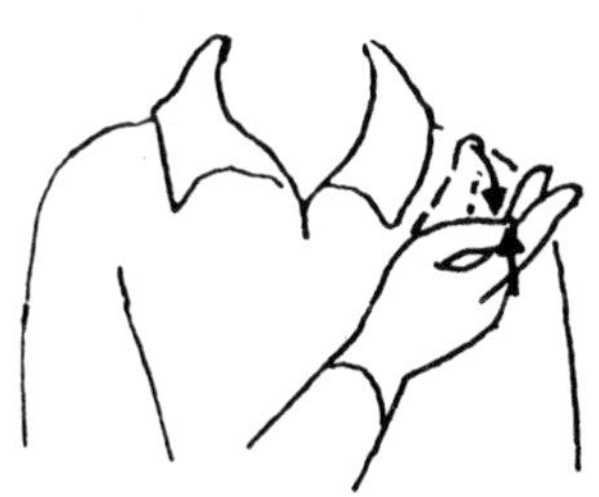

**shot (hypodermic needle)**
Place back of right V, thumb extended, on left upper arm. Push thumb against fingers, as if injecting needle.

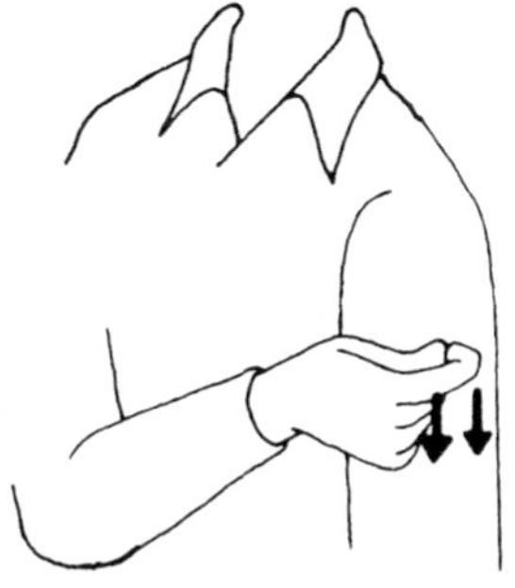

**vaccination**
Scratch left upper arm with right thumb and index finger.

**cure**
Place right C on right cheek. Move upward into A shape with thumb extended.

**X-ray**
X shape RH. Change to flat O shape, palm in. Then quickly spread into open 5 shape in front of chest.

**prescription**
Fingerspell R-X.

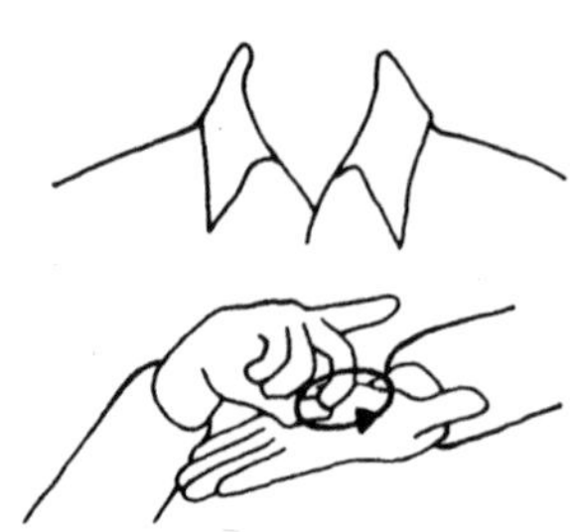

**drug**
Circle tips of right D on left palm.

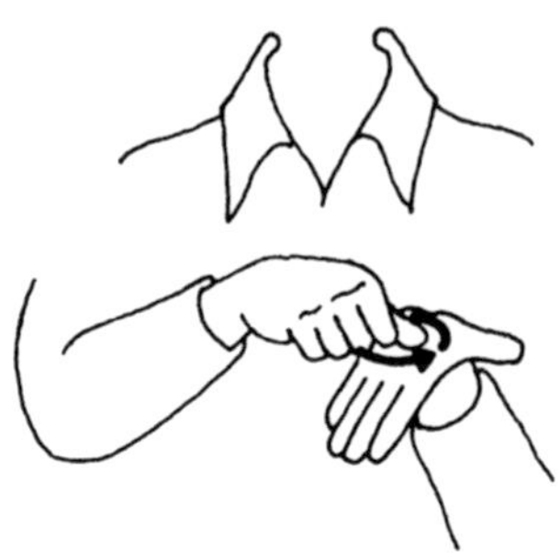

**aspirin**
A shape RH palm down, thumb extended. Place thumb in upturned left palm and circle.

**vitamin**
Shake right V from left to right.

**medicine**
Circle tip of right middle finger in upturned left palm.

**pill**
Mime popping pill in mouth with thumb and index finger.

**well (adj. & adv.)**
LH open B palm up. W shape RH palm in. Place tips on mouth, then move out and down to left palm.

**sick**
Five shape RH palm in. Tap forehead with middle finger.

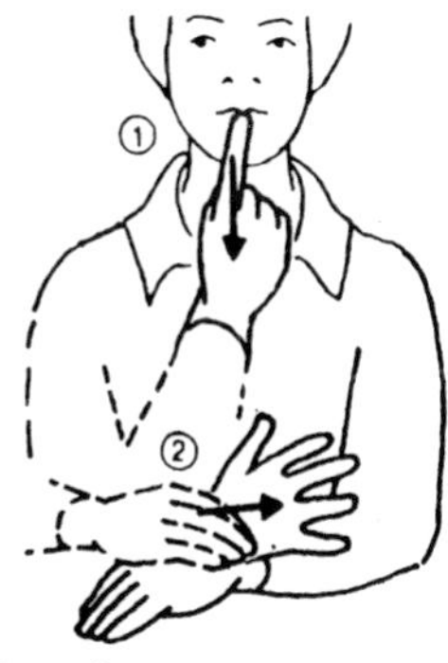


**infection**
Brush lips with tip of right index. Change to flat O, place on wrist, and spread into 5 shape while moving up arm.

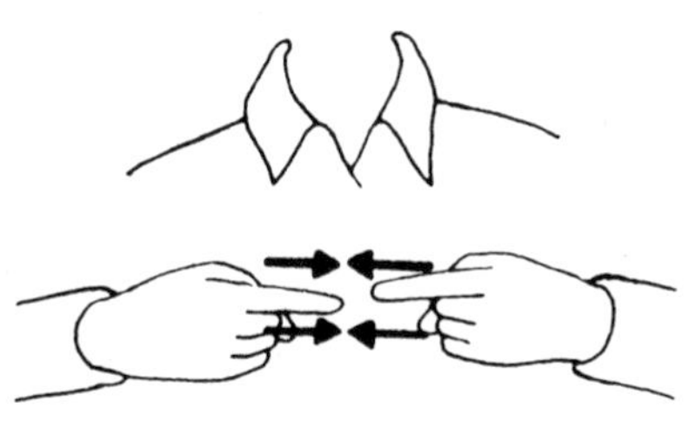

**hurt**
One shape both hands, palms in, tips facing. Move back and forth toward one another. (Sometimes made with H handshapes.)

**headache**
One shape both hands, tips facing. Move back and forth in front of forehead.

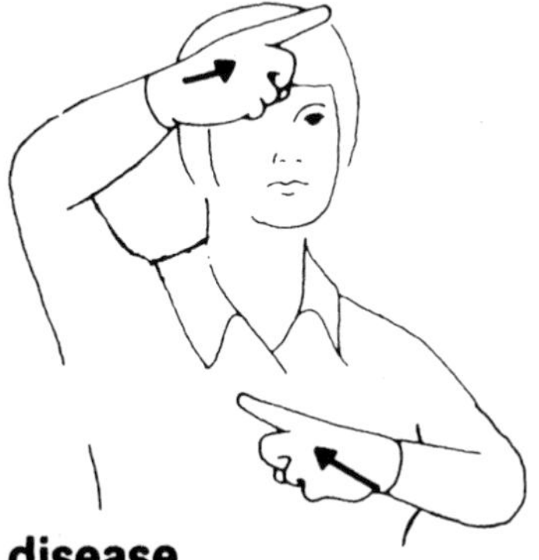

**disease**
D shape both hands, palms in. Place right D on forehead and left D on chest.

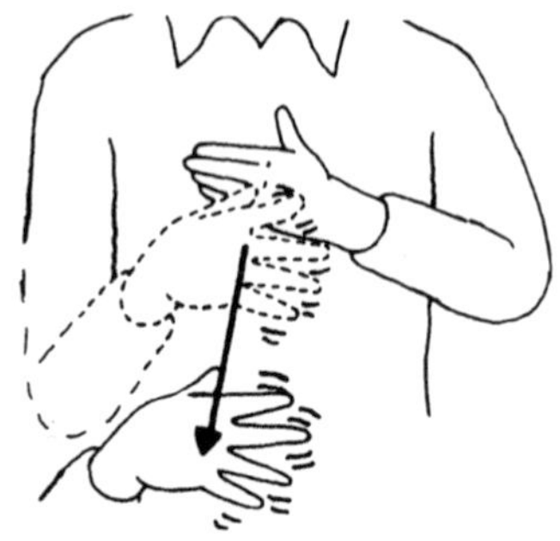

**blood**
LH open B palm in, tips right. Trickle right fingers down back of left (to indicate blood dripping).

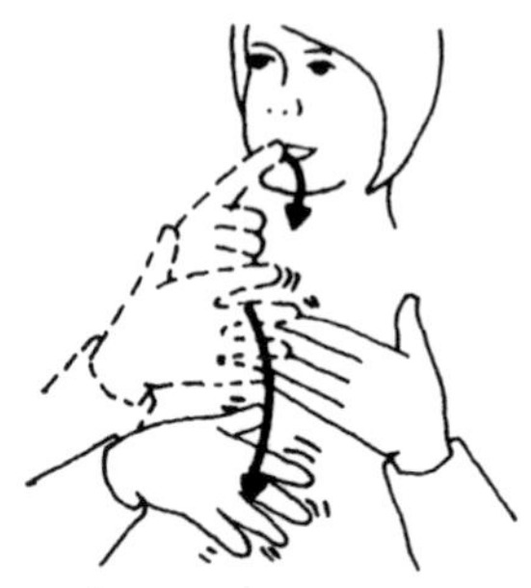

**bleed**
LH open B palm in, tips right. Place right index finger on lips then flutter right fingers across back of left fingers.

**Band-Aid**
S shape LH knuckles down. Draw right H over back of left S.

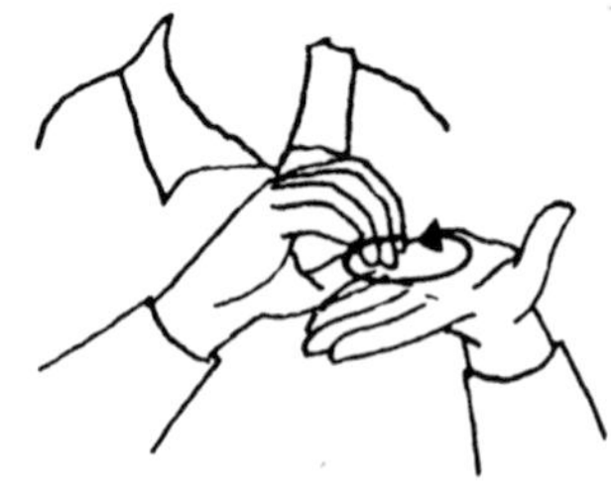

**ointment**
Circle thumb of right O counterclockwise in palm of LH.

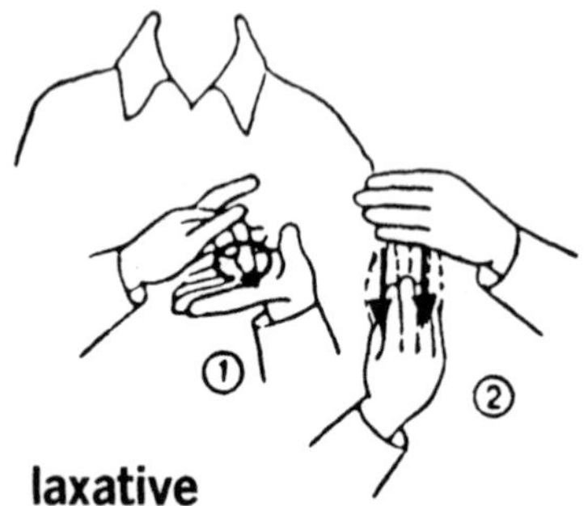


**laxative**
Circle tip of right middle finger in upturned left palm. Then place fingers of right hand in cupped LH and draw down. Repeat motion.

**enema**
Tap lips (or chin) twice with index finger of right W shape. Insert thumb of RH twice into bottom of loose S shape LH.

**cold (noun)**
Place right thumb and index on nose, then draw away as if using handkerchief.

**cough**
C shape RH palm in. Place under throat with index and thumb touching chest. Rock up and down.

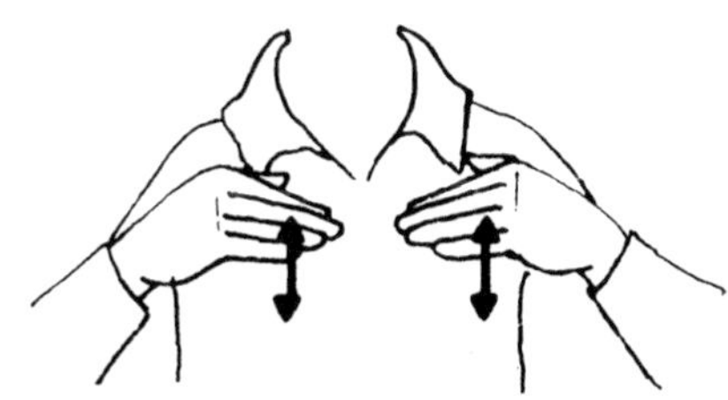

**bronchitis**
Bent open B both hands, palms in. Place tips on chest and move up and down.

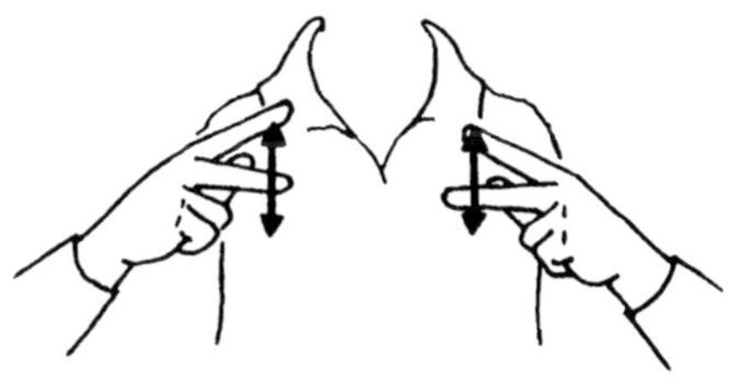

**pneumonia**
Rub middle fingertips of P shape hands up and down on chest.

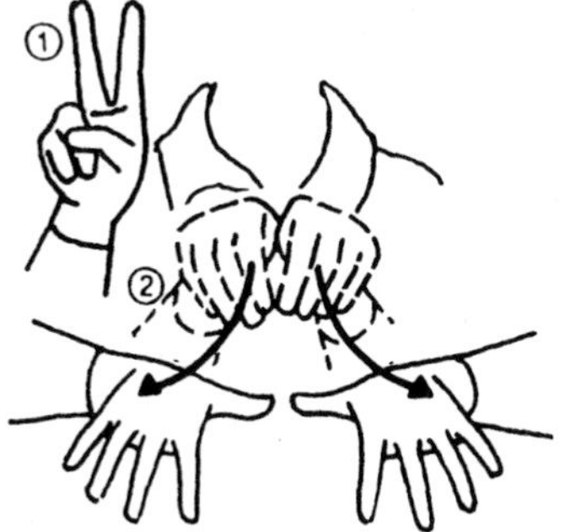


**virus**
V shape RH. Then place thumb and index tips of flat O shapes together and spread apart.

**flu**
Place back of right F on forehead.

**rectum**
Point to rectum with right index finger then form the letter F with RH.

**flatulence (passing gas)**
Place back of flat O on buttocks then rapidly open into 5 shape.

**constipate**
A shape both hands, left palm right, right palm left, thumbs extended. Place right thumb in left A and shake slightly.

**diarrhea**
C shape LH palm right. Place 5 shape RH, palm in, in left C then draw down quickly into flat O shape. Repeat several times.

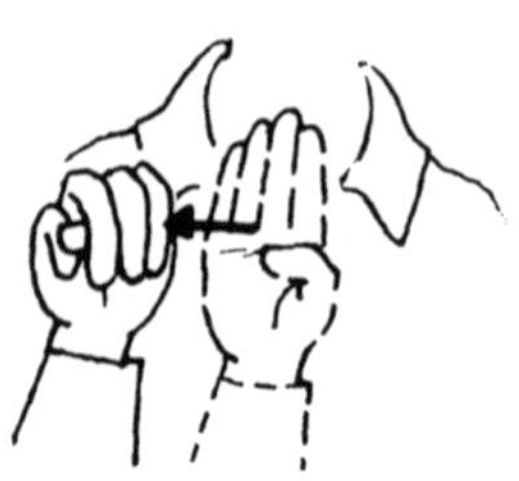

**bowel movement**
Fingerspell B-M.

**bowel movement (alt.)**
C shape LH palm right. Place right 5, palm in, in left C then draw into flat O shape.

**dizzy**
Circle right claw hand, palm in, clockwise in front of forehead.

**fever**
RH open B palm out, tips left. Place back of hand on forehead.

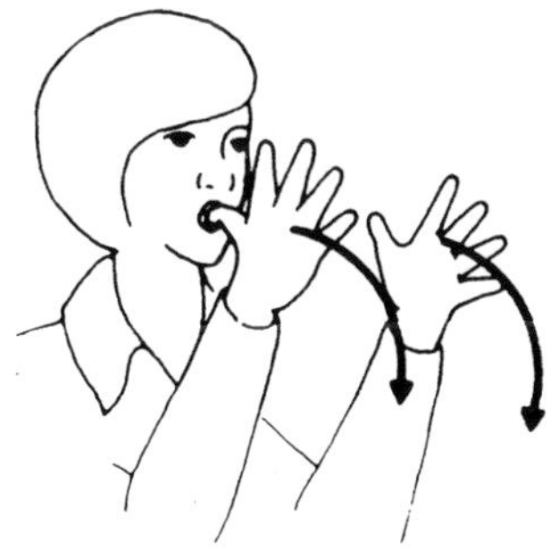

**vomit (throw up)**
Five shape both hands, palms facing, right thumb on mouth. Move both hands forward and down in sudden motion.

**chill**
Place right bent V on top of left bent V with thumbs touching. Rub back and forth (as if teeth chattering).

**flushed**
Move both five shape hands upward and apart to sides of face.

**pale**
RH flat O palm in, held in front of chin. Move upward in front of face, spreading into 5 shape.

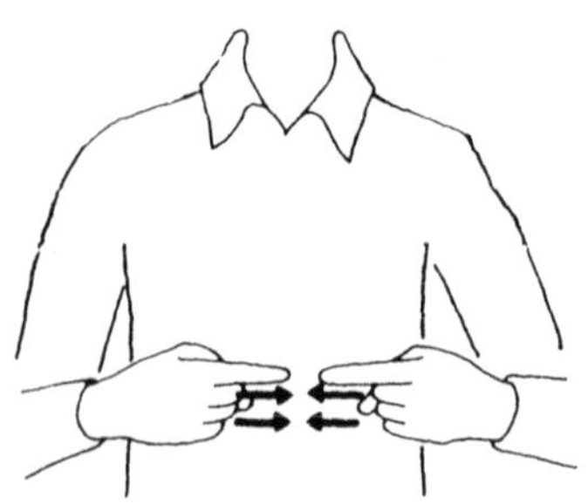

**stomachache**
One shape both hands, palms in, tips facing. Move back and forth toward one another in front of stomach.

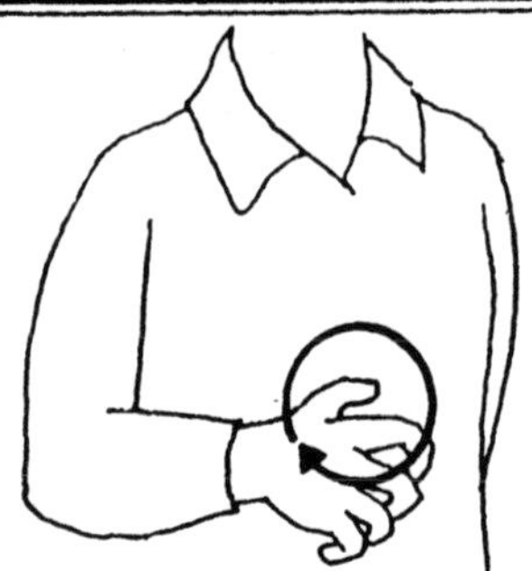

**nauseous**
Circle right claw shape, palm in, clockwise at stomach.

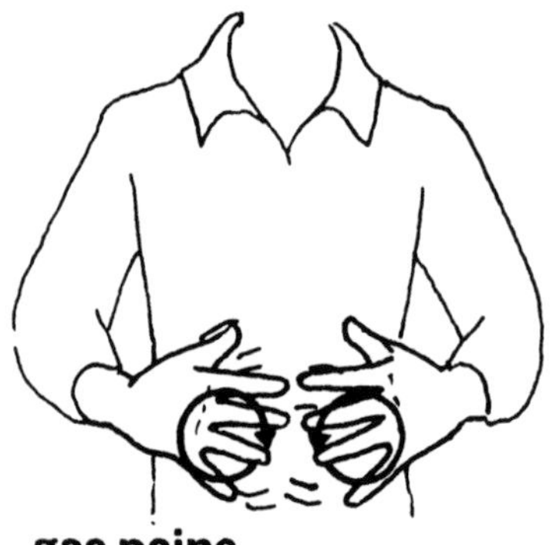

**gas pains**
Five shape both hands, palms in, tips facing. Rotate hands in front of stomach in small circles while fluttering fingers.

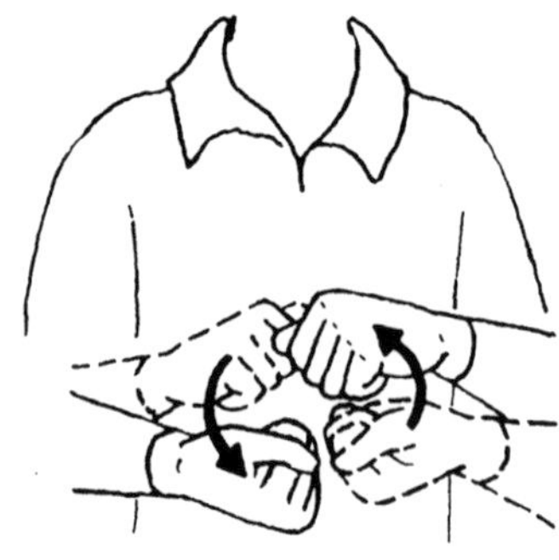

**cramp**
A shape both hands, right knuckles down, left knuckles up. Hold at stomach level and twist.

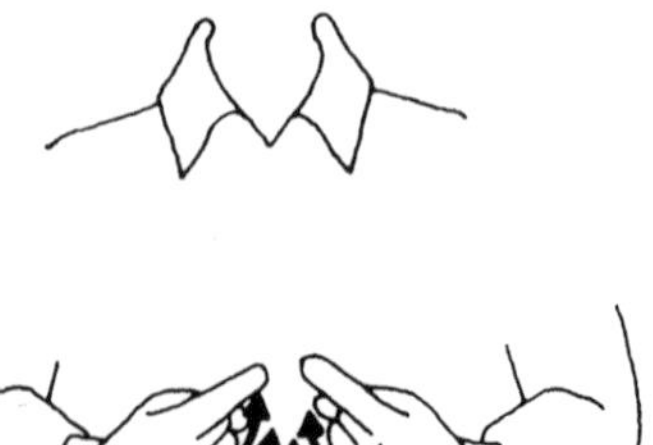

**pain**
One shape both hands, palms in, tips facing. Move toward one another while arcing upward. Repeat motion.

**urinate**
Tap nose twice with middle fingertip of P shape RH, palm in.

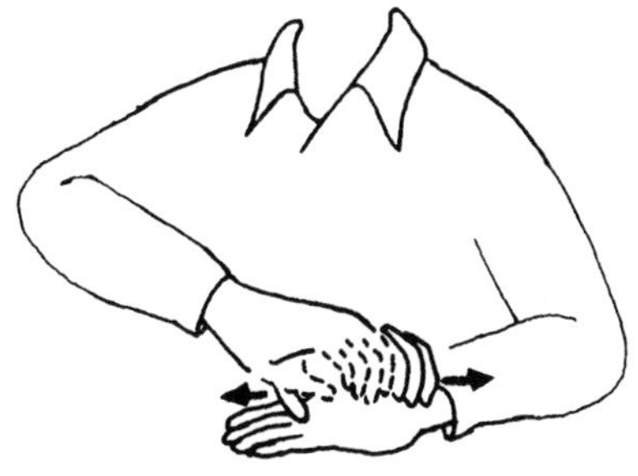

**blister**

LH open B palm down, tips out. Place tips of right flat O on back of LH and spread slightly.

**burn**

One shape LH palm down, tip right. Flutter fingers of RH beneath left index.

**sprain**

Bent V shape both hands, left palm in, right palm down. Twist left V down and right V up.

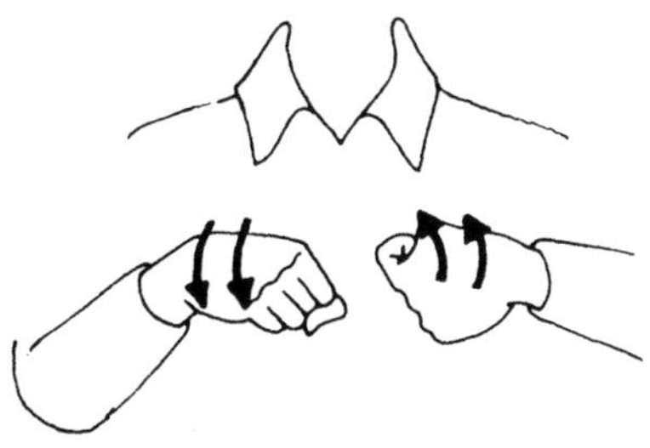

**sore**

S shape both hands, palms down. Twist in opposite directions while moving toward each other. Repeat motion.

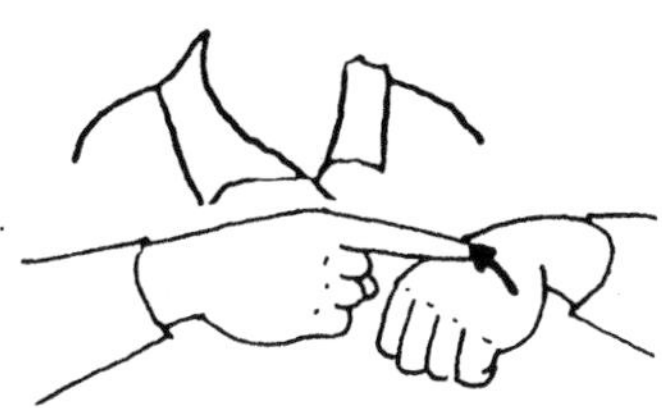

**cut (noun)**

S shape LH palm down. Draw right index to the right across back of left S.

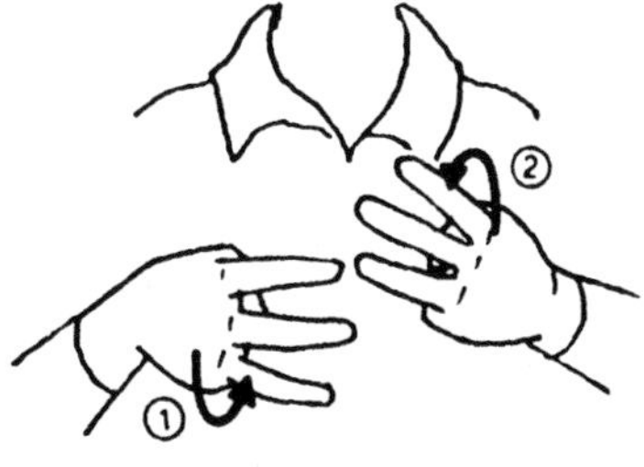


**wound**

W shape both hands, tips facing. Twist wrists in opposite directions while moving fingers toward one another.

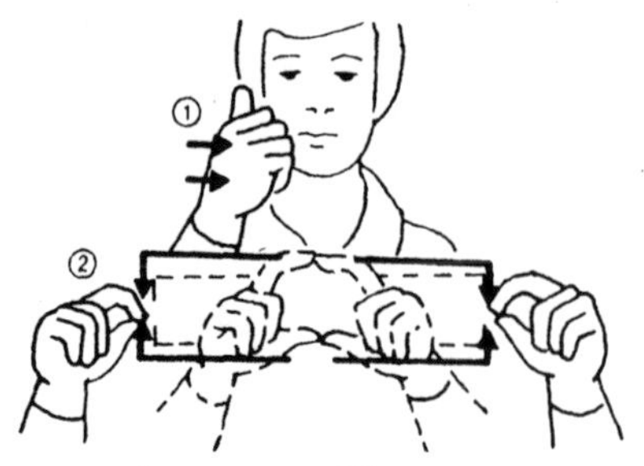


**sanitary napkin**
Tap knuckles of right A on right cheek twice. Then place tips of index fingers and thumbs together. Draw apart and close, outlining napkin.

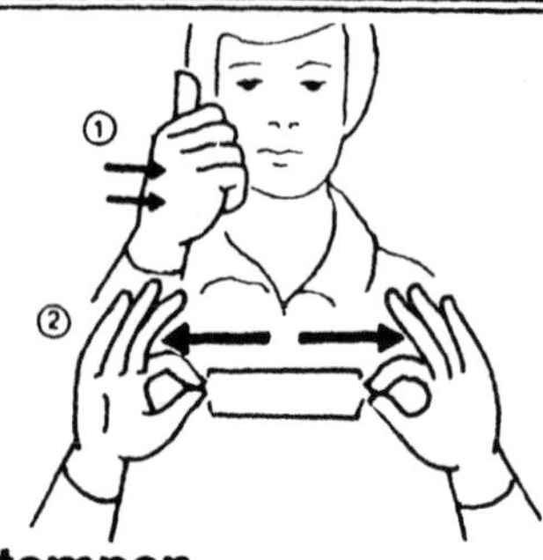


**tampon**
Tap right cheek with knuckles of right A twice. Form F shapes, tips touching, and draw apart, outlining shape of tampon.

**menstruation (period)**
Tap right cheek twice with flat fingers of right A.

**pregnant**
Intertwine fingers of both hands. Place in front of stomach then move out.

**breast**
Bent RH open B palm in. Place tips on left breast then on right breast.

**nipple**
Place F shape on left nipple. Move to right nipple.

**vagina (vulva)**
Place index tips and thumb tips together with index tips pointing down.

**virgin**
Move V shape RH over head and down right side of face (as if outlining shawl).

**penis**
One shape RH palm down. Support right wrist with left index while wiggling right index up and down slightly.

**testicle**
C shape both hands, palms up. Alternately move hands up and down.

**erection**
One shape both hands. Place index finger LH at base of RH. Flip up right index finger.

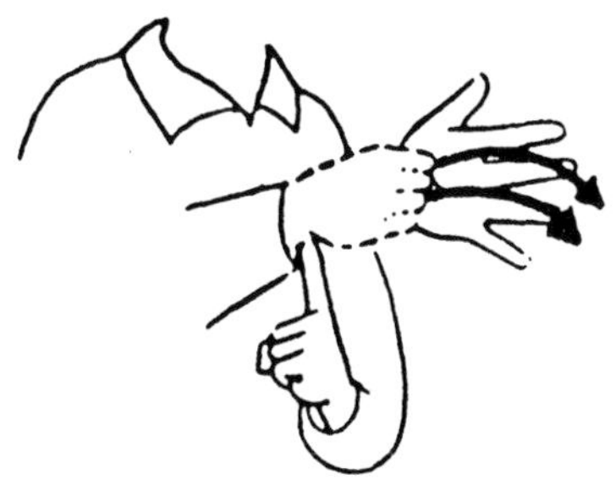

**ejaculate**
Place left index finger at base of right S. Quickly fling right S forward into 5 shape. Repeat.

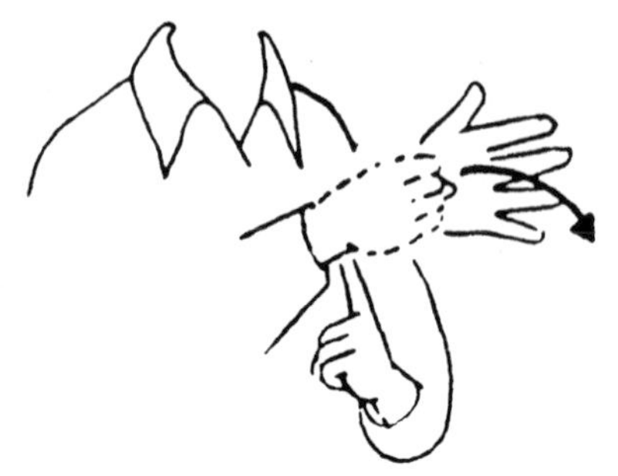

**semen/sperm**

Place left index finger at base of right S. Quickly fling right S forward into 5 shape.

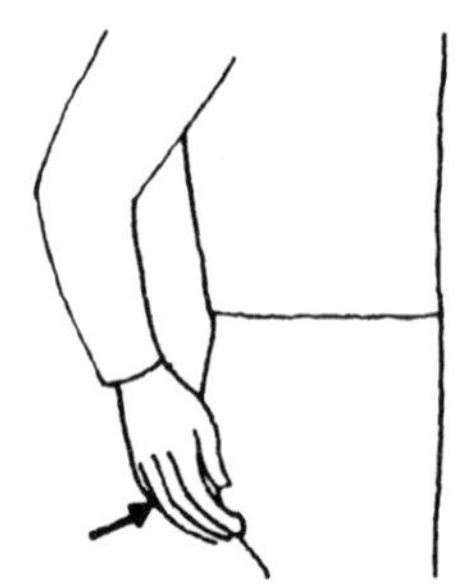

**buttock**

Place right hand on buttock.

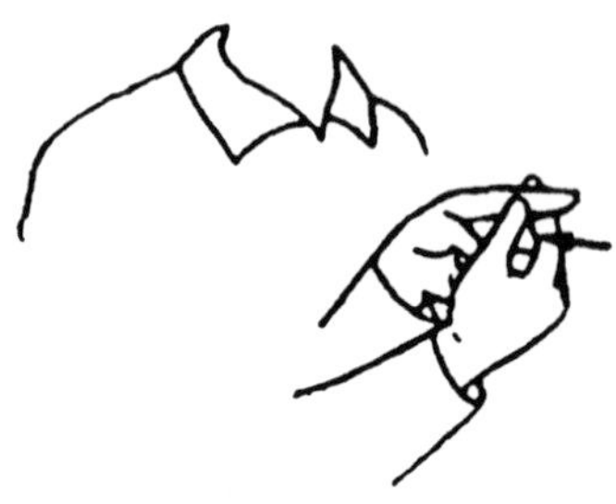

**condom**

One shape LH, pointing. Slide RH thumb and index finger down left index finger.

**birth control**

Spell the letters B and C.

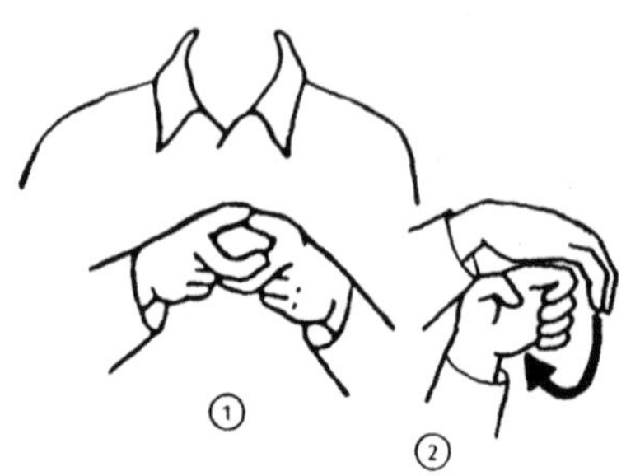


**diaphragm**

Form a small circle with thumb and index fingers of both hands. Mime insertion by slipping right fingertips into bottom of left C.

**masturbate**

B shape LH. Rub tips of M shape RH up and down left index finger.

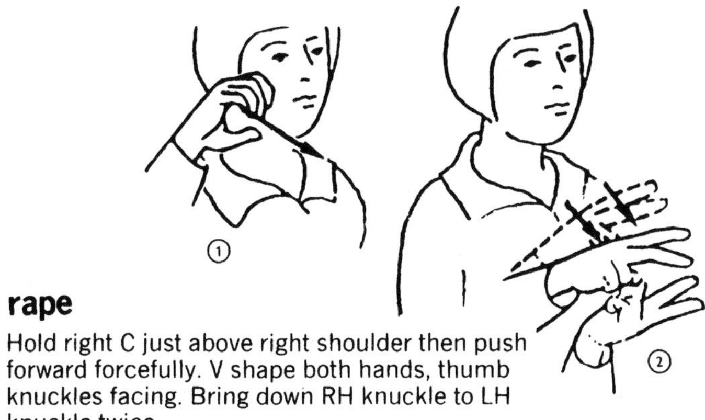


**rape**

Hold right C just above right shoulder then push forward forcefully. V shape both hands, thumb knuckles facing. Bring down RH knuckle to LH knuckle twice.

**intercourse**

V shape both hands, thumb knuckles facing. Bring down RH knuckle to LH knuckle twice.

**kiss**

Place tips of right open B on mouth and move back to cheek.

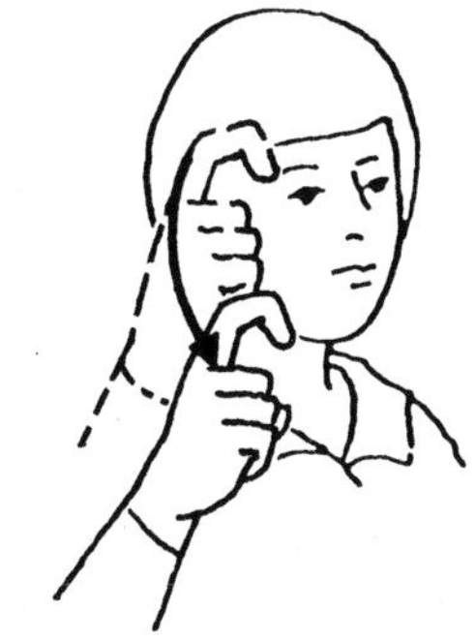

**sex**

Touch right temple, then right cheek, with right X.

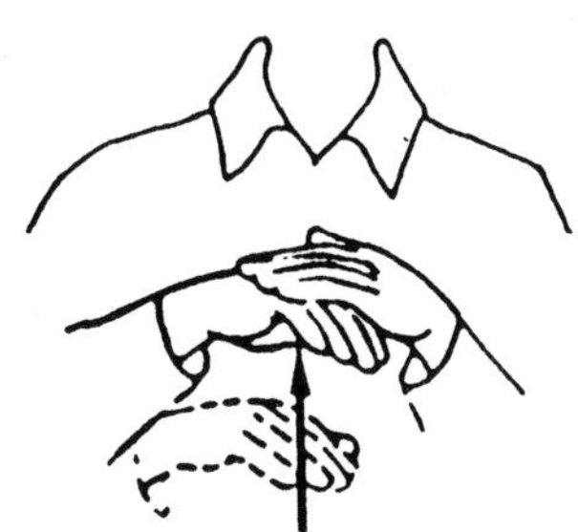

**orgasm**

Open B both hands, palms down, right under left. Slowly raise RH up against left palm of open B shape LH.

## PRACTICE SENTENCES

Repeat each of the following phrases or sentences several times. Start forming each sign at the same time you begin to speak its corresponding word.

After you can sign, and simultaneously say, each phrase or sentence comfortably, pair each incomplete phrase with every appropriate sign in this chapter.

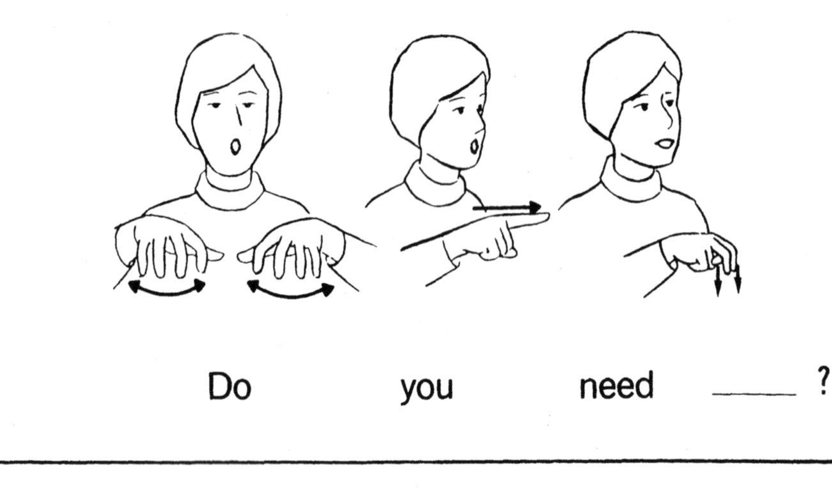

Do you need ____ ?

I have a headache.

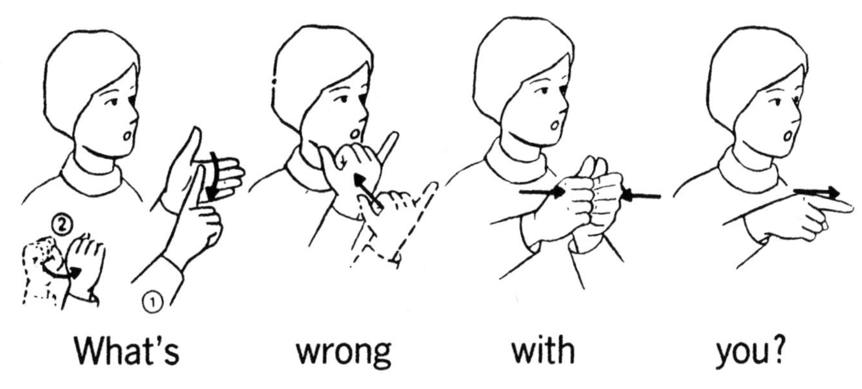
What's
wrong
with
you?

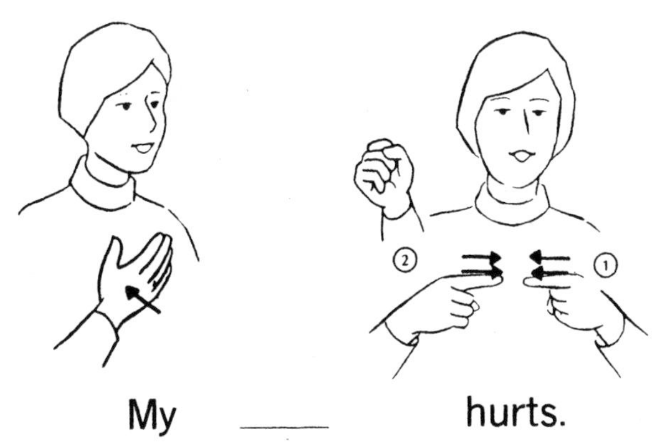
My
___
hurts.

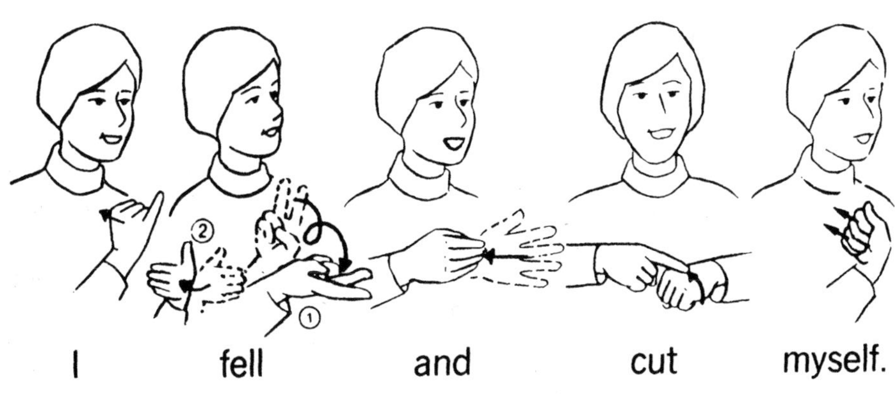
I
fell
and
cut
myself.

# REFERENCES


Bornstein, H. (1973). A description of some current sign systems designed to represent English. *American Annals of the Deaf, 118,* 454-463.

———(1974). Signed English: A manual approach to English language development. *Journal of Speech and Hearing Disorders, 39,* 330-343.

———(1979). Systems of sign. In L. Bradford and W. Hardy (eds.) *Hearing and hearing impairment.* (pp. 333-361). New York: Academic Press.

———(1982). Towards a theory of use for Signed English: From birth through adulthood. *American Annals of the Deaf, 127,* 26-31.

Bornstein, H., Saulnier, K., & Hamilton, L.B. (1980). Signed English: A first evaluation. *American Annals of the Deaf, 126,* 69-72.

Bornstein, H., & Saulnier, K. (1981). Signed English: A brief follow-up to the first evaluation. *American Annals of the Deaf, 126,* 69-72.

Rawlings, B. (1973). *Characteristics of hearing impaired students by hearing status,* U.S. 1970-71 (Series D, No. 10). Washington, D.C.: Gallaudet University Center for Assessment and Demographic Studies.

Shroyer, E. and Shroyer, S. (1982). *Signs Across America.* Washington, D.C.: Gallaudet University Press.

Trybus, R., & Jensema, C. (1978). *Communication patterns and educational achievement of hearing impaired students (Series T. No. 2).* Washington, D.C.: Gallaudet University Center for Assessment and Demographic Studies

# INDEX

WORDS

## A



## B



## C

# D

# E



# F

# G



# H



# I



# J



# K



# L

# M



# N

# O



# P



# Q



# R

# S

# T



# U



# V

## W

## Z

## SENTENCES

# More Signed English Books and Videotapes

For ordering information, call toll-free 1-800-621-2736 V, 1-888-630-9347 TTY, 1-800-621-8476 FAX.

Or write to: Gallaudet University Press
Chicago Distribution Center
11030 South Langley Avenue
Chicago, IL 60628

## Reference Books and Videotapes

| Title | ISBN |
|---|---|
| The Comprehensive Signed English Dictionary | 0-913580-81-3 |
| The Signed English Schoolbook | 0-930323-30-0 |
| The Signed English Starter | 0-913580-82-1 |
| Signed English for the Classroom | 0-913580-37-6 |

### Flash Cards

| | |
|---|---|
| Sign/Word Flash Cards | 0-930323-31-9 |

### Instructional Videotapes

| | |
|---|---|
| The Signed English Starter Part I Videotape | 1-56368-038-6 |
| The Signed English Starter Part II Videotape | 1-56368-040-8 |

### Signed English Storybooks

| | |
|---|---|
| Goldilocks and the Three Bears | 1-56368-057-2 |
| Little Red Riding Hood | 0-930323-63-7 |
| The Night Before Christmas | 1-56368-020-3 |
| Nursery Rhymes from Mother Goose | 0-930323-99-8 |

## Signed English for Children Softcover Books

### Beginning Books

*Basic vocabulary, phrases, and simple sentences related to daily activities.*

| | |
|---|---|
| A Book about Me | 0-913580-19-8 |
| Circus Time | 0-913580-51-1 |
| Fire Fighter Brown | 0-913580-50-3 |
| My Animal Book | 0-930323-38-6 |
| My Toy Book | 0-913580-22-8 |
| The Pet Shop | 0-913580-54-6 |
| Police Officer Jones | 0-913580-53-8 |
| With My Legs | 0-913580-42-2 |

## Growing Up Books and Stories

*High interest-level topics presented in simple straightforward sentences.*

| | |
|---|---|
| The Clock Book | 0-913580-48-1 |
| The Holiday Book | 0-913580-30-9 |
| I Want to Be A Farmer | 0-913580-14-7 |
| The Ugly Duckling | 0-913580-29-5 |

## More Stories and Poems

*Advanced language patterns. Classic fairy tales, some with complicated plots and more sophisticated vocabulary.*

| | |
|---|---|
| Be Careful | 0-913580-55-4 |
| Jack and the Beanstalk | 0-913580-47-3 |
| Little Poems for Little People | 0-913580-31-7 |
| Mouse's Christmas Eve | 0-913580-28-7 |
| The Three Little Pigs | 0-913580-09-0 |
| We're Going to the Doctor | 0-913580-26-0 |

## Coloring Book

| | |
|---|---|
| Don't be a Grumpy Bear | 0-930323-26-2 |

To request a catalog, write to:

Gallaudet University Press
800 Florida Avenue NE
Washington, DC 20002-3695